ORGANIZE
MY
KINGDOM

ORGANIZE MY KINGDOM

A HISTORY OF RESTORED PRIESTHOOD

John A. Tvedtnes

CORNERSTONE

Published by:
Cornerstone Publishing & Distribution, Inc.
50 South 500 West
Bountiful, Utah 84011

First Printing: November 2000

Printed in the United States of America
04 03 02 01 00   10 9 8 7 6 5 4 3 2 1

ISBN: 1-929281-08-0

Cover Design by Adam R. Hopkins

Contents

ABOUT THE AUTHOR

John A. Tvedtnes was born in 1941. At an early age, he developed an interest in the Bible, which he read at the age of eight. By that time, his Roman Catholic family had moved to Salt Lake City where he was introduced to The Church of Jesus Christ of Latter-day Saints by friends at school who invited him to Primary. He was taught by stake missionaries and baptized. New Year's Day 2000 marked fifty years since he was confirmed a member of the Church.

His grandfather, though a devout Catholic, sent him a copy of the Book of Mormon left by missionaries. This led to a new world of scripture that John continues to explore today as Associate Director of Research at the Foundation for Ancient Research and Mormon Studies (FARMS) now a part of BYU.

After earning a BA in anthropology at the University of Utah in 1969, John received a Graduate Certificate in Middle East area studies and an MA in Linguistics, with a minor in Arabic. In 1971, he received a second MA in Middle East Studies (Hebrew), with a minor in anthropology. He has taken courses at the University of California (Berkeley) and the BYU Salt Lake Center, and did extensive graduate work at the Hebrew University in Jerusalem, studying Egyptian and Semitic languages.

John taught Hebrew and linguistics at the University of Utah for three years and Hebrew and anthropology at the BYU Salt Lake Center for five years. During more than eight years in Israel, he was with the BYU Jerusalem program, where he taught Hebrew, anthropology, ancient Near Eastern history and archaeology, and historical geography of Israel and the Near East. He has also taught special CES courses for Gospel Doctrine teachers, including the course that led to this volume.

PREFACE

I twice had the opportunity to teach a weeknight course for gospel doctrine teachers on the Doctrine and Covenants and the History of the Church. Though I felt myself well prepared to teach the course, I found that preparing materials for a two-hour class each week for two years gave me additional insights that had previously escaped my attention. Out of this came the present book, *Organize My Kingdom: A History of Restored Priesthood.*

The title is inspired by Joseph Smith's introduction to D&C 103:35, in which the Lord said, "pray earnestly that peradventure my servant Joseph Smith, Jun., may go with you, and preside in the midst of my people, and *organize my kingdom* upon the consecrated land, and establish the children of Zion upon the laws and commandments which have been and which shall be given unto you."

On April 6, 1830, the day the Church was organized, the assembled members acknowledged the authority of section 20 of the Doctrine and Covenants, which guided the establishment of priesthood offices. Of this action, Joseph Smith later wrote:

> In this manner did the Lord continue to give us instructions from time to time, concerning the duties which now devolved upon us; and among many other things of the kind, we obtained of Him the following, by the spirit of prophecy and revelation; which not only gave us much information, but also pointed out to us the precise day upon which, according to His will and commandment, we should proceed to organize His Church once more here upon the earth. (*History of the Church* 1:64)

During the fourteen years that followed, the Lord gave many more revelations to the prophet Joseph Smith regarding the organization of the Church and the officers who would serve its people.

These revelations did not cease with the death of the prophet Joseph. They continued with each of his successors and are still with us today. Indeed, with the ever-increasing pace of growth in the number of Latter-day Saints throughout the world, there is as much need for such revelation in our day as there was when the Church was first restored 170 years ago.

It is my sincere hope that readers will see the hand of the Lord in the evolution of the Church of Jesus Christ of Latter-day Saints since 1830 and that, knowing how the Lord operates, they will be willing to sustain actions taken by present-day leaders of the Church. President Gordon B. Hinckley expressed it best when he addressed the Saints in the conference of April 1995, the first in which he spoke as President of the Church:

> This church does not belong to its President. Its head is the Lord Jesus Christ, whose name each of us has taken upon ourselves. We are all in this great endeavor together. We are here to assist our Father in His work and His glory, "to bring to pass the immortality and eternal life of man" (Moses 1:39). Your obligation is as serious in your sphere of responsibility as is my obligation in my sphere. No calling in this church is small or of little consequence. All of us in the pursuit of our duty touch the lives of others. To each of us in our respective responsibilities the Lord has said: "Wherefore, be faithful; stand in the office which I have appointed unto you; succor the weak, lift up the hands which hang down, and strengthen the feeble knees" (D&C 81:5). (*Ensign* 25/5 [May 1995], 71)

—John A. Tvedtnes

Chapter 1

THE CALLING OF JOSEPH SMITH

Wherefore, I the Lord, knowing the calamity which should come upon the inhabitants of the earth, called upon my servant Joseph Smith, Jun., and spake unto him from heaven, and gave him commandments; And also gave commandments to others, that they should proclaim these things unto the world. (D&C 1:17-18)

In the spring of 1820, the Lord began to reveal his will to the earth through a modern prophet named Joseph Smith, Jr. Joseph was born in Sharon, Vermont, on December 23, 1805, the third son of Joseph Smith, Sr., and Lucy Mack Smith. At the age of fourteen, he received his first heavenly manifestation when, after praying in a wooded area near his father's home, he saw the Father and the Son.

"My object in going to inquire of the Lord," he later wrote, "was to know which of all the sects was right, that I might know which to join . . . I was answered that I must join none of them, for they were all wrong" (*Joseph Smith-History* 1:18-19).

Three years later, a heavenly messenger showed Joseph the location of a hidden record kept by an ancient Israelite people who once inhabited the American continent. Beginning in 1827, the young prophet translated the record into English by the gift and power of God. The result was the Book of Mormon, which was declared to be the word of God, alongside the Bible (*Joseph Smith-History* 1:29-54, 59-67).

Following the restoration of ancient priesthood authority from heaven, Joseph and others proceeded to re-establish the true and authorized church of Christ on the earth.

The Priesthood

The *priesthood* has often been defined as the power to act in the name of God. At a conference held in New York City on August 17,

1843, Brigham Young (who later succeeded Joseph Smith) "spoke of the Priesthood, and said that it was a perfect system of government" (*History of the Church* 5:550). Another of Joseph's successors, John Taylor, defined the priesthood in similar terms:

> It is the government of God, whether on earth or in the heavens, for it is by that power, agency, or principle that all things are governed on the earth and in the heavens, and by that power that all things are upheld and sustained. It governs all things—it directs all things—it sustains all things—and has to do with all things that God and truth are associated with. It is the power of God delegated to intelligences in the heavens and to men on the earth. (*Millennial Star* 9:321)

> What is the kingdom of God? It is God's government upon the earth and in heaven.
> What is his Priesthood? It is the rule, authority, administration, if you please, of the government of God on the earth or in the heavens; for the same Priesthood that exists upon the earth exists in the heavens, and that Priesthood holds the keys of the mysteries of the revelations of God; and the legitimate head of that Priesthood, who has communion with God, is the Prophet, Seer and Revelator to his Church and people on the earth.
> When the will of God is done on earth as it is in heaven, that Priesthood will be the only legitimate ruling power under the whole heavens; for every other power and influence will be subject to it. (*Journal of Discourses* 6:25)

The teachings of the Prophet Joseph Smith on this subject are essential in order to fully understand the meaning of the term priesthood. He declared:

> The Priesthood is an everlasting principle, and existed with God from eternity, and will to eternity, without beginning of days or end of years. The keys have to be brought from heaven, whenever the Gospel is sent. When they are revealed from heaven, it is by Adam's authority. (*Journal of Discourses* 6:237)

Joseph Smith Foreordained to the Priesthood

Joseph Smith's call to restore the priesthood and the Church was foreseen by the Lord. Indeed, Joseph was foreordained in the premortal celestial world to perform this work. This was attested in a revelation given to President John Taylor in Salt Lake City on June 27, 1882:

> Behold, I raised up my servant Joseph Smith to introduce my Gospel, and to build up my Church and establish my Kingdom on the earth; and I gave unto him wisdom and knowledge and revelation, and intelligence pertaining to the past, the present, and the future, even to that extent which was not known among men; and I endowed him with power from on high, and conferred upon him the Priesthood of Aaron, and also the Priesthood of Melchizedek, which is after the order of the Son of God, even the holiest of all, and after the power of an endless life, and administereth forever in this world and the world to come. He was called and ordained to this office before the world was. He was called by me, and empowered by me, and sustained by me to introduce and establish my Church and Kingdom upon the earth; and to be a Prophet, Seer, and Revelator to my Church and Kingdom; and to be a King and Ruler over Israel.[1]

President Taylor further stated, "Joseph Smith, in the first place, was set apart by the Almighty, according to the councils of the Gods in the eternal worlds, to introduce principles of life among the people, of which the Gospel is the grand power and influence" (*Journal of Discourses* 21:94). Other Church leaders have confirmed this teaching.[2]

The idea that priesthood leaders are foreordained is suggested in Abraham 3:22-24. Under the date of May 12, 1844, Joseph Smith expressed the concept in these words:

> Every man who has a calling to minister to the inhabitants of the world was ordained to that very purpose in the Grand Council

---

1 Revelation to John Taylor, June 27, 1882, John Taylor Papers, LDS Church Archives.

2 For some statements on Joseph Smith's foreordination to the priesthood, see the appendix to this volume.

of heaven before this world was. I suppose that I was ordained to this very office in that Grand Council. (*History of the Church* 6:364)

The importance of this principle is found in the confusion surrounding two of Joseph Smith's revelations, in which the Lord explained that it was necessary to have the Melchizedek Priesthood in order to see God (D&C 84:19-22; 107:18-19). In view of the fact that Joseph had not yet received that authority at the time of his first vision, some wonder how he could have seen God.

This was explained by Elder Orson Pratt, who discussed in detail the question of Joseph's priesthood authority in a discourse delivered October 10, 1880:

> The Lord did not see proper to organize the authority of this Church all at once in all the various councils and authorities that, from time to time, have been ordained among this people; it was a gradual work. Authority was bestowed before there was any Church. First (not the authority of the Priesthood) but the authority to bring forth the plates of the Book of Mormon and to translate them by the Urim and Thummim, by the inspiration of the Holy Ghost . . .
>
> Joseph Smith, when he translated these records by the aid of the Urim and Thummim, had not yet received any Priesthood, so far as his temporal existence was concerned. But now, do not misunderstand me in regard to this position. He did hold the Priesthood before he came here upon the earth. I remarked that Joseph, so far as having any ordination here in the flesh was concerned, held no Priesthood at the time that he brought forth the plates of the Book of Mormon and translated them; but he did hold the Priesthood, which was conferred upon him in the councils of eternity, before this world was formed. You will find this recorded in a sermon delivered by the Prophet Joseph, showing that not only he, but also all of the faithful that have received the Priesthood here in this life, were ordained before the foundation of the world. Consequently, they had the ordination; that ordination was after the order of Him who is from all eternity to all eternity, an everlasting Priesthood, without father, without mother, without beginning of days or end of years; having been handed

down from all eternity. That Priesthood was conferred upon Joseph Smith before he came here; he was among those that are spoken of in "The Pearl of Great Price" . . . Abraham saw them. (*Journal of Discourses* 22:28)

Elder Pratt went on to explain that this is how Joseph Smith, at age fourteen, could see God despite the revelation of September 22, 1832, which taught that the priesthood was necessary for such a privilege (*Journal of Discourses* 22:29). He then continued:

He was not without the Priesthood in reality; but was a man chosen, a man ordained, a man appointed from before the foundation of this world, to come forth in the fulness of times to introduce the last dispensation among the children of men; to come in order to organize that kingdom that was predicted by the ancient Prophets . . . [The speaker here refers to the restoration of the priesthood by John the Baptist and Peter, James and John, then continues:] . . . having all these preparations here in the flesh as well as having been preordained to this mission. (*Journal of Discourses* 22:29-30)

From Small Beginnings

The beginnings of the restored Church were small. At the Church's inaugural meeting on April 6, 1830, there were only six elders in attendance, though approximately seventy persons had been baptized. In a revelation dated September 11, 1831, the Lord told the prophet Joseph, "ye are laying the foundation of a great work. And out of small things proceedeth that which is great" (D&C 64:33). By the year 2000, the Church had nearly eleven million members.

The rapid growth experienced in the work initiated by Joseph Smith a little more than a century and a half ago was foreseen 2500 years beforehand by an Israelite prophet. Daniel, interpreting a dream the Lord had given to the king of Babylon, spoke of "a stone . . . cut out of the mountain without hands," a kingdom set up by the God of heaven to replace all worldly governments in the last days. The stone, though small when first cut out, grew in size and "became a great mountain, and filled the whole earth" (Daniel 2:31-45).

Today, members of The Church of Jesus Christ of Latter-day Saints tend to think that the Church has always been as it is now, with its First Presidency, quorums of the Twelve and Seventy, Presiding Bishopric, stake presidencies and high councils, bishoprics, and various priest-hood offices. But the Church had small beginnings, with just a few of these offices, and grew into the organization we know today.

The words of Brigham Young, from a discourse delivered May 7, 1861, are helpful in understanding the process by which this growth took place:

> How came these Apostles, these Seventies, these High Priests, and all this organization we now enjoy? It came by rev-elation . . . In the year 1831 the Prophet Joseph Smith went to Ohio . . . and arrived in Kirtland sometime in May. They held a General Conference, which was the first General Conference ever called or held in Ohio. Joseph then received a revelation and ordained high priests . . . These were the first that were ordained to this office in the Church. I relate this to show you how Joseph proceeded step by step in organizing the Church. At that time there were no Seventies nor Twelve Apostles. (*Journal of Discourses* 9:88-89)

The purpose of the leadership structure of the restored Church is to assist us in our return to the presence of our Heavenly Father. Knowing that this is best accomplished when human beings are free to choose good over evil, Joseph Smith, under the date of January 27, 1832, recorded these words:

> It was my endeavor to so organize the Church that the brethren might eventually be independent of every incumber-ence beneath the celestial kingdom by bonds and covenants of mutual friendship and mutual love. (*History of the Church* 1:269)

In this book, we will examine how the Church came to be orga-nized by means of periodic revelations, step by step, "line upon line, precept upon precept, here a little and there a little" (D&C 128:21). We will also learn that this process is unlikely to cease before the coming of the Lord in glory. In other words, as the Church continues to grow, we can expect to see further modifications in its organizational structure to meet present needs and population size.

Brigham Young stated, "Joseph Smith has laid the foundation of the Kingdom of God in the last days; others will rear the superstructure" (*Journal of Discourses* 9:364). In 1877, Brigham instituted a "reformation" in the Church, during which much reorganization was undertaken. This was not to be the last reorganization of the priesthood and the restored Church in which it is housed. Speaking of the work then in progress, Elder Orson Pratt said:

When we have done all we can do, towards organizing as far as possible, according to the written law of God, as given to us, in our weakness, have we completed the organization? By no means. The organization is only perfect as far as the people are prepared to receive it, and no further. To say that there will be a stated time, in the history of this Church, during its imperfections and weakness, when the organization will be perfect, and that there will be no further extension or addition to the organization, would be a mistake. Organization is to go on, step after step from one degree to another, just as the people increase and grow in the knowledge of the principles and laws of the kingdom of God, and as their borders shall extend. (*Journal of Discourses* 19:12)

Three years later, Elder Pratt expressed similar views:

The Lord made manifest these things not all at once, but from time to time, as the people progressed and were counted worthy in His sight to receive further knowledge upon these things. You may ask, why it was that the Lord did not give the whole pattern at once, why He did not unfold everything all in a moment. It was because we were as little children then...and we could not bear all things at once; therefore He revealed unto us enough from time to time, to set our minds reflecting; He revealed sufficient to cause us to be stirred up in our minds to pray unto Him; and when we prayed unto Him about any of the duties of the Priesthood, then He would reveal it. But He would be sought unto by His people before He would reveal a fulness of knowledge upon these important subjects. This seeking unto the Lord to obtain little by little, and precept by precept in the knowledge of the things of God, is just the way a wise parent would instruct his own sons. (*Journal of Discourses* 22:31)

The principle of continuing revelation to govern the kingdom of God was expressed by Joseph Smith in the ninth Article of Faith: "We believe all that God has revealed, all that He does now reveal, and we believe that He will yet reveal many great and important things pertaining to the Kingdom of God."

Sources

In determining the development of priesthood organization in the restored Church, one must go beyond a mere reading of the standard history books and even the Doctrine and Covenants (D&C). In part, this is because some of the revelations published in the D&C reflect later changes that were not in effect at the time the original instructions came from the Lord. This becomes particularly evident when one examines earlier versions of those revelations, such as those found in the Book of Commandments (BC), published in 1833, and in the first edition of the D&C, published in 1835. Some of the earliest revelations were published in the Church's newspaper, the *The Evening and Morning Star*.[3]

In some cases, original documents have survived and can be used as reference material.[4] Some are also available in the Kirtland Revelation Book, a handwritten notebook from the mid-1830s held by the LDS

---

3 This official Church publication was initially edited at Independence, Missouri, by William W. Phelps, who printed issues 1-14 (June 1832 through July 1833). After the Saints were forcibly removed from Jackson County, Oliver Cowdery took up editorship of the paper, publishing issues 15-34 (December 1833 through September 1834) in Kirtland, Ohio.

4 In the past couple of decades, some of the early historical documents have been published. See, for example, the following: Andrew F. Ehat and Lyndon W. Cook, *The Words of Joseph Smith: the Contemporary Accounts of the Nauvoo Discourses of the Prophet Joseph* (Orem: Grandin, 1991); Dean C. Jessee, *The Personal Writings of Joseph Smith* (Salt Lake City: Deseret, 1984); Dean C. Jessee, *The Papers of Joseph Smith, Volume 1: Autobiographical and Historical Writings*, (Salt Lake City: Deseret, 1989); Dean C. Jessee, *The Papers of Joseph Smith, Volume 2: Journal, 1832-1842*. (Salt Lake City: Deseret, 1992).

Church.[5] Another useful source is the Far West Record, which contains historical and revelatory information from both Kirtland, Ohio, and from the LDS settlements in Missouri.[6]

The effect of Church growth is reflected in variant versions of the revelations, where the later editions were changed to reflect subsequent organizational developments. Consequently, we will not merely accept the "date" of the revelation assigned to it in the Doctrine and Covenants,[7] but will, rather, examine the changes made to those sections from a chronological point-of-view.[8] This does not mean that we wish to downplay the importance of revelation. Rather, we will attempt to illustrate how revelation has worked in the organizing of the Church. The flexible nature of Church organization does not detract from its divine origins and purposes, but actually enhances them.

We will also have recourse to other early publications of the Church, such as the *Journal of Discourses*. The *History of the Church*, of which the first six volumes are based on the work begun by Joseph Smith and

---

5 For a summary of the history and contents, see John A. Tvedtnes, "Historical Perspectives on the Kirtland Revelation Book," in Stephen D. Ricks, Donald W. Parry, and Andrew H. Hedges, *The Disciple as Witness: Essays on Latter-day Saint History and Doctrine in Honor of Richard Lloyd Anderson* (Provo: FARMS 2000).

6 The Far West Record comprises the high council minutes from Far West, Missouri, from April 6, 1838 through the Nauvoo period (1844), and also includes copies of minutes from earlier conferences and high councils from 1830 onward. A printed edition is Donald Q. Cannon and Lyndon W. Cook, *Far West Record* (Salt Lake City: Deseret, 1983).

7 When the *Doctrine and Covenants* was republished in 1981, some of the erroneous dates that appeared in previous editions were corrected by referring to the Book of Commandments, early editions of the Doctrine and Covenants, the Kirtland Revelation Book, and other dated copies from the time of Joseph Smith. As a result, the current edition is more accurate than any of its predecessors.

8 Elder B. H. Roberts, who edited the *History of the Church* in its final form, included footnotes indicating some of the rewording or additional verbiage in later versions of Joseph Smith's revelations. For example, D&C 20 (*History of the Church* 1:68, 173) and D&C 42 (*History of the Church* 1:150, 152). In most cases, he was incorporating notes previously prepared by Elder Orson Pratt for the history as published in the *Deseret News*. In Joseph Smith's diary for December 1, 1832, he noted, "wrote and corrected revelations &c." (cited in Dean C. Jessee, *The Papers of Joseph Smith* 2:4). In a letter to W. W. Phelps, dated June 25, 1833, the prophet included a small list of corrections to "errors in the [Book of] Commandments, as printed" (*History of the Church* 1:364). Changes to the revelations are discussed in Lyndon W. Cook, *The Revelations of the Prophet Joseph Smith* (Salt Lake City: Deseret, 1985) and Robert J. Woodford, The Historical Development of the Doctrine and Covenants (PhD dissertation, Brigham Young University, 1974), 2 volumes.

his scribes, is used extensively but with care in those areas where later editing has led to anachronisms.[9] Other early Church records that have found their way into print in recent years are also used.

Most histories of the LDS Church have tended to reflect current reality and to either ignore, or at least pass over, developments that led to that reality. In the opinion of the present author, this has obscured the method by which the Lord works in revealing his will to his chosen prophets. It has left us in a position where many Church members feel that the Church is inflexible and incapable of change and further development. Were this so, the very existence of living prophets would be superfluous.

Only by understanding how the Lord has worked through his prophets over the past century and a half can we truly appreciate what he is doing today and what he will yet accomplish in the years to come. Therefore, this work is not a critical approach to Mormon history, but rather, a realistic one with the additional purpose of providing an anchor for the faith of the Saints, an anchor that will keep them securely attached to the Lord's Church as it approaches what promises to be an era of many more revelations and refinements.

---

9 For example, the *History of the Church* was compiled from the Manuscript History begun by Joseph Smith, with some changes by Brigham Young and others. The Manuscript History was the source for earlier publications on the history of the Church in such periodicals as *The Times and Seasons* (published in Nauvoo, Illinois), the *Millennial Star* (published in Great Britain), and the *Deseret News* (published in Utah). In some cases, there have been modifications to the earlier printed versions in the published *History of the Church*.

Chapter 2

THE RESTORATION

Behold, I will reveal unto you the Priesthood, by the hand of Elijah the prophet, before the coming of the great and dreadful day of the Lord. (D&C 2:1)

When the angel Moroni appeared for the first time to young Joseph Smith on the evening of September 21, 1823, he quoted a number of biblical prophecies that he said were about to be fulfilled. One of these was from Malachi 4:5, which he read differently, suggesting that Elijah the prophet would come and "reveal unto you the Priesthood" (Joseph Smith-History 1:38).

This is the earliest mention made to the boy prophet of the priesthood, and it may not have made much sense to him at the time. It was a promise that was to be fulfilled in the years to come.

While translating the Book of Mormon, Joseph Smith received further indications that he would receive priesthood authority from God. In May of 1829, the Lord revealed that Joseph and his brother Hyrum were not to preach until they were called (D&C 11:15-16).[1]

The Aaronic Priesthood

The translation and publication of the Book of Mormon occupied much of Joseph Smith's time during the early part of his ministry in 1829-30. Having discovered mention of baptism for the remission of sins in the translation from the plates, he and Oliver Cowdery were desirous to inquire of the Lord about the matter. On May 15, 1829,

---

1 This verse corresponds to Book of Commandments 10:8. In D&C 5:6, 17, a revelation dated to 1829, Joseph was promised an ordination to preach. The words were inserted into the revelation in the 1835 edition of the D&C (32:2-3), and are not found in the parallel chapter of the Book of Commandments (BC 4), published in 1833. Nevertheless, the promise was made, as the context of the original shows. It may be that the term "priesthood" had no meaning to Joseph Smith at the time the revelation was received and consequently was not added until a later date, when he knew of the principle and remembered the Lord's promise.

while praying near the Susquehanna River, they received a visit from the resurrected John the Baptist, who laid his hands on their heads and ordained them with these words:

> Upon you my fellow servants, in the name of Messiah, I confer the Priesthood of Aaron, which holds the keys of the ministering of angels, and of the gospel of repentance, and of baptism by immersion for the remission of sins; and this shall never be taken again from the earth, until the sons of Levi do offer again an offering unto the Lord in righteousness. (D&C 13; Joseph Smith-History 1:68-71)

Joseph further recorded that

> The messenger who visited us on this occasion and conferred this Priesthood upon us, said that his name was John, the same that is called John the Baptist in the New Testament, and that he acted under the direction of Peter, James and John, who held the keys of the Priesthood of Melchizedek, which Priesthood, he said, would in due time be conferred on us, and that I should be called the first Elder of the Church, and he (Oliver Cowdery) the second. (Joseph Smith-History 1:72; cf. D&C 27:7)[2]

The Apostleship

On a subsequent occasion, Peter, James and John did, indeed, appear to Joseph Smith and Oliver Cowdery and ordained them to the apostleship. The exact date of this event was never recorded in the early history of the Church. Nevertheless, Larry C. Porter has presented evidence that the ordination of these two young men to the higher office took place sometime between May 15 and May 29, 1829.[3] Porter cites D&C 27:12-13, dated August 1830, as evidence that the apostleship had already been conferred by that date:

---

2 The modern printed editions of the *Pearl of Great Price* also include (as a footnote) a version of the event written and published by Oliver Cowdery in *Messenger and Advocate* 1:14-16 (October 1834). For other accounts of this event recorded by Oliver, see the appendix.

3 Larry C. Porter, "Dating the Restoration of the Melchizedek Priesthood," *Ensign*, June 1979, 5-10. Larry C. Porter, "The Restoration of the Aaronic and Melchizedek Priesthoods," *Ensign* December 1996, 30-47.

And also with Peter, and James, and John, whom I have sent unto you, by whom I have ordained you and confirmed you to be apostles, and especial witnesses of my name, and bear the keys of your ministry, and of the same things which I revealed unto them;

Unto whom I have committed the keys of my kingdom, and a dispensation of the gospel for the last times, and for the fulness of times.

While this statement truthfully reflects an historical event, it did not form part of the original revelation dated August 1830, for it does not appear in chapter 28 of the Book of Commandments (BC) published in 1833. It was first added to the revelation when it appeared again in the 1835 printing of the D&C (as 50:3).[4]

When he later began writing the history of the Church, Joseph Smith had the following to say about the restoration of the Melchizedek Priesthood:

We now became anxious to have that promise realized to us, which the angel that conferred upon us the Aaronic Priesthood had given to us, viz., that provided we continued faithful, we should also have the Melchizedek Priesthood, which holds the authority of the laying on of hands for the gift of the Holy Ghost. We had for some time made this matter a subject of humble prayer, and at length we got together in the chamber of Mr. Whitmer's house [see D&C 128:21.], in order more particularly to seek of the Lord what we now so earnestly desired; and here, to our unspeakable satisfaction, did we realize the truth of the Savior's promise—"Ask, and it shall be given you; seek, and ye shall find; knock, and it shall be opened unto you"—for we had not long been engaged in solemn and fervent prayer, when the

---

4 Indeed, verses 5 through 13 of that section (beginning with the words "with Moroni") were not part of the original revelation, though the information they contain may have been known in its entirety to Joseph Smith at the earlier date. These verses are also missing in the revelation as published in *The Evening and Morning Star* 1:10 (March 1833). The 1835 edition of the Doctrine and Covenants dates the revelation to the month of September rather than August, as subsequent editions did. The current (1981) edition notes that part was written in August, part in September of 1830. To this, we should add that part was written after the 1833 publication.

word of the Lord came unto us in the chamber, commanding us that I should ordain Oliver Cowdery to be an Elder in the Church of Jesus Christ; and that he also should ordain me to the same office; and then to ordain others, as it should be made known unto us from time to time. We were, however, commanded to defer this our ordination until such times as it should be practicable to have our brethren, who had been and who should be baptized, assembled together, when we must have their sanction to our thus proceeding to ordain each other, and have them decide by vote whether they were willing to accept us as spiritual teachers or not. (*History of the Church* 1:60-61)[5]

The prophet subsequently described the events of April 6, 1830, when the Church was officially organized and he and Oliver Cowdery ordained each other to the office of elder in the new organization. Some critics have assumed from this—as also from the absence of a recorded date—that Peter, James and John never did appear to the two young men to ordain them to the Melchizedek Priesthood, and that Joseph Smith merely took authority to himself. This is contradicted by Oliver Cowdery's supporting testimony as given at a conference held at Mesquito Creek, Council Bluffs, Iowa, on October 21, 1848, upon his return to the Church, a decade after having been excommunicated:

I was present with Joseph when an holy angel from God came down from heaven and conferred or restored, the Aaronic Priesthood, and said at the same time that it should remain upon the earth while the earth stands. I was also present with Joseph when the Melchisedek Priesthood was conferred by the holy angels of God from on high. This Priesthood we then conferred on each other, by the will and commandment of God. This Priesthood is also to remain upon the earth until the last remnant of time. This holy Priesthood, we then conferred upon many and is just as good and valid as if God had done it in person.[6]

---

5 This entry in Joseph Smith's history is undated, but was placed by him just before a revelation dated June 1829.

6 Reuben Miller Diary, of the same date, in LDS Church Historian's Office; see also *Deseret News*, April 13, 1859.

It may be that the reason Joseph omitted reference to the ordination by Jesus' chief apostles was that this claim would have brought even greater persecution on his head. It was perhaps for the same reason that he referred, in his official account of the first vision, to "two personages" who appeared to him in the grove, without naming them.[7]

That the apostleship, which presides over the Melchizedek Priesthood, had already been bestowed upon Joseph and Oliver by June of 1829 is indicated in a revelation given during that month found in D&C 18 and also published in chapter 15 of the Book of Commandments:

> And now, Oliver Cowdery, I speak unto you, and also unto David Whitmer . . . even as unto Paul mine apostle, for you are called even with that same calling with which he was called. (D&C 18:9; also BC 15:10-11)

In the verses that follow, the Lord instructs these men that they have been called to preach. He then speaks of

> others who are called to declare my gospel . . . Yea, even twelve; and the Twelve shall be my disciples, and they shall take upon them my name; and the Twelve are they who shall desire to take upon them my name with full purpose of heart. (D&C 18:26-27; also BC 15:27-29)

Though the quorum of the Twelve Apostles was not organized for another five and a half years, the Lord continued his revelation by giving instructions as follows: "And now I speak unto (you), the Twelve." (D&C 18:31 adds the word "you," which was not in BC 15:33, published before the call of the Twelve, nor in the 1835 D&C 43:5.)

Confirmation of Oliver Cowdery's calling to the apostleship is found in a revelation addressed to him in 1829, from which the following quotes are drawn:

---

7 In his 1832 account of his first vision, Joseph mentioned having seen "the Lord." See Dean C. Jessee, *The Papers of Joseph Smith, Volume 1: Autobiographical and Historical Writings* (Salt Lake City: Deseret, 1989), 6. Critics have suggested that this and other minor variants invalidate the first vision story, but it was merely his first attempt to tell what happened. Presumably, "the Lord" refers to Christ, with whom Joseph conversed at the time. The Father merely introduced his Son. He didn't respond to the young boy's questions.

> Behold I am Oliver—I am an Apostle of Jesus Christ by the will of God the Father and the Lord Jesus Christ.
>
> A commandment from God unto Oliver, how he should build up His Church and the manner thereof . . .
>
> I speak unto you even as unto Paul mine Apostle for ye are called even with that same calling with which he was called.[8]

The last of these paragraphs is worded in the same way as D&C 18:9, in which Oliver Cowdery and David Whitmer are both designated apostles.

The ordination of Joseph and Oliver to the apostleship is noted in BC 24:2-3, where each is called "an apostle of Jesus Christ, an elder of this church." D&C 20:2-3 adds that they were, respectively, "the first elder" and "the second elder." In his pamphlet, "An Address to All Believers in Christ," David Whitmer wrote that he had been ordained an elder by Joseph Smith during the month of June 1829, the date of D&C 18, in which he is said to be an apostle.[9] D&C 20:38 informs us that "an apostle is an elder."

Brigham Young later declared that "Joseph Smith, Oliver Cowdery and David Whitmer were the first Apostles of this dispensation" (*Journal of Discourses* 6:320).[10] By virtue of the apostolic authority which they received, Oliver Cowdery and David Whitmer— two of the Three Witnesses to the Book of Mormon—were instructed "that you shall search out the Twelve" (D&C 18:37; BC 15:42). At the time these instructions were given (June 1829), Martin Harris, the third witness, was not worthy of the same calling, though he later joined the others in the selection and ordination of the first Quorum of the Twelve Apostles.[11] For a discussion of the twelve, see chapter 6.

---

8 Revelation through Oliver Cowdery, 1829, in Joseph Smith Collection, LDS Church Historian's Office, cited in Robert J. Woodford, "The Historical Development of the Doctrine and Covenants" (PhD dissertation, Brigham Young University, 1974), 1:287-90.

9 David Whitmer, "An Address to All Believers in Christ" (privately published, Richmond, Missouri, 1887), 32.

10 The passage is cited more extensively below. Other statements by early Church leaders confirm that Joseph and Oliver received the apostleship from Peter, James and John. Some of these are included in the appendix to this volume.

11 It is not impossible that Martin Harris was ordained an apostle, though it has not generally been recognized in the Church. Years later, Brigham Young noted, "Peter comes along with James and John and ordained Joseph to be an Apostle, and then Joseph ordained Oliver and David Whitmer and Martin Harris; and then they were

Establishing the Church

The authority received by Joseph Smith and Oliver Cowdery under the hands of Peter, James and John was, as the Lord stated (D&C 27:12), the apostleship, which holds the right of presidency in the priesthood and the Church. Brigham Young declared

> The Priesthood which Peter, James and John held while in the flesh was the highest ever bestowed upon the children of men, and it was conferred upon Joseph and Oliver, and without it they never could have built up the kingdom.[12]

He also testified:

> I know that Joseph received his Apostleship from Peter, James, and John, before a revelation on the subject was printed, and he never had a right to organize a Church before he was an Apostle." (*Journal of Discourses* 1:137)

On another occasion, he explained his reasoning:

> Could [Joseph Smith] have built up the kingdom of God without first being an apostle? No, he never could. The keys of the eternal priesthood, which is after the order of the Son of God, is comprehended by being an apostle. All the priesthood, all the keys, all the gifts, all the endowments, and everything preparatory to entering back into the presence of the Father and of the Son is in, composed of, circumscribed by, or I might say incorporated within the circumference of the apostleship.[13]

Having received the keys of the priesthood, Joseph and Oliver proceeded to baptize, confirm and ordain others and to restore the church

---

ordered to select twelve more and ordain them" (*Journal of Discourses* 6:29). Since Oliver Cowdery was ordained by the same messengers as Joseph Smith, one wonders how literally one should take President Young's statement, for he has Joseph ordaining Oliver. It may be that he is referring not to ordination to the apostleship, but rather to a setting apart (the two terms were often used synonymously in the early Church) of the Three Witnesses to call the Twelve, for which see the discussion in chapter 6.

12 *Deseret News Weekly*, June 6, 1877.
13 *Millennial Star* 15:489, reporting a discourse of April 6, 1853.

of Christ to the earth. David Whitmer, writing in 1887, half a century after he left the Church, stated:

> In this month [June, 1829] I was baptized, confirmed, and ordained an Elder in the Church of Christ by Bro. Joseph Smith. Previous to this, Joseph Smith and Oliver Cowdery had baptized, confirmed and ordained each other to the office of an Elder in the Church of Christ. I was the third person baptized into the church. In August, 1829, we began to preach the gospel of Christ. The following six Elders had then been ordained: Joseph Smith, Oliver Cowdery, Peter Whitmer, Samuel H. Smith, Hyrum Smith and myself. The Book of Mormon was still in the hands of my brother, but my brother, Christian Whitmer, had copied from the manuscript the teachings and doctrine of Christ, being the things which we were commanded to preach. We preached, baptized and confirmed members into the Church of Christ, from August, 1829, until April 6th, 1830, being eight months in which time we had proceeded rightly; the offices in the church being Elders, Priests and Teachers.
>
> Now, when April 6, 1830, had come, we had then established three branches of the "Church of Christ," in which three branches were about seventy members: One branch was at Fayette, N. Y.; one at Manchester, N. Y., and one at Colesville, Pa. It is all a mistake about the church being organized on April 6, 1830, as I will show. We were as fully organized—spiritually—before April 6th as we were on that day.[14]

The date set by revelation for the official organization of the Church was April 6, 1830. On that day, Joseph Smith, Oliver Cowdery and four

---

14 David Whitmer, *An Address to All Believers in Christ* (Richmond, Missouri, 1887), 32-33. Regarding the first conference of the Church, held on June 9, 1830, *History of the Church* 1:84 reads, "Our numbers were about thirty." The 1981 Church Almanac says there were 27 members at the time of this conference. This is contradicted by David Whitmer, who wrote that there were about 70 by the time of the formal organization on April 6, 1830. The official History notes that, prior to the official organization, "occasionally we administered the ordinance of baptism" (*History of the Church* 1:59; the reception of the Melchizedek Priesthood, the organization of the Church and giving of the Holy Ghost are noted on page 60). In the first printed version of the history, the text read, "almost daily we administered the ordinance of baptism" (*Times and Seasons* 3:915).

others assembled at the home of Peter Whitmer, Sr., and formally organized what ultimately came to be known as The Church of Jesus Christ of Latter-day Saints. Half a century after leaving the Church, David Whitmer looked back at the events of April 6, 1830. (His recollection reflects the fact that he had come to believe that none of Joseph's revelations were from God except those that came "through the stone." Though his story must be viewed in the light of his later bitterness, it nevertheless sheds some light on the history of the time.) He commented on those events as follows:

> The reason why we met on that day was this; the world had been telling us that we were not a regularly organized church, and we had no right to officiate in the ordinance of marriage, hold church property, etc., and that we should organize according to the laws of the land. On this account we met at my father's house in Fayette, N. Y., on April 6, 1830, to attend to this matter of organizing according to the laws of the land; you can see this from Sec. 17 Doctrine and Covenants: the church was organized on April 6th "agreeable to the laws of our country." [D&C 20:1]
>
> It says after this, "by the will and commandments of God" [D&C 20:1]; but this revelation came through Bro. Joseph as "mouthpiece." Now brethren, how can it be that the church was any more organized—spiritually—on April 6th, than it was before that time? There were six elders and about seventy members before April 6th, and the same number of elders and members after that day. We attended to our business of organizing according to the laws of the land, the church acknowledging us six elders as their ministers; besides, a few who had recently been baptized and not confirmed were confirmed on that day; some blessings were pronounced, and we partook of the Lord's supper.
>
> I do not consider that the church was any more organized or established in the eyes of God on that day than it was previous to that day . . .
>
> Just before April 6, 1830, some of the brethren began to think that the church should have a leader, just like the children of Israel wanted a king. Brother Joseph finally inquired of the Lord about it . . . Joseph received a revelation that he should be the leader; that he should be ordained by Oliver Cowdery as

"Prophet Seer and Revelator" to the church, and that the church should receive his words as if from God's own mouth . . . We had all confidence in Brother Joseph, thinking that as God had given him so great a gift as to translate the Book of Mormon, that everything he would do must be right.[15]

At the same time, the Articles and Covenants of the church (from the preface to BC 24), which later became D&C 20, were accepted as binding on the Church. This section outlines the duties of some of the offices of the priesthood. The previous year, the Lord mentioned the offices of priest and teacher (D&C 18:32; BC 15:35), which are also described in D&C 20:46-56, along with the offices of deacon and elder (D&C 20:38-39, 57-59; BC 24:31-32, 40-41). All these offices required ordination (D&C 20:60; BC 24:42; D&C 20:48; BC 24:32).[16] Some of the more important verses follow:

> The priest's duty is to preach, teach, expound, exhort, and baptize, and administer the sacrament,
> And visit the house of each member, and exhort them to pray vocally and in secret and attend to all family duties.
> And he may also ordain other priests, teachers, and deacons.
> And he is to take the lead of meetings when there is no elder present;
> But when there is an elder present, he is only to preach, teach, expound, exhort and baptize,
> And visit the house of each member, exhorting them to pray vocally and in secret and attend to all family duties.
> In all these duties the priest is to assist the elder if occasion requires. (D&C 20:46-52)[17]

---

15 David Whitmer, *An Address to All Believers in Christ* (Richmond, Missouri, 1887), 32-34.

16 A revelation given to Oliver Cowdery in 1829 is closely related to D&C 20 and shares some verbiage with the latter. Portions are included in the appendix.

17 This is paralleled by BC 24:36-37, where the idea is essentially the same, though the wording is a little different. From D&C 20:49-51, BC 24:37 reads "and take the lead of meetings; but none of these offices is he to do when there is an elder present, but in all cases is to assist the elder." The change in wording was already present in the 1835 edition of the Doctrine and Covenants. *The Evening and Morning Star*, which published the revelation in its first and thirteenth issues (June 1832 and June 1833), reads the same as the BC.

The teacher's duty is to watch over the church always, and be with and strengthen them;

And see that there is no iniquity in the church, neither hardness with each other, neither lying, backbiting, nor evil speaking;

And see that the church meet together often, and also see that all the members do their duty.

And he is to take the lead of meetings in the absence of the elder or priest—

And he is to be assisted always, in all his duties in the church, by the deacons, if occasion requires.

But neither teachers nor deacons have authority to baptize, administer the sacrament, or lay on hands;

They are, however, to warn, expound, exhort, and teach, and invite all to come unto Christ. (D&C 20:53-59)[18]

An apostle is an elder, and it is his calling to baptize;

And to ordain other elders, priests, teacher, and deacons; And to administer bread and wine—the emblems of the flesh and blood of Christ—

And to confirm those who are baptized into the church, by the laying on of hands for the baptism of fire and the Holy Ghost, according to the scriptures;

And to teach, expound, exhort, baptize, and watch over the church; And to confirm the church by the laying on of the hands, and the giving of the Holy Ghost;

And to take the lead of all meetings.

The elders are to conduct the meetings as they are led by the Holy Ghost, according to the commandments and revelations of God. (D&C 20:38-45)[19]

---

18 This corresponds to BC 24:38-41, where in verses 40-41 (D&C 20:57; 1835 D&C 2:11), the words "if occasion requires" and "or lay on hands" were added later, and are not in the version of the revelation published in issues 1 and 13 of *The Evening and Morning Star* (June 1832 and June 1833).

19 The corresponding passage in BC 24:32-35 is basically the same, and reads the same as the version of the revelation published in issues 1 and 13 of *The Evening and Morning Star* (June 1832 and June 1833). However, note that D&C 20:41, 43 is almost identical (the same thought), and that verse 41 is not found in BC. The difference may derive from a later attempt to emphasize the idea by repetition, or may be a printer's error, a case of dittography.

It is interesting that this passage says "an apostle is an elder." The apostle Peter wrote, "The elders which are among you I exhort, who am also an elder" (1 Peter 5:1). At the time the Church was organized in 1830, there were three apostles, Joseph Smith, Oliver Cowdery and David Whitmer. Yet the first two of these were ordained elders in the new Church, as Joseph Smith records:

> We proceeded, according to previous commandment, to call on our brethren to know whether they accepted us as their teachers in the things of the Kingdom of God, and whether they were satisfied that we should proceed and be organized as a Church according to said commandment which we had received. To these several propositions they consented by a unanimous vote. I then laid my hands upon Oliver Cowdery, and ordained him an Elder of the "Church of Jesus Christ of Latter-day Saints;" after which, he ordained me also to the office of an Elder of said Church. (*History of the Church* 1:76-77)[20]

The First Elder

Provision was made, at the outset, that "one of the elders" should be chosen as membership clerk for the entire Church (D&C 20:82; BC 24:61). Even at this early stage, the necessity for keeping records was expressed. The importance of records is noted in the very first verse of a revelation received on the date the Church was organized:

> Behold, there shall be a record kept among you; and in it thou shalt be called a seer, a translator, a prophet, an apostle of Jesus Christ, an elder of the church through the will of God the Father, and the grace of your Lord Jesus Christ. (D&C 21:1; BC 22:1)

The precise nature of Joseph Smith's calling is reflected in the order in which these titles are given. He was first a seer, when he saw God the Father and his Son Jesus Christ in the Sacred Grove in the spring of 1820. He then became a translator, commissioned to produce the

---

20 Since this was not the Church's official title at the time of its organization, the words, here placed in quotes by the Prophet, reflect the name given it at a later stage, as recorded in D&C 115:4.

English version of the Book of Mormon, beginning in 1827. During the course of that translation, he became a prophet, receiving revelations (which he recorded) pertaining to the latter-day restoration (some of them in the D&C). Subsequently, he was ordained an apostle in May 1829 and on April 6, 1830, he was sustained as the First Elder of the Church, with Oliver Cowdery being the Second Elder.

This latter calling is reflected in the Lord's words addressed to Oliver Cowdery on the day of his ordination:

> Wherefore it behooveth me that he [Joseph Smith] should be ordained by you, Oliver Cowdery mine apostle;
>
> This being an ordinance unto you, that you are an elder under his hand, he being the first unto you, that you may be an elder unto this church of Christ, bearing my name—
>
> And the first preacher of this church unto the world. (D&C 21:10-12; BC 22:13-15)[21]

The call to be the first two elders in the restored Church was further reflected in these words:

> Joseph, who was called of God and ordained an apostle of Jesus Christ, an elder of this church...
>
> Oliver, who was also called of God an apostle of Jesus Christ, an elder of this church, and ordained under his [Joseph's] hand. (BC 24:3-4)[22]

---

21 This may imply that while the office of apostle (which Joseph and Oliver already held) could exist outside the Church (and, indeed, was necessary for its restoration), the office of elder is a calling within the organized Church. John A. Widtsoe wrote,

> On April 6, 1830, when the Church was organized, the Prophet Joseph Smith and his associate, Oliver Cowdery, who had previously received the Melchizedek Priesthood, were ordained elders in the newly formed Church. Only then could the power delegated to them be made to function acceptably to the Lord. Offices in the Priesthood, such as Elder, Seventy, or High Priest, appear only in connection with the organized Church.

See his *Evidences & Reconciliations* (Salt Lake City: Bookcraft, 1943), 178. This would explain the statement that "an apostle is an elder" and would also perhaps be the reason Joseph referred (as we have noted earlier) to the fact that he and Oliver were looking forward to being ordained on April 6, 1830. I.e., while they had already received the priesthood keys from Peter, James and John, they had not yet been authorized to function within an organized Church.

22 This is also the wording of the revelation as published in issues 1 (June 1832) and 13 (June 1833) of *The Evening and Morning Star*.

The original version, cited here, did not reflect the terms "first elder" and "second elder," which were added to D&C 2:1 in the 1835 publication, corresponding to our D&C 20:2-3. It is not known whether the term "we the elders of the church" in D&C 20:16 (BC 24:12) refers to these two men only or to the six elders present at the inaugural meeting on April 6, 1830. But it is nevertheless true that Joseph Smith was ordained as First Elder and Oliver Cowdery as Second Elder on that date, as Joseph Smith clearly indicated.[23]

The Lord instructed Oliver Cowdery, "Make known thy calling unto the church, and also before the world" (D&C 23:2; BC 17:4).[24] He evidently became over-zealous in this and came to believe that he had the same authority as Joseph Smith, despite the Lord's earlier instructions in D&C 21:11.

Consequently, in September 1830, the Lord told Oliver that only Joseph Smith was authorized to write commandments for the Church (D&C 28:1-7; BC 30:1-6), "for I have given him the keys of the mysteries, and the revelations which are sealed, until I shall appoint unto them another in his stead" (D&C 28:7; BC 30:6).

This idea has been frequently repeated in Church history. An October 8, 1877, statement by Elder George Q. Cannon, who later became a member of the First Presidency, will illustrate:

> The Church . . . is governed by men who hold the keys of the Apostleship, who have the right and authority. Any one of them, should an emergency arise, can act as President of the Church, with all the powers, with all the authority, with all the keys, and with every endowment necessary to obtain revelation from God, and to lead and guide this people . . . but there is only one man at a time who can hold the keys, who can dictate, who can guide, who can give revelation to the Church. The rest must acquiesce in his action, the rest must be governed by his counsels, the rest must receive his doctrines. It was so with Joseph. Others held the Apostleship—Oliver received the Apostleship at the same time

---

23 In D&C 20:5, Joseph is referred to as "this first elder" (the wording being the same in *The Evening and Morning Star*, issues 1 and 13). However, this may simply have reference to the fact that he was the first one named in the preceding passage.

24 Note that BC chapters 17-21 were combined as section 45 in the 1835 edition of D&C and are section 23 in our current edition.

that Joseph did, but Joseph held the keys, although Oliver held precisely the same authority. There was only one who could exercise it in its fullness and power among the people. (*Journal of Discourses* 19:234)

Oliver's position in the Church was further clarified in a revelation of September 1830, in which the Lord said of him, "And none have I appointed to be his counselor over him in the church, concerning church matters, except it is his brother, Joseph Smith, Jun" (D&C 30:7).[25]

On December 18, 1833, Oliver Cowdery wrote of Joseph Smith as the "first elder" of the Church, in the narration written prior to the entry of the patriarchal blessing given by the prophet to his father, Joseph Smith Sr., at Kirtland.[26] He reiterated the same in the preface to the patriarchal blessing which he (Oliver) pronounced on Joseph Smith on September 22, 1835, in Kirtland, and recorded by him on October 3 of that year.[27]

Priesthood as a Prerequisite to Organizing the Church

In a discourse delivered April 7, 1852, Brigham Young declared:

Joseph Smith was a Prophet, Seer, and Revelator before he had power to build up the kingdom of God, or take the first steps towards it. When did he obtain that power? Not until the angel had ordained him to be an Apostle. Joseph Smith, Oliver Cowdery, and David Whitmer were the first Apostles of this dispensation, though in the early days of the Church David Whitmer lost his standing, and another took his place... When a man is an Apostle, and stands at the head of the kingdom of God on the earth and magnifies his calling, he has the keys of all the power that ever was bestowed upon mortal man for the building up of the kingdom of God on the earth. (*Journal of Discourses* 6:320)

---

25 BC 31:5 read, "And none have I appointed to be over him in the church, except it is his brother Joseph." The minor change in wording was made in the 1835 edition (52:2).

26 Patriarchal Blessings Book, 1:8, in LDS Church Historian's Office.

27 Patriarchal Blessings Book, 2:28, in LDS Church Historian's Office.

Other presidents of the Church who had known the prophet Joseph made similar declarations. John Taylor declared:

[God] selected Joseph Smith to be the first Apostle in his Church . . . He was endowed with power and authority which was given him for that purpose, that he might be the legitimate representative of God upon the earth. He also taught him how to organize his Church, and put him in communication with many of the ancient Prophets who have long since passed away. (*Journal of Discourses* 19:303)

Wilford Woodruff noted:

In these last days the Lord called upon Joseph Smith, gave him power and authority to organize His Church and kingdom again upon the earth, and gave him the Holy Priesthood and the keys of the kingdom of God. Joseph was ordained to the Apostleship under the hands of men holding the keys of the kingdom of God in the days of Jesus— namely, Peter, James and John. (*Journal of Discourses* 13:321)

But Joseph Smith's calling to the apostleship was just the beginning. During his lifetime and during the presidencies of his successors, there would be many new revelations concerning the organization and operation of the Church. Elder Orson Pratt put it this way:

The Lord called him [Joseph] to lay the foundation of this work; he gave him revelations before the rise of the Church. He ordained him and Oliver Cowdery to the Apostleship, giving them the authority, and power, and office, and Priesthood, to perform the things necessary in the future organization of the Church, giving line upon line, precept upon precept, from time to time, to instruct the various Councils of the Church in regard to their several duties. (*Journal of Discourses* 19:113)

In subsequent chapters, we will examine the process of the restoration and organization of the Church in detail.

Chapter 3

THE KIRTLAND PERIOD

And also those to whom these commandments were given, might have power to lay the foundation of this church, and to bring it forth out of obscurity and out of darkness, the only true and living church upon the face of the whole earth. (D&C 1:30)

Only six elders were in attendance at the first meeting of the Church on April 6, 1830. They were Joseph Smith Jr., Oliver Cowdery, Peter Whitmer, John Whitmer, David Whitmer, and Ziba Peterson. At this, the first conference of the Church, it was agreed that Samuel H. Smith, Joseph's brother, should also be ordained an elder.[1]

A second conference of the Church was held on September 26, 1830, at which Joseph Smith Jr. "was appointed leader of the Conference by vote" and "was appointed by the voice of the Conference to receive and write Revelations & Commandments for this Church."[2]

A dramatic increase in the number of Church members soon followed. One of the early converts was Parley P. Pratt, a "Campbellite" preacher. The Campbellites were officially known as the Disciples of Christ, founded in the state of Ohio by Alexander Campbell, Walter Scott, and Sidney Rigdon. The group believed in the imminent return of Jesus Christ and in the restoration of the priesthood with all of its powers, as reflected in the Bible.

Through the efforts of Parley P. Pratt, Sidney Rigdon, pastor of a Campbellite congregation in Mentor, Ohio, not only joined the restored Church in the fall of 1830, but brought some of his flock with him.[3] The growth of the Church in Ohio was so rapid that the small

---

1 Donald Q. Cannon and Lyndon W. Cook, *Far West Record* (Salt Lake City: Deseret, 1983), 1.

2 *Ibid.*, 3; see D&C 26.

3 Indeed, Sidney Rigdon and one of his followers, Frederick G. Williams, were later to become Joseph Smith's counselors when the First Presidency was organized. It was Rigdon who brought Edward Partridge—The Church's first bishop—to meet Joseph Smith in Fayette, New York, in December 1830, and had him baptized.

congregations in New York paled by comparison. Joseph Smith received a commandment from the Lord to go to Ohio (D&C 37; 38:32; 39:14-15) and arrived there at the beginning of February 1831, settling in the town of Kirtland (*History of the Church* 1:145).

As Church membership grew, branches were established in various towns throughout the northern Ohio region. Following instructions given at the Church's first meeting (D&C 20:44-45), elders were ordained and appointed to lead each of these branches (cf. D&C 41:2-3; BC 43:3-4). From time to time, these elders met in conference.

At one of these early conferences, held on February 9, 1831[4], it was noted that the elders, priests and teachers were responsible for teaching the principles of the gospel (cf. D&C 20:42, 50, 59). Consequently, a number of the brethren holding these offices were called upon to go out and teach as missionaries (D&C 42:4, 12; BC 44:5, 13).

The February 1831 conference also laid down guidelines for ordination of men to the priesthood:

> It shall not be given to any one to go forth to preach my gospel, or to build up my church, except he be ordained by some one who has authority and it is known to the church that he has authority and has been regularly ordained by the heads of the church. (D&C 42:11; BC 44:12)

At the same conference, it was determined that two or more elders should be called when a sick member requires a blessing (D&C 42:43-44; BC 44:35; cf. James 5:14-15). In a section recorded the following month, Joseph Smith further clarified the role of elders by saying that they were to lay on hands for the Holy Ghost (D&C 49:14; BC 52:15).

The Bishop

During the first ten months of the Church's existence, those holding the priesthood restored by Peter, James and John were simply called "elders." Except for the designation of the First and Second Elder and an occasional reference to the office of apostle, there was no attempt at specialization in the office of elder. This was to change,

---

4 See D&C 42:1; BC 44:1, where some of the men listed were apostles.

however, in Kirtland, beginning with the introduction of the office of bishop. The first mention of the title "bishop" came in a revelation dated February 4, 1831:

> I have called my servant Edward Partridge; and I give a commandment, that he should be appointed by the voice of the church, and ordained a bishop unto the church, to leave his merchandise and to spend all his time in the labors of the church;
>
> To see to all things as it shall be appointed unto him in my laws in the day that I shall give them. (D&C 41:9-10; BC 43:11)

The English title "bishop" comes from the New Testament Greek term *episkopos,* meaning "overseer." When Edward Partridge was ordained as the first latter-day bishop on February 4, 1831, the Lord had not yet revealed what he was to oversee. Five days later, a revelation instructed Bishop Partridge to stand in his appointed office (D&C 42:10; BC 44:10), then proceeded to indicate that the bishop's duty was to collect for the poor (D&C 42:30-32; BC 44:26). In an earlier revelation dated January 2 of the same year, the Lord called for the appointment of men to look after the poor of the Church, telling them to leave the state of New York (D&C 38:34-36; BC 40:30). In a discourse delivered nearly fifty years later, Elder Orson Pratt rightly pointed out that, while these men performed the duties normally assigned to bishops, there were, as yet, no individuals holding that office in the Church.[5]

In the revelation of February 9, 1831, the Lord instructed that goods were to be laid before "the bishop of my church, and two of the elders, such as he shall appoint and set apart for that purpose" (BC 44:26). The later version, in D&C 42:31 (1835 D&C 13:8) reads, "the bishop of my church and his counselors, two of the elders, or high priests." At the time of the original revelation, there was no mention of "counselors" for the bishop, nor did the office of high priest exist. These were both to come at a conference held five months later. For

---

5 *Journal of Discourses* 22:3. His comments are included in the appendix to this volume.

the moment, the term "elder" referred to one holding the priesthood restored by Peter, James and John.[6]

Continuing the 1831 revelation on the duties of the bishop, we read:

> And the residue shall be kept in my storehouse, to administer to the poor and needy, as shall be appointed by the elders of the church and the bishop. (BC 44:29)[7]

> And the elders are to assist the bishop in all things, and he is to see that their families are supported . . . as may be thought best by the elders and bishop. (BC 44:54)[8]

Following these verses, the revelation in its earlier form (in the BC), and that given in the D&C, go their separate ways, discussing different matters. D&C 42 (from verse 78) is the same as BC Chap. 17 (the amalgamation of the two was made in the 1835 edition), while BC 44:56-57 includes some priesthood matters not included in the 1835 or later editions, as follows:

> And again, the elders and bishop, shall counsel together, and they shall do by the direction of the Spirit as it must needs be

---

6 In a discourse delivered on April 6, 1879, Erastus Snow indicated that, in the revelation of April 6, 1830 (D&C 20), the term "elder" embraced the offices that later became elder, apostle, high priest, high councilor, seventy, and even the First Presidency (*Journal of Discourses* 20:182). It is for this reason that it is perfectly in order, even today, to call a General Authority, regardless of his priesthood office, "Elder."

7 The 1835 edition of D&C 13:10 (1981 D&C 42:34) reads, "Therefore the residue shall be kept in my storehouse to administer to the poor and needy, as shall by appointed by the High Council of the church, and the bishop and his council." This wording was significant after the organization of high councils and after the bishop had gained counselors, but it had no meaning in February 1831. Whether the term "elders" here refers to the First and Second Elder or to elders in general or to the elders specifically chosen to assist the bishop is uncertain, though the latter is likely, as appears from the quote that follows, taken from the same revelation.

8 The revised version, in D&C 42:71-73 (1835 D&C 13:19), reads:
> And the elders or high priests who are appointed to assist the bishop as counselors in all things, are to have their families supported . . . as may be thought best or decided by the counselors and bishop. And the bishop, also, shall receive his support, or a just remuneration for all his services in the church.

Again, the terms "high priest" and "counselor" could have had no meaning at the time the original revelation was given and were inserted only after these offices had been instituted in the Church. As for the "remuneration" paid to the bishop and his counselors, with the exception of later Presiding Bishoprics, this was discontinued when the united order ceased.

necessary. There shall be as many appointed as needs be necessary to assist the bishop in obtaining place for the brethren from New York, that they may be together as much as can be, and as they are directed by the Holy Spirit; and every family shall have a place, that they may live by themselves—

And every church shall be organized in as close bodies as they can be; and this for a wise purpose—even so. Amen.

The "wise purpose" probably refers to the Lord's ultimate plan to organize wards and stakes from these branches. The men appointed to "assist the bishop in obtaining place for the brethren from New York" are obviously the same ones mentioned in the revelation from the previous month, to which we have alluded above. In subsequent revelations, such men are termed "agents" for the bishop.

In a revelation dated March 8, 1831, the Lord spoke of the various gifts of the Spirit, and indicated that the bishop and the (presiding) elders were to have the power of discerning gifts, in order that no one make any unsupported claims before the Church (D&C 46:27-29; BC 49:23-24).

The "elders" in this and other passages cited above must refer to the presiding elders and not to elders in general. That this is the case is reflected in another revelation given the same month, in which there is mention of "the bishop and the elders of the church" (BC 51:6). In D&C 48:6 (1835 D&C 64:2), this was changed to read "the presidency and the bishop of the church." At the time the revelations were received, the Church was under the direction of the First and Second Elder, Joseph Smith and Oliver Cowdery. Later, when the First Presidency was organized, it became appropriate to make a change in the text to keep current with the government of the expanding Church.

In later years, Brigham Young found it significant that the first office in the Church was that of Apostle, while the second was that of Bishop, thus representing the spiritual and temporal heads of the kingdom.[9]

_____

9 *Journal of Discourses* 1:135. Extracts from his discourse are included in the appendix to this volume.

High Priests

It was in the midst of the organization of the bishopric that the first high priests were ordained in the restored Church. The occasion was a conference held in Kirtland, Ohio, June 3-6, 1831, at which time some of the elders were called to go on missions to Jackson County, Missouri.[10] The official history of the Church reads:

> On the 3rd of June,[11] the Elders from the various parts of the country where they were laboring, came in; and the conference before appointed, convened in Kirtland; and the Lord displayed His power to the most perfect satisfaction of the Saints. The man of sin[12] was revealed, and the authority of the Melchisedek Priesthood was manifested and conferred for the first time upon several of the Elders. (*History of the Church* 1:175-176)[13]

Some modern critics of the LDS Church have used this passage to argue that Joseph Smith never laid claim to having the "Melchizedek Priesthood" (as opposed to the lesser or Aaronic Priesthood) prior to June of 1831. They further contend that this implies he did not receive nor claim to have received the apostleship from Peter, James and John, until after that date. They seem to be unaware (or at least unwilling to recognize) that the terms "Melchizedek Priesthood" and "High Priesthood" were, in the early days of the Church, used in reference to priests of the order of Melchizedek as opposed to priests of the order of Aaron. It was only later that the term "priesthood" came to be used in its more general meaning of divine authority, referring to all of those who received such authority, regardless of their title.[14] What is meant

---

10 In May of that year, the prophet Joseph received the following revelation for Ezra Booth: "Let my servant Ezra humble himself and at the conference meeting he shall be ordained unto power from on high and he shall go from thence if he be obedient unto my commandments and proclaim my gospel unto the western regions with my servants" (Kirtland Revelation Book, 91-92).

11 According to the manuscript history by Joseph Smith, this took place on June 6, but according to the record kept by by then-Church Historian, John Whitmer, the conference began on the third, with the revelation concerning the priesthood being given on the sixth.

12 This refers to Satan, who attempted to thwart the Lord's plans.

13 On 7 May 1861, Brigham Young discussed the events of these early days. His comments, taken from *Journal of Discourses* 9:88-89, are included in the appendix to this volume.

14 There are many examples of the term "high priesthood" in early documents later being changed to read "high priest" or "high priests." For examples, see the appendix to this volume.

is that some of the elders present at the 1831 conference were ordained to the office now referred to as "high priest" (or Melchizedek priest).

Of the institution of the office of high priest, John Whitmer, then Church Historian, recorded:

> June 3, 1831. A general conference was called . . . the Lord made manifest to Joseph that it was necessary that such of the elders as were considered worthy, should be ordained to the high priesthood.[15]

Parley P. Pratt also recalled the events of that day:

> On the sixth of June, 1831, a general conference was convened at Kirtland, consisting of all the Elders, far and near, who could be got together . . .
>
> Several were then selected by revelation, through President Smith, and ordained to the High Priesthood after the order of the Son of God; which is after the order of Melchizedek. This was the first occasion in which this priesthood had been revealed and conferred upon the Elders in this dispensation, although the office of an Elder is the same in a certain degree, but not in the fulness. On this occasion I was ordained to this holy ordinance and calling by President Smith.[16]

The order of ordination is given in the Far West Record.[17] Joseph Smith "laid his hands upon Lyman Wight and ordained him to the High Priesthood",[18] then ordained John Murdock, Reynolds Cahoon, Harvey Wheelock and Hyrum Smith. Lyman Wight then ordained Joseph Smith Sr., Joseph Smith Jr., Parley P. Pratt, Thomas B. Marsh, Isaac Morley, Edward Partridge, Joseph Wakefield, Martin Harris, Ezra Thayre, Ezra Booth, John Corrill, Samuel H. Smith, John

---

15 John Whitmer's History, Chapter 7. See also John Corrill, *A Brief History of the Church of Jesus Christ of Latter Day Saints* (ms., 1839), 18, where he records that "About fifty elders met, which was about all the elders [who] then belonged to the church . . . the Malchisedic [*sic*] priesthood [again referring to the office of high priest] was then for the first time introduced, and conferred on several of the elders."

16 Parley P. Pratt (Jr.), ed.,*Autobiography of Parley Parker Pratt* (Salt Lake City: 1873; 3rd ed., Deseret Book Co., 1938), 68.

17 Donald Q. Cannon and Lyndon W. Cook, *Far West Record*, 7.

18 Wording from *John Whitmer's History,* Chapter 5.

Whitmer and Sidney Rigdon. All of those thus ordained as high priests were then blessed by Bishop Edward Partridge.

More than two decades later, George A. Smith, referring to one of these men, Ezra Booth, said, "He was present when the elders first received the ordination of the high priesthood. They met together in June, 1831 . . . the manifestation of God being on Joseph, he set apart some of the elders to the High Priesthood" (*Journal of Discourses* 2:4).

Oliver Cowdery, the Church's Second Elder, was not to receive this blessing until nearly three months later. Under the date of August 28, 1831, we read, "At a Church meeting held in Kirtland, Ohio, Oliver Cowdery was ordained to the High Priesthood by the voice of the Church & command of the Lord under the hand of br. Sidney Rigdon."[19]

Some years later, David Whitmer criticized the innovation brought into the Church in June of 1831, believing it to be a false doctrine "introduced at the instigation of Sydney [*sic*] Rigdon." He claimed "the office of high priest was never spoken of, and never thought of being established in the church until Rigdon came in . . . During 1829, several times we were told by Brother Joseph that an elder was the highest office in the church."[20]

Evidently, David Whitmer felt that Sidney Rigdon persuaded Joseph Smith to add an extra priesthood office in order that some of the elders might be considered higher or more important than the others. His reaction shows a resistance to change that is typical of some today who also find it difficult to accept organizational changes, even when they are clearly necessary in a rapidly expanding church.

In his discussion of the high priesthood, Whitmer expressed his belief that the idea of the office of high priest had been taken by Sidney Rigdon from the Old Testament and the Book of Mormon. The principal Book of Mormon reference to the subject is Alma 13, where we find that those who attained to the high priesthood in ancient times were translated (cf. JST Genesis 14:26-36). This ties in with Joseph

---

19 Donald Q. Cannon and Lyndon W. Cook, *Far West Record,* 10.

20 Some of David Whitmer's remarks on this subject—all drawn from his "An Address to All Believers in Christ" (Richmond, Missouri, 1887)—are cited in the appendix to this volume.

Smith's explanation of the office, given in a discourse delivered in Kirtland on October 25, 1831:

> Br. Joseph Smith jr. said that the order of the Highpriesthood [*sic*] is that they have power given them to seal up the Saints unto eternal life. And said it was the privilege of every Elder present to be ordained to the Highpriesthood.[21]

Herein lies a glimpse into the future of the priesthood, with the promise that men and women can, if faithful, become kings and queens, priests and priestesses unto God.[22] In a revelation dated February 10, 1832, the Prophet records that the heirs of the celestial kingdom are "priests and kings . . . priests of the Most High, after the order of Melchizedek, which was after the order of Enoch, which was after the order of the Only Begotten Son" (D&C 76:56-57; 1835 D&C 91:5).

As for David Whitmer's claim that the high priest was more important than the elder and thus an office available only to the elite, it appears to be refuted by Joseph Smith's statement that "every Elder present" might be ordained to the high priesthood.[23] Indeed, as we learn from subsequent revelations, the office of elder is the general office of the higher priesthood, while that of high priest is specially provided for those elders who are called to administrative duties in the Church, as will be discussed later.

After the June 1831 conference, it appears to have been standard Church practice to call high priests, rather than elders, to head the various branches of the Church, wherever possible. And while previous revelations had been addressed to "the elders assembled,"[24] the revelation of December 4, 1831 is addressed to "the high priests assembled" (D&C 72:1; 1835 89:1; see also D&C 89:1, dated February 27, 1833).

---

21 Donald Q. Cannon and Lyndon W. Cook, *Far West Record*, 20-21; see D&C 68:12.

22 Cf. Exodus 19:6; 1 Peter 2:9; Revelation 1:6; 5:10; 20:6.

23 Note the following entries in the *Far West Record:* October 5, 1832: "certain Elders present should express their minds concerning ordination to the Highpriesthood." (Donald Q. Cannon and Lyndon W. Cook, *Far West Record*, 57) September 10, 1834: "Application made by James Emmet Elder to be promoted to the highpriesthood." (ibid., 98)

24 D&C 41:2; 42:1; 43:1; 44:1; 50:1; 52:1; 57:1; 58:1; 60:1; 61:2; 64:1; 67:1.

Concerning the relationship of the high priests to the elders, Joseph Smith wrote to the brother of Jared Carter on April 13, 1833, as follows:

> The duty of a High Priest is to administer in spiritual and holy things, and to hold communion with God; but not to exercise monarchial government, or to appoint meetings for the Elders without their consent. And again, it is the High Priests' duty to be better qualified to teach principles and doctrines than the Elders; for the office of Elder is an appendage to the High Priesthood, and it concentrates and centers in one. (*History of the Church* 1:338)

This statement clarifies the use of the term "appendage to the high priesthood" as it appears in the D&C 84:29-30, under the date of September 22-23, 1832, where we read, "And again, the offices of elder and bishop are necessary appendages belonging unto the high priesthood. And again, the offices of teacher and deacon are necessary appendages belonging to the lesser priesthood."

By "high priesthood" was meant, at that time in Church history, the office of high priest. Therefore, we are to understand that the office of elder is an "appendage" to the office of high priest, just as the offices of teacher and deacon are "appendages" to the office of priest of the Aaronic order.

Four years later, the Lord clarified this subject (in D&C 85:1-12) by showing that the high priest's office is principally for presiding officers, while the elder is a more general office, having the same power and authority, but presiding only when there is no high priest present. Even after the calling of high priests, however, men holding this office were sometimes called by the more general title of "elder."[25]

---

25 For example, under the date of March 17, 1834, we read of "Elders Sidney Rigdon and Lyman Wight," who were two of the very first high priests ordained in June 1831 (*History of the Church* 2:44).

The Bishopric

At the June 1831 conference, "br. John Corrill & Isaac Morley were ordained assistants to the bishop under the hand of Lyman Wight."[26] This constituted the first complete bishopric in the Church. During the same month, Algernon Sidney Gilbert was ordained an elder and appointed an agent to the Church by Bishop Partridge (D&C 53:3-4; BC 55:4).[27]

The choice of the bishop's counselors appears to have been made during the preceding month. In a revelation dated to May 1831, the Lord instructed Edward Partridge to organize the people (D&C 51:1-2).[28] He and "those whom he has chosen" (evidently his counselors, and possibly the "bishop's agents" as well) were to administer the law of consecration and stewardship (D&C 51:3-20), while the bishop or his designated agent was to handle financial matters for the Church (D&C 51:12).

In a revelation dated August 1, 1831, there is mention of Bishop Partridge and his "counselors" (D&C 58:24; BC 54:30). It is at this time we learn that the one appointed to this office (Edward Partridge, from verse 14), with his counselors, is to be a judge in Israel, judging according to the laws given to the prophets (D&C 58:17-18; BC 54:21). The role of the bishop as a judge was also noted in a revelation of the following month (D&C 64:40). Subsequently, when one of the earliest revelations (given February 9, 1831) concerning the role of the bishop was republished in the 1835 D&C (13:22; 1981 D&C 42:82), it was noted that the bishop should be at the church court, if possible—a fact not mentioned in the earliest version (BC 47).

This was a new role for the bishop. The original intent of naming the bishop as a "judge in Israel" was to empower him to assign stewardships, in much the same way Joshua divided up land inheritances among the tribes of Israel (Joshua 18-19).

During the fall of 1831, Bishop Edward Partridge moved to Missouri to preside over the Saints gathering there to the land denominated

---

26 Donald Q. Cannon and Lyndon W. Cook, *Far West Record*, 7.

27 Brother Gilbert's calling is mentioned in D&C 57, July 20, 1831, and in D&C 58, August 1, 1831.

28 This revelation was not included in the Book of Commandments in 1833. It first shows up as Section 23 in the 1835 D&C.

"Zion." It was about this time that another bishop's agent was called: "Br. Newel K. Whitney was ordained an agent unto the Disciples in this land under the hand of br. Oliver Cowdery."[29] Brother Whitney (who later became second bishop of the Church) was called to head a mercantile establishment that, under the economic system then being instituted in the Church, constituted an ecclesiastical calling for the administration of the law of consecration and stewardship (see D&C 63:45).

During the month of November 1831, Joseph Smith received two revelations concerning the role of the bishop. One spoke of the bishop, of the agent over the Lord's storehouse and of the stewards over temporal things (D&C 70:11; 1835 26:3). The other notes that additional bishops are to be called (D&C 68:14; 1835 D&C 22:2).

A second bishop was, indeed, appointed—for the Kirtland area—from among the high priests, as the Lord indicated in a revelation given the following month, December 4, 1831 (D&C 72:2; 1835 89:1).[30] Newel K. Whitney, who had been serving as a bishop's agent in Missouri, was called to fill this position and received his ordination on December 31, 1831.

In the revelation calling Bishop Whitney, we find more about the duty of the bishop's office. Elders were to render an account of their stewardships (under the law of consecration and stewardship) to the bishop, with all records going to the bishop in Zion, i.e., to Edward Partridge (D&C 72:5-6, 16, 19; 1835 D&C 89:2, 4). Members of the Church going to Zion (Missouri) were to have a certificate from the bishop (in Kirtland) or three elders (D&C 72:24-25; 1835 D&C 89:5).

The duty of the bishop was to be made known by the commandments already given and by decisions made by the Church membership assembled in conference (D&C 72:7, 9ff; 1835 D&C 89:1, 3ff). Nevertheless, insofar as the law of consecration and stewardship was concerned, the bishop was to be judge (D&C 72:17; 1835 D&C 89:4).

From this time on, we read of two bishops in the records of the Church, the Bishop in Zion and the Bishop in Kirtland (see e.g., D&C

---

29 Donald Q. Cannon and Lyndon W. Cook, *Far West Record*, 11.

30 As with D&C 68:15, 22, the original revelation, as published in *The Evening and Morning Star* 1:7, December 1832, had the bishop chosen by the high priests, not the first presidency (which did not yet exist) in what corresponds to D&C 72:2 (cf. verse 7).

84:104). At a conference held in Zion on April 26, 1832, a revelation spoke of the Lord's storehouse (D&C 82:18) and commanded that Edward Partridge, Newel K. Whitney, Sidney Rigdon, Joseph Smith, Oliver Cowdery, and Martin Harris and others were "to manage the affairs of the poor, and all things pertaining to the bishopric both in the land of Zion and in the land of Kirtland" (D&C 82:11-12).

Instructions for Bishop Whitney came on September 22-23, 1832. He was to travel and minister to the poor in the churches (branches), and was to employ an agent for secular business (D&C 84:112-113).[31] A revelation received on March 8, 1833 also instructed the bishop to obtain an agent, who should be a rich and faithful man (D&C 90:22-23). This requirement may have been an attempt to avoid placing someone who would be easily tempted by the riches of the world into a position where he could defraud the Church of offerings received from the faithful.

In March of 1832, a set of instructions concerning the bishops was revealed to Joseph Smith and Sidney Rigdon:

> Verily thus saith the Lord unto you my servant Sidney and Joseph: I reveal unto you for your own profit and instruction concerning the Bishops of my Church—What is their duty in the Church. Behold, it is their duty to stand in the office of their Bishopric and to fill the judgment seat which I have appointed unto them—to administer the benefits of the Church or the overplusses of all who are in their stewardships, according to the commandments as they are severally appointed. And the property or that which they receive of the Church is not their own but belongeth to the Church. Wherefore, it is the property of the Lord and it is for the poor of the Church, to be administered according to the law—For it is the will of the Lord that the Church should be made equal in all things. Wherefore the Bishops are accountable before the Lord for their stewardships, to administer of their stewardship (in the which they are appointed by commandment jointly with you my servants) unto the

---

31 When written in the Kirtland Revelation Book, this passage did not include the name of Newel K. Whitney. It was subsequently added above the line and marked for insertion. (The omission may have been due to a scribal error.) The word "bishop" in D&C 84:114 read "bishops" on the same page (Kirtland Revelation Book, 30).

Lord, as well as you my servants or the rest of the Church, that the benefits of all may be dedicated unto the Lord, that the Lord's storehouse may be filled always, that ye may all grow in temporal as well as spiritual things. And now verily I say unto you, the Bishops must needs be separated unto their Bishopric and judgment seats from [the] care of business.[32]

On November 27, 1832, Joseph Smith wrote a letter to W. W. Phelps, an assistant to Bishop Edward Partridge in Zion (Independence, Missouri), in which he spoke of "the Bishop, the man that God has appointed in a legal way, agreeably to the law given to organize and regulate the Church, and all the affairs of the same" (*History of the Church* 1:298). From this letter came D&C 85, which deals with Bishop Edward Partridge and his responsibilities in relation to the law of consecration and stewardship in the land of Zion.

---

32 Revelation to Joseph Smith, March 1832, Newel K. Whitney Papers, Harold B. Lee Library at Brigham Young University.

Chapter 4

GOVERNMENT OF THE EARLY CHURCH

Hearken, O ye elders of my church whom I have called, behold I give unto you a commandment, that ye shall assemble yourselves together to agree upon my word; And by the prayer of your faith ye shall receive my law, that ye may know how to govern my church and have all things right before me. (D&C 41:2-3)

By June 1831, there were five basic priesthood offices in the Church: high priest, elder, priest, teacher and deacon. In addition, there were special administrative officers such as the "First Elders" (who were apostles) and the bishopric and agents. Presiding officers had been chosen for various "churches" after Joseph Smith moved to Ohio. For example, Newel Knight remained in Colesville, New York, to preside over the Saints there. Following instructions from the prophet, the entire group moved as a body to Ohio, where they began settling in Thompson. A wealthy Church member living in Thompson had promised to provide land for these Saints, but later withdrew his offer.

In June 1831, Newel Knight and other elders from the Thompson group came to Joseph Smith in Kirtland and the Lord revealed his will concerning them (History of the Church 1:180-1). This revelation became D&C 54 (note especially verse 2, which speaks of Elder Knight's "office").

In consequence of the instructions received, the group left the next month to settle in Missouri.[1] In mid-July, Joseph Smith brought others to Missouri as well, including Bishop Edward Partridge (*History of the Church* 1:188, 191), and the settlement of Zion began to take shape.

---

1 John Whitmer's History, Chapter 8.

As other members of the Church moved to Missouri over the next few years, it became necessary to more fully organize them into administrative bodies. Prior to this time, local groups were called "churches." Now, for the first time, we read of "branches" of the Church:

> Minutes of a special Conference held in Zion July 13, 1832 at the house of Joseph Knight in Kaw Township for the purpose of dividing the Church on the land of Zion, into branches for the better convenience of holding meetings & organizing the Church &c.[2]

At a conference of high priests held the following December 4, two high priests were "appointed to go forth and set in order the different Branches of the Church of Christ in the land of Zion & see that there are High Priests or Elders set apart to see that meetings are held & the officers & members do their duties."[3]

Though most of the "presiding elders" after 1831 appear to have been high priests, there were some who were, in fact, elders. In a letter addressed to the "Church of Christ in Thompson, Geauga County Ohio," the First Presidency, on February 6, 1833, wrote of "Salmon Gee . . . who has been ordained by us, in obedience to the commandments of God, to the office of Elder to preside over the Church in Thompson." He is thereafter referred to as "Salmon Gee, Elder of the Church in Thompson" (*History of the Church* 1:324-5).

The First Presidency

In November 1831, the prophet Joseph Smith recorded three revelations dealing with the Presidency of the High Priesthood. One of these revelations comprises pages 84-86 of the Kirtland Revelation Book (KRB), which became D&C 107:59-92, 99-100. In D&C 107, it is appended to a later revelation, one verse of which (58) referred to that which followed as "the revelation which says." The KRB version has a preface reading, "Revelation given November 1831 . . . regulat-

---

2 Donald Q. Cannon and Lyndon W. Cook, *Far West Record* (Salt Lake City: Deseret, 1983), 52.

3 *Ibid.*, 58.

ing the Presidency of the Church." Some verses (e.g., 76) refer to "a President of the High Priesthood after the order of Melchizedek" being tried by the bishop. In one case, the word "President" in the Kirtland Revelation Book was changed to "Presidency" in D&C 107:79.

Another revelation of November 1831 is D&C 68. The 1835 edition (22:2) speaks of the "First Presidency of the Melchizedek Priesthood," while subsequent editions reworded this to read "First Presidency of the Church" (D&C 68:19).

On January 25, 1832, Joseph Smith was sustained as President of the High Priesthood (i.e., of those holding the office of high priest) in a conference held at Amherst, Ohio.[4] At the time he had not yet chosen counselors. This took place two months later, as the prophet noted in Kirtland Revelation Book, 10-11:

> March 8th 1832
> Chose this day and ordain[ed] brother Jesse Gause and broth[er] Sidney to be my counsellors of the ministry of the presidency of [the] high Priesthood.

The action taken at the Amherst conference was subsequently ratified by the Church at a conference in Zion, Missouri on April 26, 1832. The minutes of the conference note that Joseph Smith was "acknowledged by the High Priests in the land of Zion to be President of the High Priesthood, according to commandment and ordination in Ohio, at the Conference held in Amherst Jan 25 1832."[5]

Sidney Rigdon, Joseph's first counselor, had, from the time of his conversion in the Kirtland area in 1830, played an important role in the leadership of the Church. In a revelation dated December 1830, the Lord told him, "Thou art blessed, for thou shalt do great things. Behold thou wast sent forth, even as John, to prepare the way before me, and before Elijah which should come, and thou knewest it not" (D&C 35:4; BC 37:5-6). The same revelation speaks of the calling of Joseph Smith:

---

4 See preface to D&C 75.

5 Donald Q. Cannon and Lyndon W. Cook, *Far West Record*, 44; see also *History of the Church* 1:267.

And I have sent forth the fulness of my gospel by the hand of my servant Joseph; and in weakness have I blessed him;

And I have given unto him the keys of the mystery of those things which have been sealed, even things which were from the foundation of the world, and the things which shall come from this time until the time of my coming, if he abide in me, and if not, another will I plant in his stead.

Wherefore, watch over him that his faith fail not, and it shall be given by the Comforter, the Holy Ghost, that knoweth all things. (D&C 35:17-19; BC 37:18-20)

Sidney Rigdon is mentioned together with Joseph Smith in revelations dated February 9, 1831 (D&C 42:4; BC 44:5), June 1831 (D&C 53:5; BC 55:5), August 1831 (D&C 63:65; BC 64:77), December 1, 1831 (D&C 71:1; 1835 D&C 90:1) and January 10, 1832 (D&C 73:3; 1835 D&C 29:2), indicating the interest the Lord had in this man who was to become Joseph Smith's first counselor. In two revelations from August 1831, Joseph Smith, Oliver Cowdery and Sidney Rigdon were named together (D&C 60:6, 17; BC 61:9, 24; D&C 61:23, 30; BC 62:25, 31). In a revelation dated November 1831, these three are named along with Martin Harris, John Whitmer and William W. Phelps (all of them former scribes to Joseph Smith) as stewards over the revelations (D&C 70:1-3; 1835 D&C 26:1). On February 16, 1832, while Joseph Smith and Sidney Rigdon were engaged in the Bible translation project (see verse 15), the two received the revelation known as "The Vision" (D&C 76:11). In March of 1832, the Lord commanded Newel K. Whitney (bishop in Kirtland), Joseph Smith and Sidney Rigdon to sit in council with the saints in Zion.[6]

Joseph's second counselor was Jesse Gause, whose name has been variously spelled in the early records. In the minutes of the conference of April 26, 1832, he is listed among the high priests who were pre-

---

6 D&C 78:9. A similar listing is found in D&C 82:11 (BC 86:4), where the original revelation of April 26, 1832 listed a number of individuals by code names. Here, we find together Bishop Edward Partridge, Bishop Newel K. Whitney, Sidney Rigdon, Oliver Cowdery, and Martin Harris.

sent in Zion with Joseph Smith and Sidney Rigdon.[7] In subsequent minutes, similar lists appear.[8]

The revelation confirming the calling of the First Presidency was given in March 1832 and is now D&C 81. In the first verse, we read that Frederick G. Williams was called "to be a high priest in my church, and a counselor unto my servant Joseph Smith, Jun." This, however, is anachronistic, for it was Jesse Gause's name that appeared in earlier versions of the revelation, as the preface to the 1981 edition of D&C 81 indicates.[9] On page 17 of the Kirtland Revelation Book, we find a handwritten version of the revelation contained in D&C 81. For verse 1, the name "Jesse" has been blotted out and the name "Frederick G. Williams" added to the page in another hand. Gause was excommunicated from the Church in December of 1832, and was replaced by Williams in March of the following year. As a result, when the revelation was published in the 1835 edition of D&C (see 79:1), Frederick G. Williams's name was substituted. Several other entries in the Kirtland Revelation Book list Williams as a counselor to Joseph Smith.[10]

The First Presidency and the Keys

In the revelation calling Jesse Gause to be Joseph's counselor, the Lord spoke of the prophet as the one "unto whom I have given the keys of the kingdom, which belong always unto the Presidency of the

---

7 Donald Q. Cannon and Lyndon W. Cook, *Far West Record*, 44, where his name is spelled Gauss.

8 E.g., under the date of April 30, 1832, minutes of the "Council of the literary Firm of Zion" (for publishing Church works), there are listed "Joseph Smith jr. President, Sidney Rigdon, John Whitmer, Oliver Cowdery, William W. Phelps and Jesse Gauss, one of the President's Councillors" (ibid., 46). Under the same date we have the minutes of the "United Firm" (United Order, or Order of Enoch, designed to generate Church revenues), indicating the presence of "Joseph Smith jr. President of Conference also of the Highpriesthood, Edward Partridge Bishop, Newel K. Whitney Bishop of Kirtland, Sidney Gilbert, Agent in Zion, Sidney Rigdon, Counsillor of President, John Whitmer, Lord's Clerk, Jesse Gauss, Counsillor to the President" (ibid., 47).

9 For a discussion, see Robert J. Woodford, "Jesse Gause, Counselor to the Prophet," *BYU Studies* 15 (Spring 1975), 362-364.

10 A note to the end of revelation of December 6, 1832 (D&C 86) on page 32 of the KRB notes that it was transcribed by Frederick G. Williams, who is said to be "counselor." A note appended to the revelation of December 27, 1832 (D&C 88:1-126) refers to Williams as "scribe counselor to Joseph" (KRB, 46). At the end of the next revelation of January 3, 1833 (D&C 88:127-137), he is also called "Counselor" (KRB, 48).

High Priesthood" (D&C 81:12).[11] Another revelation received the same month (March 1832) describes the nature of these keys:

> And unto the office of the Presidency of the High Priesthood I have given authority to preside with the assistance of his councilors over all the concerns of the Church . . . For unto you I have given the keys of the kingdom and if you transgress not they shall never be taken from you. Wherefore feed my sheep, even so, Amen.[12]

These keys are mentioned several times in a major revelation on the calling of the First Presidency, given a year later, on March 8, 1833, from which we extract the following:

> Therefore, thou art blessed from henceforth that bear the keys of the kingdom given unto you; which kingdom is coming forth for the last time.
>
> Verily I say unto you, the keys of this kingdom shall never be taken from you, while thou art in the world, neither in the world to come;
>
> Nevertheless, through you shall the oracles be given to another, yea, even unto the church . . .
>
> And again, verily I say unto thy brethren, Sidney Rigdon and Frederick G. Williams, their sins are forgiven them also, and they are accounted as equal with thee in holding the keys of this last kingdom;
>
> As also through your administration the keys of the school of the prophets,[13] which I have commanded to be organized . . .

---

11 The passage reads the same in the Kirtland Revelation Book (p. 18) and in 1835 D&C 79:1. A similar thought is found in the patriarchal blessing pronounced on the head of Joseph Smith by Oliver Cowdery in Kirtland, on September 22, 1835: "By the keys of the kingdom shall he lead Israel into the land of Zion, while the house of Jacob shouts in the dance and in the song—"Joy O my soul in that day, for thou shalt be with him and bear thy part in the keys which are confirmed upon thee for an everlasting priesthood, forever and ever." (Patriarchal Blessings Book 2:28, LDS Church Historian's Office)

12 Revelation to Joseph Smith, March 1832, Newel K. Whitney Papers, Harold B. Lee Library, Brigham Young University.

13 The school of the prophets is discussed later in this chapter.

I give unto you a commandment that you continue in the ministry and presidency . . . preside over the affairs of the church and the school;

And from time to time, as shall be manifested by the Comforter, receive revelations to unfold the mysteries of the kingdom;

And set in order the churches . . .

And this shall be your business and mission in all your lives, to preside in council, and set in order all the affairs of this church and kingdom. (D&C 90:2-4, 6-7, 12-16)

From these passages, it is clear that the "First Presidency of the High Priesthood" was to preside not only over the high priests, but also over the "school" of the Elders or of the Prophets and over the entire Church. The same revelation names both Sidney Rigdon (verse 21) and Frederick G. Williams (verse 19) as counselors to Joseph Smith. Ten days later, they received their ordinations. Joseph Smith recorded the event under the date of March 18, 1833:

Elder Rigdon expressed a desire that himself and Brother Frederick G. Williams should be ordained to the offices to which they had been called, viz., those of Presidents of the High Priesthood, and to be equal in holding the keys of the kingdom with Brother Joseph Smith, Jun., according to the revelation given on the 8th of March, 1833. Accordingly I laid my hands on Brothers Sidney and Frederick, and ordained them to take part with me in holding the keys of this last kingdom, and to assist in the Presidency of the High Priesthood, as my Counselors." (*History of the Church* 1:334)

Thereafter, we find revelations mentioning not only Joseph Smith, but also his counselors.[14]

Though Sidney Rigdon and Frederick G. Williams were "counselors" to Joseph Smith, they are also called "Presidents." Thus, in a letter sent by Joseph Smith and Frederick G. Williams to John Smith on July 1, 1833, they call themselves "Presidents of the High

---

14 Cf. D&C 93:41, 44-45, 51-52 (dated May 6, 1833) and 100:1, 9, (dated October 12, 1833).

Priesthood" and place the title "Presidents" after their signatures (*History of the Church* 1:370). Under the date of November 19, 1833, Joseph termed Sidney Rigdon "a President of the Church of Christ" (*History of the Church* 1:443) and wrote of Frederick G. Williams that he "seeks with all his heart to magnify his Presidency in the Church of Christ" (*History of the Church* 1:444).

The First Presidency, as the highest authoritative body in the Church, replaced the offices of First and Second Elder, which Joseph Smith and Oliver Cowdery had held from 1830. In consequence of this, some changes had to be made in the wording of some of the earlier revelations when they were republished. A prime example is BC 51:6, in which we read of "the bishop and elders of the church." In the 1835 edition of the D&C (64:2), this was changed to read "the presidency and the bishop of the church," which is the text found in our current D&C 48:6.

By the same token, BC 49:23-24 (D&C 46:27-29) should also have been changed, for the "elders" who are there said to have the power of discerning gifts, along with the bishop, are the presiding elders of the Church, not all those holding the office of elder.

Though Joseph Smith was initially called "President of the High Priesthood of the Church; or, in other words, the Presiding High Priest over the High Priesthood of the Church" (D&C 107:65-66), it was clear from the beginning that he, along with his counselors, presided not just over the high priests, but over the Church as well. This had already been stated in the revelation of November 1831 that called for the establishment of the Presidency:

> And again, the duty of the President of the office of the High Priesthood is to preside over the whole church, and to be like unto Moses—
>
> Behold, here is wisdom; yea, to be a seer, a revelator, a translator, and a prophet, having all the gifts of God which he bestows upon the head of the church. (D&C 107:91-92)

Today, we call this the First Presidency because other presidencies were established, beginning in 1834, to preside over what became the stakes of the Church. This is discussed in Chapter 5, Organizing the Church

Quorums

With the organization in 1832 of the First Presidency to preside over the high priests of the Church, we see the beginning of what later came to be known as "quorums." During that same year certain men were chosen to preside over groups of high priests and elders in the Church. These callings came as a result of a revelation in November 1831. It called for elders to be appointed to preside over the priests, teachers, and deacons. By the time the revelation was published in 1835 D&C 3:31, the Church was sufficiently organized that the Lord had given new instructions, making it necessary to modify this passage to indicate that elders would preside over elders, priests over priests, and deacons over deacons (see D&C 107:60-63).

Some idea of the importance of quorums is found in Joseph Smith's 1833 description of "the house of the Lord for the Presidency," to be built in Zion, in which there would be a pulpit on the west end of the house "to be occupied by the High Priesthood as follows:"

1. the President and his council
2. the Bishop and his council
3. the High Priests
4. the Elders.

The pulpit on the east end was "to be occupied by the Lesser Priesthood":

1. the Presidency of the Lesser Priesthood
2. the Priests
3. the Teachers
4. the Deacons

(*History of the Church* 1:360)

At the same time, the prophet gave a list of names of temples to be built in Zion. They included:

the Presidency of the High and most Holy Priesthood, after the order of the Son of God

the Sacred Apostolic Repository, for the use of the Bishop

the Evangelical House, for the Priesthood of the Holy Order of God

the Elders of Zion

the Presidency of the High Priesthood, after the Order of Aaron
the Highest Priesthood after the Order of Aaron
the Teachers in Zion, Messenger to the Church
the Deacons in Zion, Help in Government
(*History of the Church* 1:359)

Of interest is that there are separate listings for a temple for the "the Bishop," for the "Presidency of the High Priesthood, after the Order of Aaron," and for "the Highest Priesthood after the Order of Aaron." Exactly what was meant by these terms is unknown, though there are some hints in the organization of the Aaronic Priesthood leaders established later at Nauvoo (discussed in Chapter 9, The Nauvoo Era).

School of the Prophets

The full organization of quorums, however, was not to come until 1835-36, when the Kirtland Temple was being completed. The revelation commanding the construction of the Temple came on December 27, 1832, in the section today known as D&C 88. Addressed to the elders returning from missions, the revelation also calls for the organization of a school of the prophets, complete with a presidency (with the President as teacher), for "those who are called to the ministry in the church, beginning at the high priests, even down to the deacons" (D&C 88:119-120, 122, 127:128, 132). The First Presidency was to be the Presidency of this School (D&C 90:6-7, 13), and a portion of the Temple was to be set aside "for the school of mine apostles" (D&C 95:17). On other occasions, the school is called a "school for the Elders" (*History of the Church* 2:169, 175, 180).

The function of the School of the Prophets was to teach principles of the Gospel and priesthood duties to men who had been ordained to various priesthood offices. In a very real sense, the School was a forerunner to the modern priesthood quorums.

Though Joseph Smith was instructed that the School was to be established in the Temple in Kirtland, the earliest "school of Elders" was actually organized in Zion, Missouri, in the late summer or fall of 1833, with Parley P. Pratt (later of the quorum of the Twelve) presiding.[15]

---

15 HC 1:400-401, fn citing the *Autobiography of Parley P. Pratt*, p. 100. See also D&C 97:3-5.

The organization of the school of the prophets did not take place until a number of months after the calling of the Twelve and the Seventy. On October 5, 1835, Joseph Smith "attended a Council of the Twelve Apostles . . . told them that it was the will of God they should take their families to Missouri next season; also this fall to attend the solemn assembly of the First Elders, for the organization of the School of the Prophets" (*History of the Church* 2:287).

The first meeting of this "Elders' School" was held on November 2, 1835, with a "lecture on the theory and practice of physics" (*History of the Church* 2:299-300). Joseph formally organized the school and dedicated it the following day (*History of the Church* 2:301). In the early stages, the school was held in a room over the Prophet's store. But when the Temple was completed, it officially became the "School of the Prophets" and held its first meetings in the new structure at the time of its dedication on March 27, 1836 (D&C 109:6-9 and subsequent verses).

Patriarchs

The year 1833 saw the introduction of the office of patriarch. The term has the literal meaning of "father-ruler" and refers to the role of the father in the family. In ancient times, as Joseph Smith was later to teach (D&C 107:39-57), this priesthood descended from father to son within the family. It authorized the head of the family to perform necessary ordinances (such as sacrifice), to preside in his family and to pronounce blessings on his posterity. The Old Testament has several examples of such blessings given by ancient patriarchs to their sons.

On December 18, 1833, the Prophet Joseph Smith gave the first patriarchal blessings of modern times to a group of assembled elders. In the minutes of the meeting, he is referred to as the first patriarch of the Church.[16] He blessed Oliver Cowdery, Joseph Smith Sr. and his wife Lucy, along with their sons Hyrum, Samuel and William. Oliver Cowdery also gave some patriarchal blessings on that occasion.

---

16 The narration was written by Oliver Cowdery as a preface to the patriarchal blessing pronounced by the Prophet Joseph on the head of his father, Joseph Smith Sr., and was included in the Patriarchal Blessings Book, Vol. 1:8 (LDS Church Historian's Office). For extracts from the blessing, see the appendix.

Following the pronouncement of the blessings, Joseph Smith Sr. was "ordained to the Patriarchal Priesthood, to hold keys of blessings on the heads of all the members of the Church, the Lord revealing that it was his right to hold this authority."[17]

The exact nature of the patriarchal office was not as yet fully revealed to the Church, however; this was to come later. When we re-examine the office of patriarch in subsequent chapters, we shall see that, aside from the Second Elder, those who received patriarchal blessings first in the Church were members of the Smith family. It is significant that the head of that family, Joseph Smith Sr., was at that time ordained as the first Patriarch in the Church.[18]

On the day Joseph Smith Sr. was ordained to the office of Patriarch, he was also set apart as an Assistant Counselor to his son, Joseph Jr., in the Presidency of the High Priesthood. Later the same day, Joseph's elder brother, Hyrum, and their uncle John were set apart to the same office. It is likely that these callings to the First Presidency reflected the Prophet's knowledge concerning the patriarchal authority of his family—a subject on which he did not elaborate until after the move to Nauvoo (discussed later in this volume).

Building up Zion

The year 1833 saw tremendous growth in the membership and organization of the Church in the state of Missouri. The first steps at organizing the members there took place in the spring of that year:

> On the 26th of March a council of High Priests, twenty-one in number, convened for the general welfare of the Church, in what was then called Zion, in Jackson County, Missouri . . . At the sitting of the council of the 26th of March, according to the plan taught at the solemn assembly, which was, that the seven High

---

17 Joseph Fielding Smith, *Essentials in Church History* (copyrighted by the Church of Jesus Christ of Latter-day Saints, 1950, published by Deseret Book Co., 23rd ed., 1969), p. 142. According to Heber C. Kimball, the Prophet Joseph ordained his father to the office of patriarch and later ordained his brother Hyrum to the same office (JD 5:7).

18 Brigham Young's statement that his own father was the first ordained patriarch in the Church (*Journal of Discourses* 18:240-241) is clearly in error. President Young, recalling the ordination of his father many years afterward (1874), placed the event in Missouri at the time of the Zion's Camp expedition. He was evidently unaware that Joseph Smith Sr. had been ordained patriarch the previous December. See the discussion in the appendix.

Priests who were sent from Kirtland to build up Zion, viz.—Oliver Cowdery, William W. Phelps, John Whitmer, Algernon Sidney Gilbert, Bishop Partridge and his two counselors—should stand at the head of affairs relating to the Church in that section of the Lord's vineyard; and these seven men, with the common consent of the branches comprising the Church were to appoint presiding Elders to take the watchcare of the several branches, as they were appointed. (*History of the Church* 1:335-6)

The "presiding Elders" of the branches were, in fact, high priests, as we learn from the minutes of the conference, in which we read, "Resolved that the Churches meet according to the appointments of the several highpriests [*sic*] stationed over their respective branches."[19]

Had Joseph Smith gone to Zion at this time, it is likely that these brethren would not have been appointed to head the Church in that region. Instead, they would have recognized Joseph as their President. However, in his absence, it was necessary that there be someone to carry out his instructions and to accomplish the Lord's will. By the fall of 1833, the Church in Missouri had decided that Edward Partridge would be their presiding official. Under the date of September 11, 1833, we read:

Bishop Partridge was acknowledged by the council in Zion to be the head of the Church in Zion at that time; and by virtue of his office, was acknowledged the moderator or president of the councils or conferences. Ten High Priests were appointed to watch over the ten branches of the Church in Zion.[20]

---

19 Donald Q. Canon and Lyndon W. Cook, *Far West Record* (Salt Lake City: Deseret, 1983), 61. Generally speaking, presiding elders for the various branches in Missouri were called to their positions by the leading high priests at Zion. But there were some exceptions. For example, Warren A. Cowdery was called to be a "presiding high priest" in the area around Freedom by means of a revelation given to the prophet Joseph Smith on November 25, 1834 (D&C 106:1).

20 *History of the Church* 1:409. The *Far West Record* for this date reads, "Appointed High Priests to wach [*sic*] over the several (Churches) Branches" (Donald Q. Canon and Lyndon W. Cook, *Far West Record*, 65). The minutes of this meeting are found in ibid., 36. Among those listed to head the branches were men who later became prominent in Church history, e.g., David Whitmer (who became President in Zion), Thomas B. Marsh and Parley P. Pratt (who became apostles), Lyman Wight and Newel Knight (who were called to the Zion high council), John Corrill and Daniel Stanton (soon to become, respectively a bishop and his counselor). Some of the presiding elders of the branches retained their positions when later called to the High Council in Zion.

New Bishops

With continued growth of Church membership in Missouri and with increased participation in what later came to be known as the "United Order," it was necessary to appoint additional bishops. On June 25, 1833, the First Presidency addressed a letter to William W. Phelps and other Church leaders in Missouri. A portion of the letter reads:

> Concerning Bishops, we recommend the following: Let Brother Isaac Morley be ordained second Bishop in Zion, and let Brother John Corrill be ordained third.
>
> Let Brother Edward Partridge choose as counselors in their place, Brother Parley P. Pratt and Brother Titus Billings, ordaining Brother Billings to the High Priesthood.
>
> Let Brother Morley choose for his counselors, Brother Christian Whitmer, whom ordain to the High Priesthood, and Brother Newel Knight. Let Brother Corrill choose Brother Daniel Stanton and Brother Hezekiah Peck, for his counselors; let Brother Hezekiah also, be ordained to the High Priesthood. (*History of the Church* 1:363)

In the same letter, the Presidency noted that "When the Bishops are appointed according to our recommendation, it will devolve upon them to see to the poor, according to the laws of the Church" (*History of the Church* 1:365).

The letter also revealed some of the future plans for bishops in the Church: "In relation to the size of Bishoprics: When Zion is once properly regulated there will be a Bishop to each square of the size of the one we send you with this" (*History of the Church* 1:368). Thus, while the first Bishop of the Church, Edward Partridge, had originally an unrestricted domain, only later reduced to the land of Zion when Newel K. Whitney was called as Bishop in Kirtland, the time would come when bishops would be called to operate in rather small geographical areas, as the density of Church population increased.[21]

---

21 The current organization of the Church, of course, reflects such a state.

From the First Presidency's letter to the Missouri Saints, we note that it was a practice of the Church to ordain the bishop's counselors to the high priesthood, i.e., to the office of high priest. This appears to have been optional. When *Book of Commandments* 44:54 was reprinted in 1835 as D&C 13:19 (our D&C 42:71-73), it was changed. The original revelation read, "And the elders are to assist the bishop in all things, and he is to see that their families are supported . . . as may be thought best by the elders and bishop." The term "elders" at that time (1831) would have referred to the "First Elders," Joseph Smith and Oliver Cowdery. Following the introduction of counselors to the Bishop at the conference held in June 1831, it was no longer necessary that the presiding authorities of the Church (the First Presidency after 1832) assist the Bishop. The original text was changed in the D&C to reflect this development:

> And the elders or high priests who are appointed to assist the bishop as counselors in all things, are to have their families supported . . . as may be thought best or decided by the counselors and bishop.
> And the bishop, also, shall receive his support, or a just remuneration for all his services in the church. (D&C 42:71-73)

Though in the Church of our day bishops usually have high priests as counselors, this section makes it clear that elders may also serve in this capacity.

Under the law of consecration and stewardship, the bishop and his counselors worked full-time for the Church. This was the reason they received their support from the Church. Indeed, the work of the temporal ministry of the Church was so heavy in those days that the bishop was assisted not only by his counselors, but by the "bishop's agents." In some of the early records, these agents are referred to as those who are appointed to "gather the strength of the Lord's house" (e.g., *History of the Church* 2:136). One of the agents, Sidney Gilbert (who ran a store for the Church and from which he received his livelihood), was "keeper of the Lord's storehouse" (*History of the Church* 2:118).

Another duty that devolved upon the bishops was that of sitting in judgment on transgressors. From 1833, we read of the "bishop's court," which had authority to try even elders of the Church.[22] In the absence of a bishop, other priesthood authorities were authorized to convene courts. In a letter dated April 13, 1833, addressed to the brother of Jared Carter, the Prophet Joseph wrote, "And when there is no Bishop, they are to be tried by the voice of the Church; and if an Elder, or a High Priest be present, he is to take the lead in managing the business; but if not, such as have the highest authority should preside" (*History of the Church* 1:338-9). This was to change the following year with the institution of the high council.

---

22 E.g., *History of the Church* 1:470, where we have two such courts called during the month of December 1833.

Chapter 5

ORGANIZING THE CHURCH

Therefore, as I said unto you, ask and ye shall receive;
pray earnestly that peradventure my servant Joseph
Smith, Jun., may go with you, and preside in the midst of
my people, and organize my kingdom upon the conse-
crated land, and establish the children of Zion upon the
laws and commandments which have been and which
shall be given unto you. (D&C 103:35)

After the establishment of the high priesthood, it was the high priests who took the lead in the spiritual affairs of the Church. They would frequently assemble in "conference" or "council" in Kirtland to discuss matters of Church business, such as how "to procure money,"[1] the appointment of elders over the branches, the building of a schoolhouse for elders to prepare for missions,[2] and the building of the Kirtland Temple.[3]

On a few occasions, we find them assembling to discuss revelations. For example, on February 26, 1833, "a special council of High Priests" met in Zion to discuss the "Olive Leaf," known today as D&C 88 (*History of the Church* 1:327). The following day, Joseph Smith received the revelation known as the "Word of Wisdom" (D&C 89), given "for the benefit of the council of high priests, assembled in Kirtland, and the church, and also the saints in Zion" (D&C 89:1). Indeed, it became Joseph's practice to seek revelation from the Lord at the time of such councils.[4] In a letter written to the brother of Jared Carter on April 13, 1833, he wrote:

---

1 *History of the Church* 1:342, under date of April 30, 1833.

2 *History of the Church* 2:342, under date of May 4, 1833.

3 *History of the Church* 1:353, under date of June 6, 1833.

4 As noted below, a "conference" of high priests was assembled in Kirtland on June 4, 1833, to discuss the disposition of lands. No agreement could be reached, so the prophet Joseph asked for, and received, a revelation that became D&C 96. One of the results of this revelation (verse 6) was that John Johnson "was ordained by the conference to the High Priesthood" (*History of the Church* 1:353).

And again we never inquire at the hand of God for special revelation only in case of there being no previous revelation to suit the case; and that in a council of High Priests. (*History of the Church* 1:339)

This procedure is illustrated by the council of high priests called on June 4, 1833 to discuss the disposition of some Church property. The conference could not agree, so Joseph Smith inquired of the Lord and received the revelation known as D&C 96 (*History of the Church* 1:352-53).

The councils of high priests also became responsible for removing priesthood licenses from unfaithful brethren (e.g., *History of the Church* 1:333) and for cutting off members from the Church for transgression.[5] Ordinations to various offices were also approved by the councils of high priests and were usually performed during their meetings.[6]

On May 4, 1833, the First Presidency approved a decision made by a council held in North Township, Ohio, over which Sidney Rigdon presided. The ordination of three brethren to the office of elder and one to the office of priest was brought into question. The council "decided that their ordinations were illegal, and that the churches should not receive them in their several offices" (*History of the Church* 1:343).

A few months later, on August 8, 1833, the high priests in Missouri set a precedent by resolving "that no High Priest, Elder or Priest shall ordain any Priest, Elder or High Priest in the land of Zion, without the consent of a conference of High Priests."[7]

The elders, too, occasionally held councils. Under date of June 23, 1833, we read, "A council of the Elders of the Church was held at Westfield, New York . . . Elder Gladden Bishop was president, and Brother Chester L. Heath clerk." The council cut off Elder James Higby from the Church and "resolved that the proceedings of the

---

5 E.g., *History of the Church* 1:327, 352, 354-6. Some of the cases were heard on appeal from the Bishop's court (e.g., *History of the Church* 1:354). Often, the council would forgive the accused if he showed a repentant spirit (e.g., *History of the Church* 2:47).

6 E.g., *History of the Church* 1:327, 33, 334, 352, 353, 407, 410.

7 *History of the Church* 1:407; cf. Donald Q. Cannon and Lyndon W. Cook, *Far West Record* (Salt Lake City: Deseret, 1983), 64.

council be sent to Kirtland, that it may be known among the different branches of the church" (*History of the Church* 1:355-6). Two others "were cut off from the Church by a council of Elders in Kirtland" on December 26, 1833 (*History of the Church* 1:469). As late as August 4, 1834, we read that at Kirtland "A council of elders ordained Thomas Colburn, Elder" (*History of the Church* 2:139).

Despite these examples of elders' councils, it is clear that most priesthood ordinations and excommunications were handled by councils of high priests, even prior to the resolution passed in Zion in the fall of 1833. The high priests were the governing officers of the Church.

The number twelve played a role in some of the councils of high priests.[8] Appeal from the decision of a bishop's court appears to have always gone before a council of twelve high priests. Hence, in a letter written on June 25, 1833 by the First Presidency to Bishop Edward Partridge and others in Missouri, it is noted that if there is no agreement between the bishop and a man regarding the consecration of his property, "the case must be laid before a council of twelve High Priests, the Bishop not being one of the council" (*History of the Church* 1:365).

Four days previous to this, the Presidency had received a letter reading, in part, "I, Doctor Philastus Hurlburt [Hurlbut],[9] having been tried before the Bishop's council of High Priests . . . enter my appeal unto the President's council of high priests for a re-hearing according to the privilege guaranteed to me in the laws of the Church." The hearing was granted and "the council proceeded to ordain two High Priests, to make out the number (twelve), that the council, or Church court, might be organized." The council decided that "the Bishop's council decided correctly on the case," but restored Hurlbut after he made a confession (*History of the Church* 1:354). Soon after, when it became clear that he had not repented, he was excommunicated.[10] On

8 E.g., *History of the Church* 1:317, under the date of January 14, 1833.

9 His name is variously given as Hurlburt and Hurlbut, the latter being the correct spelling. After his excommunication for sexual promiscuity, Hurlbut became bitter and assembled material for one of the first anti-Mormon books, published in 1834.

10 *History of the Church* 1:355. On June 3, 1833, Hurlbut was excommunicated by "a conference of High Priests" called by Bishop Partridge. He appealed to a similar conference to be called by the First Presidency (*History of the Church* 1:352). The two men ordained as high priests to make the number twelve were Joseph Smith's uncle, John Smith, and his brother, William Smith, both of whom later played an important role in the Church.

the day of Hurlbut's appeal, "the President's court also took Brother Daniel Copeley's Priest's license and membership from him" (*History of the Church* 1:354).

The High Council

As Church membership increased and covered more geographic territory, it became impractical to hold councils to which all high priests would be invited. It was time to organize permanent councils, with men specifically called to serve in the principal centers of the Church.

On February 12, 1834, the prophet Joseph Smith held a "council of the High Priests and Elders" at his home in Kirtland, in order "to set before the council the dignity of the office which had been conferred on me by the ministering of the angel of God, by His own voice, and by the voice of this Church; that I had never set before any council in all the order in which it ought to be conducted, which, perhaps, has deprived the councils of some or many blessings." He then proceeded to discuss the conduct of councils in ancient times and to instruct the brethren on the purity of heart necessary to make a man "capable of judging a matter, in council" (*History of the Church* 2:25-26).

The chronological context suggests that this instructional meeting was designed to prepare the high priests and elders of the Church for the organization of the high council. Indeed, the first high council was established in Kirtland five days later, on February 17, 1834.[11] The minutes of that organizational meeting constitute Section 102 of the D&C.[12] On February 19 the minutes were read and approved in a meeting of the council "and unanimously adopted and received for a form and constitution of the High Council of the Church of Christ hereafter; with this provision, that if the President should hereafter discover anything lacking in the same, he should be privileged to supply it" (*History of the Church* 2:31).

From D&C 102, we learn that the high council was to consist of twelve high priests with a president (verses 1, 5, 9), who could be

---

11 *History of the Church* 2:28f. George A. Smith, speaking on November 15, 1864, said, "I remember very well the organization of the High Council at Kirtland as a permanent institution, there had been several Councils of twelve High Priests called for special cases, but they organized it permanently on 17th Feb. 1834" (*Journal of Discourses* 11:7).

12 Note that Joseph Smith, Sr., Church Patriarch, also served as a member of the original high council in Kirtland.

assisted by two other presidents (verses 2, 10-11), either of which could preside in his absence. The First Presidency, Joseph Smith, Sidney Rigdon and Frederick G. Williams, were acknowledged by the high council to constitute the presidency of the council (verse 3). Indeed, we read that "the President of the Church . . . is also the President of the Council, is appointed by revelation, and acknowledged in his administration, by the voice of the Church" (verses 9-10). There are also provisions for "other high priests . . . to act in the place of absent councilors" (verses 6-7), known today as "alternates." In the early years of the Church, apostles and others sometimes filled these roles.

The principal function of the high council was to serve as a judicial body, judging the actions of members of the Church and taking corrective measures where necessary, as well as hearing appeals from the bishop's council or court (D&C 102:2). Appeal from the high council's decisions could be made to "the high council at the seat of the government of the Church." On page 114 of the Kirtland Revelation Book, it reads, "the high council of the general government of the Church." The words "general government" were crossed out and "first Presidency" written in above the line in preparation for publication of the D&C in 1835 (see D&C 102:16-27). Similarly, the words "the seat of Church government" were changed in the 1835 D&C 5:14 (current D&C 102:33) to read "the First Presidency of the Church."[13]

In areas outside the organized Church (described in the text and elsewhere in the D&C as "abroad"), high priests were authorized to organize a temporary High Council when necessary for the conduct of Church courts (verses 24-32; *History of the Church* 2:220 note).

D&C 102 provides for the possibility of two assistant presidents for the president of the high council. To understand this phrase, we read under the date of September 24, 1834 that the high council of Kirtland met, "Joseph Smith, Jun., presiding, assisted by Sidney Rigdon and Frederick G. Williams, counselors." Though they are identified as "counselors," Brothers Rigdon and Williams are also termed "assistant presidents" in the minutes of the meeting (*History of the Church*

---

13 Also added to the original are verses 30-32 of our current D&C 102, which adds information on the twelve apostles as the traveling high council. This addition was first made in the 1835 edition (5:13), after the calling of the twelve.

2:165). Also, concerning the inaugural meeting on February 19, 1834, Joseph Smith recorded, "I then gave the assistant Presidents a solemn charge to do their duty in righteousness, and in the fear of God; I also charged the twelve Councilors in a similar manner" (*History of the Church* 2:32). The council then settled down to business by hearing charges brought against an elder who, following confession of his wrongdoing, was forgiven (*History of the Church* 2:33-34).

After this, it was the high council rather than an assembly of high priests that met to discuss the business of the Church. Thus, we find the council deciding, on February 20, 1834, to require Church officers to obey the Word of Wisdom (D&C 89) and sending some elders east on missions (*History of the Church* 2:34-35). Four days later, the high council met to hear a report on the state of the Church in Missouri (*History of the Church* 2:39).

On August 1, 1834, following a period of investigation, the high council of Zion (organized after the one at Kirtland) decided that an ordination performed by Samuel Brown of the Hulette Branch was "illegal therefore not acknowledged by us to be of God—Therefore is void and good for nothing." Brother Brown was required to surrender his licenses for the offices of high priest and elder for having ordained another to the priesthood without High Council approval (*History of the Church* 2:137). A year later, we find the high council in Kirtland meeting to hear an appeal from a case "from an Elders' Court in Zion" that removed the license of one of the elders (*History of the Church* 2:286). In a similar vein, we read that at a meeting held in Kirtland on September 24, 1834, the high council "decided that a notice be published to the churches and conferences abroad that High Priests be ordained hereafter in the High Council at Kirtland, and receive licenses signed by the clerk of the council" (*History of the Church* 2:165-166).

In a letter written to Hezekiah Peck from Kirtland on August 1, 1835, Joseph Smith noted that the high council was to "regulate all the affairs of Zion" and that the elders were not to "steady the ark of God . . .The high council and bishop's court have been established to do the business of Zion . . . The Elders have no right to regulate Zion, but they have a right to preach the gospel."[14]

---

14 Dean C. Jessee (ed.), *The Personal Writings of Joseph Smith* (Salt Lake City: Deseret Book Co., 1984), 346-7.

With the organization of the High Council, many of the functions formerly performed by other Church officers passed to the new organization. In consequence of this, when the Book of Commandments was revised in 1835 and published as the "Covenants" of the Church,[15] changes were made in the revelations dealing with matters now handled by the High Council. For example, the following was added to chapter 24 of the Book of Commandments, written on the day the Church was organized (April 6, 1830):

No person is to be ordained to any office in this church, where there is a regularly organized branch of the same, without the vote of that church;

But the presiding elders, traveling bishops, high councilors, high priests, and elders, may have the privilege of ordaining, where there is no branch of the church that a vote may be called.

Every president of the high priesthood (or presiding elder), bishop, high councilor, and high priest, is to be ordained by the direction of a high council or general conference. (D&C 20:65-67;1835 D&C 2:16-17)

The insertion into the original text reflects the calling of high priests, bishops, presiding elders and high councilors, none of which existed in 1830 when the Church was organized. The high council was also added to D&C 42:34 when the Book of Commandments (44:29) underwent its revision in 1835 (Section 13:10).[16]

Zion's Camp

Some months later, Joseph Smith arrived in Missouri with Zion's Camp. On June 22, 1834, he received the revelation recorded in D&C 105, commanding that some of the brethren were to go to Kirtland to receive their endowments and "power from on high" (*History of the*

---

15 The first publication of Joseph Smith's revelations, in 1833, was entitled *Book of Commandments*. When the revelations were revised and new ones added in 1835, the collection came to be known as the "Covenants." The *Doctrine and Covenants* actually comprised two parts. The "Doctrine" consisted of the "Lectures on Faith" delivered as lessons at the Kirtland School of the Prophets, while the "Covenants" consisted of the revelations given to the prophet Joseph Smith. In later editions, though the Lectures on Faith were removed, the full title continued to be used.

16 For later appraisals of these additions, see the quotes from Elder Orson Pratt and David Whitmer in the appendix to this volume.

Church 2, beginning on page 108). The following day, "a council of High Priests met according to revelation in order to choose some of the first Elders to receive their endowments being appointed by the voice of the Spirit through Br. Joseph Smith, jr. President of the Church of Christ."[17]

Of those listed as "elders," a number were high priests, including Edward Partridge, William W. Phelps, John Whitmer, David Whitmer, Algernon Sidney Gilbert, Newel Knight, Thomas B. Marsh, Lyman Wight and Parley P. Pratt. It is interesting that Joseph Smith is here called "President of the Church" and not of the High Priesthood, as in most of the earlier documents. The significance of this will become clear as we examine some of his activities while in Missouri.

Recording the events of the council of June 23, 1834, the prophet Joseph noted some special callings given to the brethren who were chosen to go up to Kirtland to receive their endowments. For example, Edward Partridge was "also to stand in his office as Bishop to purchase lands in the state of Missouri," while John Corrill, his counselor, was to "assist in gathering up the strength of the Lord's house, and preach the Gospel." The expression "gather up the strength of the Lord's house" refers to the acquisition of properties and the administration of the law of consecration and stewardship. This was also the assignment of Algernon Sidney Gilbert, who was a bishop's agent. He was told that he was "to assist in gathering up the strength of the Lord's house and to proclaim the everlasting Gospel until Zion is redeemed." He declined the missionary call, however.

Also called "to assist in gathering up the strength of the Lord's house; and to preach the everlasting Gospel" were Peter Whitmer Jr., Simeon Carter, Newel Knight, Parley P. Pratt, Christian Whitmer and Solomon Hancock. John and David Whitmer were to "continue in their offices," though, as yet, they had not been called to the Presidency in Missouri. Of Thomas B. Marsh, Joseph recorded, "his office to be made known hereafter." He became one of the original Twelve Apostles and their President. Lyman Wight, too, was to "return to Zion and have his office appointed unto him hereafter" (*History of the Church* 2:112-113).

---

17 Donald Q. Cannon and Lyndon W. Cook, *Far West Record*, 68.

During the following month, the real organization of the Church in Missouri was to begin. Joseph Smith's account reads as follows:

> On the third of July, the High Priests of Zion assembled in the yard of Colonel Arthur, where Lyman Wight lived, in Clay county, and I proceeded to organize a High Council, agreeable to the revelation and pattern given at Kirtland, for the purpose of settling important business that might come before them, which could not be settled by the bishop and his council. David Whitmer was elected president, and William W. Phelps and John Whitmer assistant presidents. The following High Priests, viz: Christian Whitmer, Newel Knight, Lyman Wight, Calvin Beebe, Wm. E. Mc'Lellin, Solomon Hancock, Thomas B. Marsh, Simeon Carter, Parley P. Pratt, Orson Pratt, John Murdock, and Levi Jackson, were appointed councilors.[18]

Interestingly, some of these brethren headed branches in Missouri at that time and were therefore serving double duty.

Four days later, on July 7, 1834, Joseph Smith again met with the Presidency and High Council of Zion. He read to them the minutes of the organization of the Kirtland High Council, now known as D&C 102. "I told them," he wrote, "that if I should now be taken away, I had accomplished the great work the Lord had laid before me, and done my duty in organizing the High Council, through which council the will of the Lord might be known on all important occasions, in the building up of Zion and establishing truth in the earth" (*History of the Church* 2:124).

The Church, it appears, was now sufficiently organized that should the prophet die, the means to receive revelation for the continued operation and growth of the organization was in place. The Prophet's words may also reflect the fact that, at this time, David Whitmer was ordained Assistant President of the Church and was therefore Joseph Smith's designated successor.[19]

President Smith then proceeded to ordain the Missouri Presidency and High Council, after which

---

18 *History of the Church* 2:122-23; see also Donald Q. Cannon and Lyndon W. Cook, *Far West Record*, 70.

19 For David Whitmer's later recollection of the event, see the appendix.

the High Priests, Elders, Teachers, Deacons and members present, then covenanted with hands uplifted to heaven, that they would uphold Brother David Whitmer as president in Zion, in my absence; and John Whitmer and William W. Phelps as assistant presidents or counselors; and myself as First President of the Church. (*History of the Church* 2:125-126)

In the minutes of the meeting, David Whitmer is called "the President of the Church in Zion."[20] His authority in that part of the Lord's vineyard was comparable to that of Joseph Smith as President in Kirtland.[21] Nevertheless, Joseph was the "First President of the Church."[22]

Stakes of Zion

The terms "First President" and "First Presidency" imply that there would be other presidencies in the Church.[23] David Whitmer was the first of these other presidents and still others were to be called in years to come. Each of these presidents took charge of what was called a "stake," a term deriving from the writings of Isaiah (33:20; 54:2). The term appears in a revelation to the prophet Joseph given in November 1831 (D&C 68:25) and in another received April 26, 1832 (D&C 82:14). In each, we read of "Zion" and "her stakes."

A "stake" is an extension of the central government of the Church. Consequently, a stake president is the presiding authority in the stake to which he is assigned, just as the "First President" presides over the

---

20 Donald Q. Cannon and Lyndon W. Cook, *Far West Record*, 73.

21 When, in May 1835, W. W. Phelps and John Whitmer, counselors to David Whitmer, arrived in Kirtland, they were termed "Presidents of the Church in Missouri" (*History of the Church* 2:227).

22 Under the date of July 1834, Parley P. Pratt wrote of one of David Whitmer's counselors, "W. W. Phelps, then President of the Church in Missouri" (Parley P. Pratt [Jr.], ed., *Autobiography of Parley Parker Pratt* (Salt Lake City, 1873; 3rd ed. Deseret Book Co., 1938), 118). A report of the minutes of a meeting held at Far West, Missouri, on April 7, 1837 begins "At a meeting of the Presidency of the Church in Missouri, the High Council, Bishop and counselors (*History of the Church* 2:481).

23 Along similar lines, Joseph Smith was earlier termed the Church's "First Elder."

entire Church.[24] In a sense, then, the stake president is the president of the Church in that area over which he is given jurisdiction.

That this was (and is) the case is reflected in the fact that in D&C 102:9, we read of "the president of the church, who is also the president of the (high) council." While Joseph Smith was, indeed, the president of the high council in Kirtland for a time, David Whitmer and others were designated as presidents of other high councils (and their stakes), as the Church grew and required further organization.

As we shall see in subsequent chapters, the officers of the earliest stakes of the Church consisted of a presidency, a high council, a patriarch, and a single bishopric. Bishops did not preside over congregations, nor did they conduct Sunday services. These were under the direction of the president. This is why, during the Kirtland era, there were only two bishops, one in Ohio and one in Missouri.

Because of the small size of the Church in its beginning, Joseph Smith, as President of the Church, was also president of its first stake, organized at Kirtland with the institution of the high council in 1834.[25] Earlier revelations alluded to the Lord's plans in this matter. For example, at the conference held in Zion on April 26, 1832, the Lord told the prophet, "I have consecrated the land of Kirtland in mine own due time for the benefit of the saints of the Most High, and for a stake of Zion" (D&C 82:13). The promised organization of the Kirtland Stake is noted in D&C 94:1 (dated May 6, 1833) and D&C 96:1 (dated June 4, 1833). It is also mentioned in a letter written by the First Presidency to the brethren in Missouri on June 25, 1833 (*History of the Church* 1:363).

While David Whitmer was president in Missouri, he was never really a stake president in the sense that we use the term today, for the

---

24 The relationship of the stake presidency to the First Presidency is comparable to that of tent stakes to the tent pole. The pole is the central governing element which gives shape and existence to the tent as a covering, while the stakes stretch out the lines that give the tent its size and flesh it out. When both are made of wood, as is still the case in the Middle East, the stake appears to be a smaller version of the tent-pole.

25 However, we should note that the high council in Kirtland, because it was under the First Presidency, was considered to be superior to the high council in Missouri. This set a precedent that continued when the Church's headquarters were in Nauvoo and early on in Salt Lake City. Though there was a regular stake presidency, the high council of the city sat on the stand with the general authorities. This will be discussed further in subsequent chapters. For John Taylor's comments about the relationship between the Kirtland and Missouri high councils, see the appendix.

Church in Missouri was not really a stake. The term "stakes of Zion" specifically excludes Zion as one of those stakes, it being the center of the tent. After the Missouri presidency was excommunicated and Joseph Smith moved there, he became not only the president of the Church, but also the president in Missouri. Likewise, during the Nauvoo period there was a separate stake presidency in Kirtland.[26]

The Assistant President

In the early days of the Church, the Lord made it clear that even though Joseph Smith had been designated to hold the keys in this last dispensation,[27] it would be possible to replace him by another if necessary.[28] In a revelation given in February 1831, it is stated that only Joseph Smith or his successor is authorized to receive revelation for the Church, but that the Prophet could, in fact, choose his own successor.[29]

Originally, Joseph's successor was the Church's second elder, Oliver Cowdery. That changed, however, when David Whitmer was selected as "President of the Church in Zion" and designated as Joseph's successor. At the conference in which David Whitmer was called to the Presidency in Zion, Missouri (September 7, 1834), he was ordained by Joseph Smith to be President of the Church.

---

26 Years later, Elder Orson Pratt spoke of this:

> Let me here take the liberty to say to this congregation that the City of Zion when it is built in Jackson County, will not be called a Stake. We can find no mention in all the revelations that God has given, that the City of Zion is to be the Centre Stake of Zion; the Lord never called it a Stake in any revelation that has been given. It is to be the head quarters, it is to be the place where the Son of Man will come and dwell, where He will have a Temple, in which Temple there will be a throne prepared where Jesus will dwell in the midst of His people; it will be the great central city, and the outward branches will be called Stakes everywhere they shall be organized as such. (*Journal of Discourses* 22:35)

27 D&C 64:5; BC 65:7, dated September 11, 1831.

28 See D&C 28:2-7 of September 1830 and D&C 35:17-18 of December 1830.

29 D&C 43:2-4; BC 45:2-4. On December 5, 1869, Elder George Q. Cannon commented of this revelation:

> The keys of this Priesthood were bestowed never more to be taken from the earth; hence, in the revelation I have read, provision was made by the Lord that Joseph, in case he should fall, should ordain another in his stead, and he should have authority only to lay hands on and set apart some one to act in his place, in case he should prove unworthy. (*Journal of Discourses* 13:49)

David Whitmer's ordination as Joseph Smith's successor is indicated in the minutes of the High Council of Zion nearly four years later. Under the date of March 15, 1838 (by which time David Whitmer had already fallen away from the Church), we read:

> President Joseph Smith jr gave a history of the ordination of David Whitmer, which took place in July 1834, to be a leader, or a prophet to this Church, which (ordination) was on conditions that he (J. Smith jr) did not live to God himself.[30]

The ordination is further confirmed in John Whitmer's manuscript, History of the Church (1831-37), 104, and in the apostate William E. M'Lellin's *Ensign of Liberty* (December 1847), 43-44, in "Testimony of 3 Witnesses," i.e., Martin Harris, Leonard Rich and Calvin Beebe.

In an account written half a century later, David Whitmer, after explaining why he and Joseph Smith disagreed on some matters (notably the printing of the Book of Commandments), wrote of his ordination:

> To show you that Brother Joseph and myself still loved each other as brethren, after this, I will tell you that he had so much confidence in me that in July, 1834, he ordained me his successor as "Prophet Seer and Revelator" to the Church. He did this of his own free will and not at any solicitation whatever on my part. I did not know what he was going to do until he laid his hands upon me and ordained me.
>
> Now, bear in mind, brethren, that I am not claiming this office; as I have told you, I do not believe in any such an office in the church. I was then in error in believing that there was such an office in the Church of Christ. I suppose this is news to many of you—that Brother Joseph ordained me his successor—but it is in your records, and there are men now living who were present in that council of elders when he did it, in the camp of Zion, on Fishing River, Missouri, July, 1834."[31]

---

30 Donald Q. Cannon and Lyndon W. Cook, *Far West Record*, 151.

31 David Whitmer, *An Address to All Believers in Christ* (Richmond, Missouri, 1887), 55.

In later years, after David Whitmer fell away from the Church and lost his position, the minutes of the July 1834 meeting were changed in *History of the Church* 2:126 to omit mention of his status as Joseph Smith's designated successor. It was undoubtedly this change in status that prompted Brigham Young to say, "Joseph Smith, Oliver Cowdery, and David Whitmer were the first Apostles of this dispensation, though in early days of the Church David Whitmer lost his standing" (*Journal of Discourses* 6:320)

Oliver Cowdery, too, was honored by the Lord during the year 1834. Under date of December 5, Joseph Smith wrote:

> According to the direction of the Holy Spirit, on the evening of the 5th of December, while assembled with Sidney Rigdon, Frederick G. Williams, and Oliver Cowdery, conversing upon the welfare of the Church, I laid my hands on Brother Oliver Cowdery, and ordained him an assistant-president, saying these words: "In the name of Jesus Christ, who was crucified for the sins of the world, I lay my hands upon thee and ordain thee an assistant-president to the High and Holy Priesthood, in the Church of the Latter-day Saints. (*History of the Church* 2:176)

Eight months previous to this time, Oliver Cowdery's name had been closely linked with that of the First Presidency. A letter dated April 7, 1834, and said by Joseph Smith to have been written by "the Presidency," is signed by "Joseph Smith, Jun., Frederick G. Williams, Oliver Cowdery" (*History of the Church* 2:48). Twelve days later, when Joseph Smith was preparing to leave for Missouri with the Zion's Camp expedition, he asked Oliver Cowdery and Zebedee Coltrin to join him in laying hands on Sidney Rigdon to bless him "to preside over the Church in my absence" (*History of the Church* 2:51). The ordination of December 5 reaffirmed Oliver Cowdery's position as the "Second Elder" in the restored Church—a position that hadn't been noted since the calling of Sidney Rigdon and Jesse Gause (later Frederick G. Williams) as counselors to Joseph Smith in the First Presidency. The minutes of the meeting of December 5, 1834, kept by Oliver Cowdery, read in part as follows:

> After addressing the throne of mercy President Smith laid hands upon High Councilor Cowdery, and ordained him to the

Presidency of the High Priesthood of the Church, saying: "Brother in the name of Jesus Christ of Nazareth, who was crucified for the sins of the world, that we through the virtue of his blood might come to the Father, I lay my hands upon thy head, and ordain thee a President of the High and Holy Priesthood, to assist in presiding over the Church, and bearing the keys of this kingdom—which Priesthood is after the order of Melchizedek—which is after the order of the Son of God."[32]

Having so done, the Prophet explained the significance of the ordination:

> The office of Assistant President is to assist in presiding over the whole Church, and to officiate in the absence of the President, according to his rank and appointment, Viz., President Cowdery, first; President Rigdon, second, and President Williams third, as they were severally called. The office of this priesthood is also to act as spokesman, taking Aaron for an example. The virtue of the above priesthood is to hold the keys of the kingdom of heaven or the Church militant.[33]

Some have presumed that this ordination made Oliver Cowdery the successor to the Prophet Joseph Smith. However, in view of the fact that David Whitmer had been so ordained just a few months

---

32 Manuscript History of the Church, Book A.1. The account from Joseph Smith's diary reads as follows:

> Friday Evening, December 5, 1834. According to the directions of the Holy Spirit breth[r]en Joseph Smith Jr., Sidney Rigdon, Frederick G. Williams, and Oliver Cowdery, assembled to converse upon the welfare of the Church, when brother Oliver Cowdery was ordained an assistant President of the High and Holy Priesthood under the hands of brother Joseph Smith Jr. saying, 'My brother, in the name of Jesus Christ who died was crucified for the sins of the world, I lay my hands upon thee, and ordain thee an assistant President of the high and holy priesthood in the Church of the Latter-day Saints'." (Dean C. Jessee, ed., *The Personal Writings of Joseph Smith* [Salt Lake City: Deseret Book Co., 1984], 37-38)

33 Manuscript History of the Church, Book A.1, in Dean C. Jessee, ed., *The Personal Writings of Joseph Smith*, 37-38. The comparison of Oliver Cowdery with Aaron alludes to earlier revelations regarding his role in the Church and its relationship to that of Joseph Smith (D&C 8:6-7; 28:2-3). Note that Sidney Rigdon, Joseph's first counselor, is designated a spokesman for the prophet in D&C 100:9-11; 124:103-104.

before and that he was still in favor with the Lord and with the Church, that seems unlikely. Rather, it would appear that David Whitmer was the designated successor to Joseph Smith should he die, while Oliver Cowdery was Assistant President, with emphasis on the word "assistant." David Whitmer, as we have noted above, was also "President of the Church in Zion."[34]

---

34 Those who held the position of Assistant Counselor to Joseph Smith were: Hyrum Smith (sustained September 3, 1837 and released November 7, 1837), Oliver Cowdery, Joseph Smith Sr. and John Smith.

Chapter 6

THE PRESIDING QUORUMS

---

*And now, verily I say unto you, I give unto you a com-
mandment that you continue in the ministry and presidency. And when you have finished the translation of the
prophets, you shall from thenceforth preside over the
affairs of the church and the school; And from time to
time, as shall be manifested by the Comforter, receive
revelations to unfold the `mysteries of the kingdom; And
set in order the churches, and study and learn, and
become acquainted with all good books, and with languages, tongues, and people. And this shall be your business and mission in all your lives, to preside in council,
and set in order all the affairs of this church and kingdom. (D&C 90:12-16)*

On May 7 ,1861, Brigham Young discussed the gradual method by
which the Church had been organized in the time of Joseph Smith:

How came these Apostles, these Seventies, these High
Priests, and all this organization we now enjoy? It came by revelation . . .

Twenty-seven years ago, on the 5th of this month, in the year
1834, a company started for Kirtland to redeem the land of Zion.
Brother Heber C. Kimball and my brother Joseph were in that
camp. There had not been ordained any Twelve Apostles, nor
any Seventies, although there was a revelation pertaining to the
Apostles and Seventies. There were High Priests, but no High
Priests' Quorum . . .

After we returned from Missouri, my brother Joseph Young
and myself had been singing after preaching in a meeting; and
when the meeting was dismissed, brother Joseph Smith said,
"Come, go down to my house with me." We went and sung to
him a long time, and talked with him. He then opened the subject of the Twelve and Seventies for the first time I ever thought

of it. He said, "Brethren, I am going to call out Twelve Apostles. I think we will get together, by-and-by, and select Twelve Apostles, and select a Quorum of Seventies from those who have been up to Zion, out of the camp boys." In 1835, the last of January or in February, or about that time, we held our meetings from day to day, and brother Joseph called out Twelve Apostles at that time. He had a revelation when we were singing to him . . . He followed up that revelation until he organized the Church, and so along until the baptism of the dead was revealed.

I relate these circumstances to show you that a person who is ordained to the office of an Elder in this kingdom has the same Priesthood that the High Priests, that the Twelve Apostles, that the Seventies, and that the First Presidency hold; but all are not called to be one of the Twelve Apostles, nor are all called to be one of the First Presidency, nor to be one of the First Presidents of all the Seventies, nor to be one of the Presidents of a Quorum of Seventies, nor to Preside over the High Priests' Quorum. (*Journal of Discourses* 9:88-89)

A revelation of November 1831 called for elders to be appointed to preside over the priests, teachers, and deacons (Kirtland Revelation Book, 84). By the time the revelation was published in 1835 as D&C 3:31 (1981 D&C 107:60-63), the Church was sufficiently organized that the Lord had given new instructions, making it necessary to modify this passage to indicate that elders should preside over elders, priests over priests, and deacons over deacons. But the most important quorums organized in 1835 were those of the Twelve and the Seventy.

The Twelve Apostles

Nearly a year before the official organization of the Church, the Lord designated Oliver Cowdery and David Whitmer to "search out the Twelve" (D&C 18:37).[1] In a revelation of September 11, 1831, there is mention of apostles and prophets (D&C 64:39). A month later, on October 26, 1831, Oliver Cowdery, serving as clerk at a Church

---

1 David Whitmer's 1887 criticism of the Church for instituting the quorum of the twelve apostles is in the appendix to this volume.

conference, "said that the directions which himself and his br. David Whitmer had received this morning respecting the choice of the twelve was that they would be ordained and sent forth from the land of Zion."[2]

On the surface, this appears to disagree with the statement found in D&C 95:4, 17 (dated June 1, 1833), that the Lord intended to prepare the twelve apostles by means of the Temple in Kirtland. In actual fact, however, both the Kirtland Temple and the land of Zion played a role in the designation of the twelve.

In January 1835, the prophet Joseph Smith wrote, "The school of the Elders will continue, and arrangements were made, according to the revelation of June, 1829, for choosing 'the Twelve Apostles' to be especial messengers to bear the Gospel among the nations" (*History of the Church* 2:180).

On February 8, 1835, Joseph Smith called Brigham and Joseph Young to his home in Kirtland and requested that they assemble the brethren for a general conference to be held the following Saturday, February 14. Joseph Young recorded the Prophet's words of that day: "'I shall then and there appoint twelve Special Witnesses, to open the door of the Gospel to foreign nations, and you,' said he (speaking to Brother Brigham) 'will be one of them.' . . . He then turned to Elder Joseph Young . . . and addressing him, said, 'Brother Joseph, the Lord has made you President of the Seventies.'"[3]

Those assembled in Kirtland on February 14, 1835 comprised mostly men who had participated in the Zion's Camp expedition during the preceding year. All of those chosen as apostles on that day had been in Missouri and were designated among the first elders sent to Kirtland to be endowed "with power from on high" at the Temple. Thus, the seemingly contradictory instructions of the Lord given during earlier years are seen to be in complete harmony one with another.

At the Saturday morning assembly, the Three Witnesses were called upon to choose the Twelve from amongst those who had gone

---

2 Donald Q. Cannon and Lyndon W. Cook, *Far West Record* (Salt Lake City: Deseret, 1983), 26.

3 Joseph Young, Sen., *History of the Organization of the Seventies* (Salt Lake City, 1878), 1-2, cited in a footnote to *History of the Church* 2:181.

up to Zion.[4] Following prayer, "these Three Witnesses were blessed by the laying on of the hands of the Presidency. The Witnesses then, according to a former commandment, proceeded to make choice of the Twelve" (*History of the Church* 2:187). Four of those chosen were members of the high council in Zion, i.e., Parley P. Pratt, Orson Pratt, William E. M'Lellin and Thomas B. Marsh.[5]

Only three of the twelve were ordained by the Three Witnesses on the day they were chosen. These were Lyman E. Johnson, Brigham Young and Heber C. Kimball. Elder Kimball later noted, "After we had been thus ordained by these brethren, the First Presidency laid their hands on us and confirmed these blessings and ordinations."[6]

The following day, February 15, 1835, a second meeting was held, at which Oliver Cowdery ordained Orson Hyde,[7] David W. Patten, Luke S. Johnson, William E. M'Lellin, John F. Boynton and William Smith to the apostleship (*History of the Church* 2:189-191). On February 21, Parley P. Pratt was "ordained one of the Twelve, by President Joseph Smith, Jun., David Whitmer, and Oliver Cowdery" (*History of the Church* 2:191).

The other two chosen apostles, Thomas B. Marsh and Orson Pratt, were absent on missions and did not return until the 25th and 26th of April, respectively, 1835 (*History of the Church* 2:193). Some time after April 27 (*History of the Church* 2:198), they were both ordained by Oliver Cowdery. We read that the ordination of Thomas B. Marsh was "sealed by President David Whitmer" and that the ordination of

---

4 Concerning the choice of the Twelve by the Three Witnesses, Elder B. H. Roberts, who edited the *History of the Church*, noted that the reason Martin Harris wasn't named in the revelation in D&C 18:37 was that he was then out of favor with the Lord, as indicated in D&C 19, a revelation given the same month (footnote to *History of the Church* 2:186). He further noted the significance of the fact that the Three Witnesses of the Book of Mormon, itself a witness of Jesus Christ, chose the twelve apostles or "special witnesses" of Christ (footnote to *History of the Church* 2:187; see D&C 107:23).

5 Donald Q. Cannon and Lyndon W. Cook, *Far West Record*, 101.

6 *Times and Seasons* 6:868, cited in a note to *History of the Church* 2:188. *Millennial Star*, 17 (July 2, 1839): 294 noted that "the President proceeded to bless two of the Twelve who had lately been ordained into the quorum." When this was republished in *History of the Church* 3:383, the word "President" was changed to "Presidency." A few statements made in later years by leaders of the Church suggest that Joseph Smith participated in the ordination of the Twelve in 1835. See quotes in the appendix to this volume.

7 For Oliver Cowdery's 1848 account of the ordination of Orson Hyde, see the appendix.

Orson Pratt was "confirmed by President David Whitmer" (*History of the Church* 2:194).

Elder Parley P. Pratt has left us an account of his ordination that is instructive. He wrote that "on the 21st day of February 1837, I took the oath and covenant of apostleship, and was solemnly set apart and ordained to that office; and as a member of that quorum under the hands of Joseph Smith, Oliver Cowdery and David Whitmer." He cited the ordination prayer by Oliver Cowdery, including the following words, "The ancients . . . had this testimony, that they had seen the Saviour after he rose from the dead. You must bear some testimony, or your mission, your labor, your toil will be in vain. You must bear the same testimony that there is but one God, one Mediator; he that has seen Him will know Him, and testify of Him."[8]

Within days after their ordination to the apostleship, the Twelve received similar instructions from Joseph Smith:

> You have been indebted to other men, in the first instance, for evidence; on that you have acted; but it is necessary that you receive a testimony from heaven for yourselves; and that you can bear testimony to the truth of the Book of Mormon, and that you have seen the face of God. That is more than the testimony of an angel. When the proper time arrives, you shall be able to bear this testimony to the world. When you bear testimony that you have seen God, this testimony God will never suffer to fall, but will bear you out; although many will not give heed, yet others will. You will therefore see the necessity of getting this testimony from heaven.
>
> Never cease striving until you have seen God face to face. Strengthen your faith; cast off your doubts, your sins, and all your unbelief; and nothing can prevent you from coming to God. Your ordination is not full and complete till God has laid His hand upon you. We require as much to qualify us as did those who have gone before us; God is the same. If the Savior in former days laid His hands upon His disciples, why not in latter days? (*History of the Church* 2:195-196)

---

8 Parley P. Pratt (Jr.), ed., *Autobiography of Parley Parker Pratt* (Salt Lake City, 1873; 3rd ed. Deseret Book Co., 1938), 118-121.

It is obvious, from these words, that the principal calling of the Twelve is to be special witnesses of Christ unto the world, to bear testimony of him. As such, they are primarily charged with the responsibility for missionary work. Nevertheless, they also have judicial and presiding authority, as we shall see later when we discuss their role as the "traveling high council."

The Seventy

The choice of the Twelve was soon followed by another meeting of the members of Zion's Camp:

> On the 28th of February (1835), the Church in council assembled, commenced selecting certain individuals to be Seventies, from the number of those who went up to Zion with me in the camp; and the following are the names of those who were ordained and blessed at that time, to begin the organization of the first quorum of the Seventies, according to the visions and revelations which I have received. The Seventies are to constitute traveling quorums, to go into all the earth, whithersoever the Twelve Apostles shall call them. (*History of the Church* 2:201-202)

The *History of the Church* then goes on to note the "names of the Presidents and Members of the First Quorum of Seventies, Ordained Under the Hand of the Prophet Joseph Smith, with his two Counselors, Sidney Rigdon and Oliver Cowdery" (*History of the Church* 2:203). When others were chosen on March 1 for the same quorum, Frederick G. Williams and Hyrum Smith were listed as participants in the ordinations (*History of the Church* 2:204).

More than half a century later, Elder Orson Pratt, one of the original apostles, noted,

> The Prophet himself, and the Twelve and all that had been called, knew nothing in relation to the duties of these Seventies until the Lord revealed what they were, and at the same time He pointed out the duties of the Presidency of the Seventies, both the duties of the seven men constituting the Presidency of the Seventies, and also those of the seven men that were to preside

over each Council of the Seventies. (*Journal of Discourses* 22:31)

The Role of Zion's Camp

The Twelve and the Seventy are essentially missionary callings, with responsibility to travel throughout the world and build up the Church. The first brethren to be called to these positions suffered many hardships during their travels in North America and Europe. Moving about without purse or scrip, they were dependent upon the generosity of members and non-members alike. Enemies of the Church lay in wait for them and two of the original Twelve were actually assassinated.

In view of the dangers and difficulties they would encounter while fulfilling their assignments, the Twelve and the Seventy had to be men of great spiritual strength and perseverance. It was important that they be characterized by faith and by an ability to withstand hardship. Knowing this, the Lord had, in 1834, commanded the organization of Zion's Camp, a group of armed men who went to assist their brethren who were being attacked by mobs in Jackson County, Missouri. During an assembly of Elders held soon after the organization of the Twelve and the Seventy, Joseph Smith discussed the role played by the Zion's Camp expedition in the organization of the Church:

> Brethren, some of you are angry with me, because you did not fight in Missouri; but let me tell you, God did not want you to fight. He could not organize His kingdom with twelve men to open the Gospel door to the nations of the earth, and with seventy men under their direction to follow in their tracks, unless He took them from a body of men who had offered their lives, and who had made as great a sacrifice as did Abraham. Now the Lord has got His Twelve and His Seventy, and there will be other quorums of Seventies called, who will make the sacrifice, and those who have not made their sacrifices and their offerings now, will make them hereafter.[9]

---

9 Joseph Young, Sen., *History of the Organization of the Seventies*, 14, cited in a note to *History of the Church* 2:182.

Critics of the Prophet might see the Zion's Camp expedition as a failure. But to Joseph Smith, the purpose of the Camp had been fulfilled in testing its participants and in preparing for the selection of the Twelve and the Seventy.[10] This would explain why President Smith was so quick to discharge the members of Zion's Camp upon their arrival in Missouri, without even a pretense of fighting.

Joseph Smith's advance knowledge on the subject of the calling of the Twelve and the Seventy is reflected in his references to a "vision" that the Lord had given him, to which he alludes in his remarks on the Seventy just cited. He first mentioned this vision on February 8, 1835, when he asked Brigham and Joseph Young to assemble the Church for the purpose of selecting the Twelve and Seventy.[11] He also spoke of it on the day the Twelve were called, as recorded in the minutes of the meeting. ("President Smith then stated that the meeting had been called, because God had commanded it; and it was made known to him by vision and by the Holy Spirit" (*History of the Church* 2:182).) It is also mentioned in connection with the calling of the Seventy in D&C 107:93, revealed on the day of their calling, March 28, 1835.

The Traveling High Council

On March 28, 1835, the day the first quorum of Seventy was organized, Joseph Smith received a revelation that comprises most of D&C 107. The revelation noted that "The Twelve are a Traveling Presiding High Council, to officiate in the name of the Lord, under the direction of the Presidency of the Church, agreeable to the institution of heaven; to build up the church, and regulate all the affairs of the same in all nations, first unto the Gentiles and secondly unto the Jews" (D&C 107:33).

In the early days of the Church, the Twelve were more frequently called "the traveling high council" than "the quorum of the twelve

---

10 The trials endured by the participants in the Zion's Camp expedition may be compared with that of Abraham, recorded in Genesis 22. Though the Lord commanded Abraham to offer Isaac as a sacrifice, he did not intend to allow the patriarch to actually kill his son. Rather, it was a test of his faith.

11 Joseph twice referred to the vision during his discussion with Brigham and Joseph Young. See Joseph Young, Sen., *History of the Organization of the Seventies*, 1-2, cited in a footnote to *History of the Church* 2:181.

apostles."[12] This title was to distinguish them from the standing high councils of the Church. After the calling of the twelve, when the 1835 edition of the Doctrine and Covenants was prepared, the following verses were added as 5:13 to the constitution of the high council, established a year earlier:

> There is a distinction between the high council or traveling high priests abroad, and the traveling high council composed of the twelve apostles in their decisions.
>
> From the decision of the former there can be an appeal; but from the decision of the latter there cannot.
>
> The latter can only be called in question by the general authorities of the church in case of transgression. (D&C 102:30-32)

Less than two weeks after the calling of the Twelve, Joseph Smith made the following comments about their office:

> What importance is there attached to the calling of these Twelve Apostles, different from the other callings or offices of the Church? . . . They are the Twelve Apostles, who are called to the office of the Traveling High Council, who are to preside over the churches of the Saints, among the Gentiles, where there is a [read "no"] presidency established; and they are to travel and preach among the Gentiles, until the Lord shall command them to go to the Jews. They are to hold the keys of this ministry, to unlock the door of the kingdom of heaven unto all nations, and to preach the Gospel to every creature. This is the power, authority and virtue of their apostleship. (*History of the Church* 2:200)[13]

---

12 In 1840, when a majority of the Twelve were in England on missions, Joseph Smith addressed an epistle "To the Traveling High Council and Elders of the Church of Jesus Christ of Latter-day Saints in Great Britain." (*History of the Church* 4:226). As late as 1843, in a proclamation to the Saints in Nauvoo, the Twelve called themselves "the Traveling High Council" (*History of the Church* 5:248).

13 These ideas are expressed in other places as well, such as the New Testament (when Christ commissioned the Twelve of his day to go throughout the world, preaching the gospel), D&C 18 (commanding the Three Witnesses to choose the Twelve) and D&C 107 (which, among other things, outlines the responsibilities of the Twelve).

Soon after being organized, the Twelve set about their duties by organizing the Church in the eastern part of the United States, outside the jurisdiction of the stakes in Kirtland and Zion. On May 14, 1835, they organized the first of several "conferences" in Dunkirk, New York, each of them comprising various branches.[14] They later organized similar conferences in England.

While the calling of the Twelve often required that they organize the Church in various parts of the world, we have but few examples of the Traveling High Council actually serving as a Church court in early days,[15] though there are records of the Twelve meeting as a high council. For example, in his diary, Joseph Smith indicated that on October 5, 1835, he attended "a high councel [sic] of the twelve apostles," but it does not appear that they held a trial.[16]

One of the early indications of the judicial role of the Twelve is in a letter written by William Smith to his brother Joseph on December 18, 1835. In it he notes that he "was called to an account, by the Twelve, yesterday, for my conduct" and that he had offered to step down from the Quorum (History of the Church 2:339). Nearly two years later, three members of the Twelve (John F. Boynton and the two Johnsons) "made their confessions and were received into fellowship by vote of the Church, also to retain their apostleship," on

---

14 The Westfield Conference comprised four branches (History of the Church 2:222). On the twenty-second of the same month, the Freedom Conference, with twelve branches, was organized in Freedom, New York (History of the Church 2:224). On June19 "nine of the traveling high council met with the church in conference at Pillow Point, New York" and organized the Black River Conference of eleven tiny branches (History of the Church 2:225). A month later (July 17), all twelve assembled at Saint Johnsbury, Vermont, and organized the Vermont Conference with ten branches (History of the Church 2:238). "Bradford, Massachusetts, August 7th. Nine of the traveling high council met and decided that the limits of the conference embrace the State of Massachusetts, to be called the Massachusetts Conference" (History of the Church 2:241). On August 28, 1835, "the traveling high council assembled in conference at Farmington, Maine, and resolved - that this be called the Main Conference," comprising four branches (History of the Church 2:253). A year later, on August 9, 1836, we read of a conference organized in New Jersey, in which nine branches were represented, from the states of New York, New Jersey, New Hampshire, Massachusetts and Pennsylvania (History of the Church 4:6).

15 For a revelation to Wilford Woodruff in which the Lord alludes to the judicial authority of the apostles, see the appendix to this volume.

16 Cited in Dean C. Jessee, ed., The Personal Writings of Joseph Smith (Salt Lake City: Deseret, 1984), 61.

recommendation of the Quorum's president, Thomas B. Marsh (*History of the Church* 2:512).

On March 17, 1839, in the midst of the exodus from Missouri, when the stakes and their high councils were disrupted by persecution, death, apostasy and flight, the Traveling High Council took charge of trying various members for their conduct. Four prominent members of the Church, including a counselor in the First Presidency (Frederick G. Williams) and the President of the Quorum of the Twelve (Thomas B. Marsh) were excommunicated at a conference conducted by Brigham Young on that date (*History of the Church* 3:283-284).

Four years later, on May 22, 1843, Joseph Smith, then residing in Nauvoo, received letters of complaint against Elder Benjamin Winchester of the Philadelphia Branch, and "directed the Twelve Apostles to act upon the matter" (*History of the Church* 5:403). The Twelve, in company with Joseph and Hyrum Smith, Bishop Newel K. Whitney, and others, held a Church court five days later. Quorum President Brigham Young announced his decision "that Elder Winchester should give up his license and cease preaching until he should reform." To this, Hyrum Smith, who had spoken for the defense, objected, believing that more testimony was needed. President Young indicated that his quorum would not hear the case again, and that, if there were to be further investigations, it would have to be done by the high council in Nauvoo. President Joseph Smith, who prosecuted the trial, "said that it was not the business of the high council. They could not try him. It belonged to the Twelve, and them alone; for it was concerning matters abroad, and not in Nauvoo. The high council was to try cases that belong to the stake, and the Twelve to regulate the churches and elders abroad in all the world; and Elder Winchester's case comes under the jurisdiction of the Twelve and theirs alone" (*History of the Church* 5:409-411).

About a year after Joseph's death, Elder Samuel Brannon, who had been disfellowshipped, appeared before "a council of the Twelve" presided by Brigham Young, and after introducing testimony to prove his innocence, was restored to fellowship (*History of the Church* 7:418). It was the Twelve who originally disfellowshipped him (*History of the Church* 7:395). In this case, however, the quorum appears to have been acting in its capacity as the Presidency of the Church, in the absence of the First Presidency.

The Twelve and the High Council

The revelation of February 1835, incorporated into D&C 107, and the additions to D&C 102 clearly established the boundaries of judicial authority of the standing high councils as opposed to the traveling high council. The standing high councils, located in what came to be called "stakes," had local jurisdiction only, in those areas of heavy concentration of Church membership. "Abroad," i.e., in areas where the Church was sparse in numbers and widely scattered, such judicial functions fell to the Quorum of the Twelve and such temporary councils of high priests or elders as they authorized to conduct that business.

Because the high council in Kirtland was headed by the Church's First Presidency, they seem to have felt from time to time that they were superior to the Quorum of the Twelve, despite the Lord's explicit statements in D&C 107. Several incidents in early Church history point out the dilemma confronting the leading quorums of the Church. For example, on August 4, 1835, the high council in Kirtland undertook to write a letter to the Twelve, in which they chided them in these words:

> We further inform the Twelve, that as far as we can learn from the churches through which we have traveled, you have set yourselves up as an independent council, subject to no authority of the Church, a kind of outlaws! This impression is wrong, and will, if persisted in, bring down the wrath and indignation of heaven upon your heads. (*History of the Church* 2:240)

One of the cases investigated by the high council was that of Gladden Bishop, who had been excommunicated by the Twelve. At a meeting of the high council held in Kirtland on September 27, 1835, Joseph Smith intervened:

> An attempt was made in the foregoing Council to criminate the Twelve before the High Council for cutting off Gladden Bishop at their Bradford conference, but their attempt totally

failed. I decided that the High Council had nothing to do with the Twelve, or the decisions of the Twelve. But if the Twelve erred they were accountable only to the General Council of the authorities of the whole Church, according to the revelations. (*History of the Church* 2:285)

The conflict between the Twelve and the Kirtland High Council over which group was second to the Presidency is understandable when one realizes that, at the time, the First Presidency presided directly over the High Council of Kirtland. Prior to the calling of the Twelve, the High Council had, in fact, been the presiding authority of the Church in the absence of the Presidency. The calling of a second high council in Zion complicated matters for some members in Kirtland, as had the calling of David Whitmer to be Joseph Smith's successor. In council with the Twelve on November 12, 1835, Joseph, referring to Whitmer's ordination in Missouri, remarked to the Apostles:

> I supposed I had established this Church on a permanent foundation when I went to Missouri, and indeed I did so, for if I had been taken away, it would have been enough, but I yet live, and therefore God requires more at my hand. (*History of the Church* 2:308)

Two months later, on January 16, 1836, the Twelve met with the First Presidency in a meeting at which the latter are significantly called "the Presidency of the High Council in Kirtland" (named as Joseph Smith, Sidney Rigdon, and Frederick G. Williams). Thomas B. Marsh, President of the Twelve, lodged some complaints on behalf of his quorum. One concerned the fact that, at a council held the previous Friday, the Twelve were placed "below the [High] Councils of Kirtland and Zion," while these latter two groups were stationed next to the Presidency. Another concern was that the decision of the Twelve (while on missions in the east) in the case of Gladden Bishop had been subsequently brought "before the High Council in Kirtland, for investigation." The Twelve felt their decision was ignored by the High Council (*History of the Church* 2:372-373).

Having heard these complaints,

President Smith next proceeded to explain the duty of the Twelve, and their authority, which is next to the present Presidency, and that the arrangement of the assembly in this place, on the 15th instant, in placing the High Councils of Kirtland next the Presidency, was because the business to be transacted, was business relating to that body in particular, which was to fill the several quorums in Kirtland, not because they were first in office, and that the arrangements were the most judicious that could be made on the occasion; also the Twelve are not subject to any other than the first Presidency, viz., "Myself" said the Prophet, "Sidney Rigdon, and Frederick G. Williams, who are now my Counselors; and where I am not, there is no First Presidency over the Twelve." (*History of the Church* 2:373-4)

To emphasize his point, the Prophet called a meeting for the following day, at which he assembled and organized the quorums by order, beginning with the First Presidency, followed by the Twelve, "the seventy who were present," then the High Councils of Kirtland and Zion (*History of the Church* 2:376). The pattern had been set.

Presiding Authority

Prior to the choosing of the Twelve and the Seventy, the High Council at Kirtland were the second council of the Church, after the First Presidency. This was to change during 1835. The revelation of February 28, 1835, the day the Seventy were selected, clearly laid down the authority of the leading quorums of the Church:

Of the Melchizedek Priesthood, three Presiding High Priests, chosen by the body, appointed and ordained to that office, and upheld by the confidence, faith, and prayer of the church, form a quorum of the Presidency of the Church.

The twelve traveling councilors are called to be the Twelve Apostles, or special witnesses of the name of Christ in all the world—thus differing from other officers in the church in the duties of their calling.

And they form a quorum, equal in authority and power to the three presidents previously mentioned.

The Seventy are also called to preach the gospel, and to be especial witnesses unto the Gentiles and in all the world—thus differing from other officers in the church in the duties of their calling.

And they form a quorum, equal in authority to that of the Twelve special witnesses or Apostles just named.

And every decision made by either of these quorums must be by the unanimous voice of the same; that is, every member in each quorum must be agreed to its decisions, in order to make their decisions of the same power or validity one with the other—

A majority may form a quorum when circumstances render it impossible to be otherwise—

Unless this is the case, their decisions are not entitled to the same blessings which the decisions of a quorum of three presidents were anciently, who were ordained after the order of Melchizedek, and were righteous and holy men. (D&C 107:22-29)

The revelation changed the order of succession and leadership in the Church. In the absence of the First Presidency, the Twelve Apostles became the presiding authority. In the absence of both of these quorums, the Seventy were to preside. Fourth in authority were the standing high councils of the Church, with the high councils of Zion having the same authority in Zion as the twelve in the stakes of Zion:

The standing high councils, at the stakes of Zion, form a quorum equal in authority in the affairs of the church, in all their decisions, to the quorum of the presidency, or to the traveling high council.

The high council in Zion form a quorum equal in authority in the affairs of the church, in all their decisions, to the councils of the Twelve at the stakes of Zion. (D&C 107:36-37)

At a meeting held in Kirtland on May 2, 1835, the matter of the role of the Twelve, the Seventy, and the High Council were discussed:

President Joseph Smith then stated that the Twelve will have no right to go into Zion, or any of its stakes, and there undertake to regulate the affairs thereof, where there is a standing high council; but it is their duty to go abroad and regulate all matters relative to the different branches of the Church. When the Twelve are together, or a quorum of them, in any church, they will have authority to act independently, and make decisions, and those decisions will be valid. But where there is no quorum, they will have to do business by the voice of the Church. No standing High Council has authority to go into the churches abroad, and regulate the matters thereof, for this belongs to the Twelve. No standing High Council will ever be established only in Zion or one of her stakes. When the Twelve pass a decision, it is in the name of the Church, therefore it is valid.

No official member of the Church has authority to go into any branch thereof, and ordain any minister for that Church, unless it is by the voice of that branch. No Elder has authority to go into any branch of the Church, and appoint meetings, or attempt to regulate the affairs of the church, without the advice and consent of the presiding Elder of that branch.

If the first Seventy are all employed, and there is a call for more laborers, it will be the duty of the seven presidents of the first Seventy to call and ordain other Seventy and send them forth to labor in the vineyard, until, if needs be, they set apart seven times seventy, and even until there are one hundred and forty-four thousand thus set apart for the ministry . . . The Twelve and the Seventy have particularly to depend upon their ministry for their support, and that of their families; and they have a right, by virtue of their offices, to call upon the churches to assist them. (*History of the Church* 2:220-221)

The diminishing role of the high council in the expanding Church was stressed by the fact that they were excluded from a special meeting held on May 5, 1835, the minutes of which record the following:

A grand council was held in Kirtland, composed of the following officers of the Church, viz: Presidents Joseph Smith, Jun., David Whitmer, Oliver Cowdery, Sidney Rigdon, Frederick G. Williams, Joseph Smith, Sen., and Hyrum Smith, with the council of the Twelve Apostles, Bishop Partridge and counselors, Bishop Whitney and counselors, and some of the Seventies with their presidents. (*History of the Church* 2:219-220)

The order in which the Presidents of the Church are listed is significant. Joseph Smith is followed by his designated successor, David Whitmer, then by the Second Elder, Oliver Cowdery, then by his original two counselors, and finally by his father and brother, who served as additional counselors to the First Presidency. During the course of the meeting:

> President Joseph Smith, Jun., said that it would be the duty of the Twelve, when in council, to take their seats together according to age, the oldest to be seated at the head, and preside in the first council, the next oldest in the second, and so on until the youngest had presided; and then begin at the oldest again.
>
> The Twelve then took their seats according to age as follows: Thomas B. Marsh, David W. Patten, Brigham Young, Heber C. Kimball, Orson Hyde, William E. M'Lellin, Parley P. Pratt, Luke S. Johnson, William Smith, Orson Pratt, John F. Boynton, and Lyman E. Johnson. (*History of the Church* 2:219-220)

This order prevailed with the original Twelve, inasmuch as they were all chosen at the same time. However, as new members were later added to the council, they took their place according to their date of ordination, so that the senior apostle served as President. This was explained in 1877 by Elder Orson Pratt, who was one of the original Twelve:

> The original Twelve, first chosen, were all made equal, by the Prophet Joseph Smith. And he said to them in the basement of the Temple as they were to be sent as a Council on their first mission, that the oldest should preside in the first Conference, in the following Conferences, the next in seniority, and so on, until all had taken their turns in presiding. And you shall be equal, showing respect to the oldest. They were arranged according to their ages, while all their successors were arranged, according to the date of their respective ordinations. (*Journal of Discourses* 19:118)

As noted earlier, D&C 107 declares that the Twelve are a body equal in authority to the First Presidency. This means that when the First Presidency is dissolved by the death of the President, it is the Twelve and not the counselors to the President who become the Presidency of the Church. At the dedication of the Kirtland Temple on March 27, 1836, the prophet Joseph further strengthened the position of the Twelve in the Church by having them sustained by the same titles as the First Presidency:

> I . . . called upon the several quorums and all the congregation of saints, to acknowledge the presidency as prophets and seers . . . I then called upon the quorums and congregation of saints to acknowledge the Twelve Apostles, who were present, as prophets, seers, revelators and special witnesses to all the nations of the earth, holding the keys of the kingdom to unlock it, or cause it to be done, among them. (*History of the Church* 2:417)

The relationship between the leading quorums was further clarified by Brigham Young in a discourse delivered May 7, 1861, in which he explained the meaning of the revelation contained in D&C 107:

> You read in the revelation alluded to that when the Twelve were called and ordained, they possessed the same power and authority as the three First Presidents; and in reading further you find that there must needs be appendages and helps growing out of this Priesthood. The Seventies possess the same power and authority; they hold the keys of establishing, building up, regulating, ordaining, and setting in order the kingdom of God in all its perfections upon the earth. We have a Quorum of High Priests, and there are a great many of them. They are a local body—they tarry at home; but the Seventies travel and preach; so also do the High Priests, when they are called upon. They possess precisely the same Priesthood that the Seventies and the Twelve and the First Presidency possess; but are they ordained to officiate in all the authority, powers, and keys of this Priesthood? No, they are not. Still, they are High Priests of God; and if they magnify their Priesthood, they will receive at some time all the authority and power that it is possible for man to receive.

Suppose that Sidney Rigdon and Frederick G. Williams had been taken away or had apostatized, as one of them did soon after the revelation I have referred to was given, and there had been only Joseph Smith left of the First Presidency, would he alone have had authority to set in order the Kingdom of God on the earth? Yes. Again: Suppose that eleven of the Twelve had been taken away by the power of the Adversary, that one Apostle has the same power that Joseph had, and could preach, baptize, and set in order the whole kingdom of God upon the earth, as much so as the Twelve, were they all together. Again: If in the providence of God he should permit the Enemy to destroy these two first Quorums, and then destroy the Quorum of Seventy, all but one man, what is his power? It would be to go and preach, baptize, confirm, lay on hands, ordain, set in order, build up, and establish the whole kingdom of God as it is now. Can we go any further? Yes; and I think you will see the reason of it, and how easy it is to be understood, and see the propriety of it . . . Suppose the Enemy had power to destroy all but one of the High Priests from the face of the earth, what would that one possess in the power of his Priesthood? He would have power and authority to go and preach, baptize, confirm, ordain, and set in order the kingdom of God in all its perfection on the earth. Could he do this without revelation? No. Could the Seventies? No. Could the Twelve? No. And we ask, Could Joseph Smith or the First Presidency do this without revelation? No; not one of them could do such a work without revelation direct from God. I can go still further. Whoever is ordained to the office of an Elder to a certain degree possesses the keys of the Melchisedek Priesthood; and suppose only one Elder should be left on the earth, could he go and set in order the kingdom of God? Yes, by revelation. (*Journal of Discourses* 9:87)

Apostleship of the Seventy

The institution of the office of Seventy in 1835 was perhaps the most surprising of all to members of the restored Church. Terms such as apostle, bishop, high priest, elder, priest, etc., were common enough in the Bible to be familiar to them. But the term "seventy" was rather obscure. There were, to be sure, a few references to a group of "seventy elders" in the time of Moses (Numbers 11:16-17, 24-30; Exodus 24:1, 9-11), but nineteenth-century Christianity knew no such office.

The only New Testament reference to the Seventy is found in Luke 10:1, where we read, "After these things the Lord appointed other seventy also, and sent them two and two before his face into every city and place, whither he himself would come." It is unfortunate that the term "other seventy" has led many Latter-day Saints to believe that Luke was speaking of a second quorum of seventy. A better translation from the original Greek would be "seventy others." The question, of course, is seventy other what?

The answer to that question is seventy other apostles. Luke's preceding chapter (9) recounts the commission of the Twelve and it is noteworthy that both the Twelve and the Seventy were "sent" out by Jesus with the same instructions. The Greek word *apostolos* means "one sent."

As we learn from the revelation of February 28, 1835 (D&C 107:34-35, 38), the Seventy are to assist the Twelve in their ministry. Like the Twelve, they "are called as special witnesses to the nations of the earth," as President John Taylor later noted (*Journal of Discourses* 24:288; see D&C 107:23, 25). There are, in fact, a number of early references in Church history in which at least the seven presidents of the Seventy (who, as we shall see, constituted the "Council of the Seventies") are called apostles. For example, exactly one year after their calling, on February 28, 1836, we find that "This day the Council of the Seventy met to render an account of their travels and ministry, since they were ordained to that Apostleship" (*History of the Church* 2:346).

On the same day that the Prophet called upon the Church to sustain the Twelve as prophets, seers and revelators (i.e., at the dedication of the Kirtland Temple on March 27, 1836), he noted:

> I next called upon the quorums and congregation of Saints to acknowledge the presidents of Seventies, who act as their representatives, as Apostles and special witnesses to the nations, to assist the Twelve in opening the Gospel kingdom among all people, and to uphold them by their prayers, which they did by rising. (History of the Church 2:418)

Subsequent Church leaders have made similar declarations. In the general conference held in October 1844, following the death of Joseph and Hyrum Smith, Brigham Young told the Seventy, "You are all apostles to the nations to carry the gospel; and when we send you to build up the kingdom, we will give you the keys and power and authority" (*History of the Church* 7:308).

Several years later, Wilford Woodruff, then one of the Twelve, spoke in Salt Lake City about "the Twelve Apostles, the Seventy Apostles, and High Priest Apostles, and all other Apostles" (*Journal of Discourses* 4:147). The "High Priest Apostles" are probably the First Presidency, while the "other Apostles" would be those ordained to the office of apostle but who were not members of the leading quorums of the Church.

Elder Orson Pratt also indicated that the Seventy were apostles. Speaking of the events of February 1835, he once said, "The Lord also, about the same time that He called the Twelve Apostles, was prepared to call Seventies to minister under the direction of the Twelve . . . and many were ordained to this Apostleship" (*Journal of Discourses* 22:30).

President Joseph F. Smith wrote, "The seventies are called to be assistants to the twelve apostles; indeed they are apostles of the Lord Jesus Christ, subject to the direction of the Twelve (*Conference Report,* April 1907, 5).

Patriarchal Authority of the Twelve

On November 3, 1835, the prophet Joseph received a revelation in which the Lord said of the Twelve Apostles,

> they must all humble themselves before me, before they will be accounted worthy to receive an endowment, to go forth in my name unto all nations . . . Therefore, verily thus saith the Lord your God, I appoint these Twelve that they should be equal in their ministry, and in their portion, and in their evangelical rights. (*History of the Church* 2:300-301)

When the 1835 *Doctrine and Covenants* was published, it added information about these "evangelical rights" to the revelation of March 28, 1835 (3:17-18) that describes the duties of the Twelve and the Seventy:

It is the duty of the Twelve, in all large branches of the church, to ordain evangelical ministers, as they shall be designated unto them by revelation. The order of this priesthood was confirmed to be handed down from father to son, and rightly belongs to the literal descendants of the chosen seed, to whom the promises were made. (D&C 107:39)

It is likely that Joseph received the revelation represented by this addition by June 21, 1835, when he noted, "I preached in Kirtland on the Evangelical Order" (*History of the Church* 2:234). Nevertheless, the revelation evidently did not read the same in its original version. At the general conference of October 5, 1877, Elder Orson Pratt noted, "When this was first given, the word 'evangelical' was not there. But Joseph was wrought upon by the Spirit to erase the word patriarchs and substitute the words 'evangelical ministers'" (*Journal of Discourses* 19:114).

The term "evangelist" is used three times in the New Testament, where the functions of the office are not described (Acts 21:8; Ephesians 4:11; 2 Timothy 4:5).[17] Article of Faith 6 declares, "We believe in the same organization that existed in the Primitive Church, namely, apostles, prophets, pastors, teachers, evangelists, and so forth." The Greek term behind "evangelist" derives from the same root as *euangelion*, meaning "good news" and generally rendered "gospel" in the King James Bible. Because of this, most Christians believe that an evangelist is a missionary, who spreads the "good news" about Christ. In the LDS view, the good news given by evangelists is in the patriarchal blessing given to members of the Church.

New Information on the Bishopric

Some time before the publication of the 1835 D&C, the Lord revealed additional information about the office of bishop that was then added to two revelations received in November 1831. These became

---

17 In 1839, the prophet Joseph discussed the meaning of Ephesians 4:11, which lists apostles, prophets, evangelists, pastors, and teachers as officers in the early Christian Church. He said, "An Evangelist is a Patriarch, even the oldest man of the blood of Joseph or of the seed of Abraham. Wherever the Church of Christ is established in the earth, there should be a Patriarch for the benefit of the posterity of the Saints, as it was with Jacob in giving his patriarchal blessing unto his sons" (*History of the Church* 3:381).

1835 D&C 3 (1981 D&C 107) and 22 (1981 D&C 68).[18] The new information indicates that a bishop, unless he is a literal descendant of Aaron (and hence a natural heir to the position, which is that of the presiding officer in the Aaronic Priesthood), must be a high priest, and that any bishop must be appointed by proper authority (D&C 68:15-21). None of this was included in the revelation as published in *The Evening and Morning Star* 1/5 of October 1832, but it was included when that issue was republished in Kirtland in June 1835. The revelation was slightly modified in the 1835 edition of the D&C, where we read that the bishop must be appointed by the "First Presidency of the Melchizedek Priesthood" (22:2). This was further modified in later editions to read "First Presidency of the Church" (D&C 68:4-22ff).[19]

At the Church's general conference of April 6, 1837, Joseph Smith wrote:

> The Bishop is a High Priest, and necessarily so, because he is to preside over that particular branch of Church affairs, that is denominated the Lesser Priesthood, and because we have no direct lineal descendant of Aaron to whom it would of right belong. This is the same, or a branch of the same, priesthood. (*History of the Church* 2:477-78)

Brigham Young later made a similar statement:

> The Bishoprick by right belongs to the literal descendants of Aaron, but we shall have to ordain from the other tribes, men who hold the High Priesthood, to act in the Lesser, until we can find a literal descendant of Aaron, who is prepared to receive it. (*Journal of Discourses* 1:136)[20]

---

18 The 1981 D&C 107 begins with a revelation of March 28, 1835, that comprises verses 1-58. To it was added a revelation received in two segments in 1831 but not previously published. See the wording of D&C 107:58.

19 As noted in Chapter 4, the quorum of the First Presidency did not exist in November 1831 when the original revelation was received. When it was organized in 1832, it constituted the presidency of the high priesthood, though it also served as the presiding authority of the Church because the high priests governed the Church. Later, the presidency of the high priesthood became the First Presidency of the Church. The two editions containing this revelation reflect this development.

20 On May 7, 1861, Brigham Young declared, "The office of a Bishop belongs to the lesser Priesthood. He is the highest officer in the Aaronic Priesthood" (Journal of Discourses 9:87).

Provisions for the trial of a member of the Presidency of the Church are outlined in D&C 107:76-83, where we learn that a council comprised of twelve high priests presided over by the bishop may conduct such a hearing. In conformity with these provisions, on August 11, 1834, a council was organized in Kirtland under the presidency of Bishop Newel K. Whitney, to hear a complaint by Sylvester Smith (a member of the Kirtland High Council) against President Joseph Smith (*History of the Church* 2:142). When the council was held on August 23, "Elder Reynolds Cahoon presided in consequence of the ill health of Bishop Whitney" (*History of the Church* 2:147).

The council decided against Sylvester Smith, but he refused to accept the decision, evidently because the bishop was absent. In consequence, Sidney Rigdon wrote a letter to Bishop Whitney on the latter date, saying, "I therefore require that you summon the High Council of this Church to investigate this case, that a final decision may be had upon the same. I say the High Council because it is a case affecting the Presidency of said Church" (*History of the Church* 2:150). The second council also decided against Sylvester Smith.

Chapter 7

THE KEYS OF THE PRIESTHOOD

The power and authority of the higher, or Melchizedek
Priesthood, is to hold the keys of all the spiritual bless-
ings of the church—To have the privilege of receiving the
mysteries of the kingdom of heaven, to have the heavens
opened unto them, to commune with the general assem-
bly and church of the Firstborn, and to enjoy the com-
munion and presence of God the Father, and Jesus the
mediator of the new covenant. (D&C 107:18-19)

As the Kirtland Temple neared completion, the early part of 1836
saw the beginnings of temple work in the restored Church, accompa-
nied by a re-emphasis on priesthood governing principles. Priesthood
leaders from Ohio and Missouri were gathered together for several
months to participate in the planned festivities.

During the previous year, the High Council of Zion lost four of its
members to the Council of the Twelve and a fifth died. At a High
Council meeting held in Kirtland on January 6, 1836, the vacancies
were filled (*History of the Church* 2:356-7).

A week later, Joseph Smith met in council with the Presidencies of
Kirtland and Zion,[1] the Twelve Apostles, the High Councils of
Kirtland and Zion, the Bishops of Kirtland and Zion, the Presidency
of the Seventy, and others (*History of the Church* 2:364). Elder Vinson
Knight was chosen to replace Hyrum Smith as a counselor to Bishop
Whitney because Hyrum "had been ordained to the Presidency of the
High Council at Kirtland." Replacements were also chosen for
"President Oliver Cowdery, who had been elected to the Presidency
of the High Council at Kirtland." Members of the Kirtland High

---

1 The Presidents are named as Joseph Smith, Sr., Sidney Rigdon, Hyrum Smith, David
Whitmer, John Whitmer, and W. W. Phelps.

107

Council who had been called to the Twelve and the Seventy were also replaced at this time (*History of the Church* 2:365-6).

On January 14, the Church adopted a set of "Rules and Regulations to be Observed in the House of the Lord in Kirtland." The rules refer to the "Presidency of the Church" and also call Joseph Smith "the presiding Elder of said Church."[2] The use of both terms was probably to emphasize the difference between Joseph Smith's position as the President of the entire Church and his position as President of the Kirtland Stake. Indeed, minutes of a meeting held the previous September 26 speak of "the Council of the Presidency of the Church, consisting of Joseph Smith, Jun., Sidney Rigdon, David Whitmer, W. W. Phelps, John Whitmer, Hyrum Smith and Oliver Cowdery," thus listing the presidencies of Kirtland and Zion together (*History of the Church* 2:283).

When the priesthood of the Church met on January 15, the rules for the temple were sustained, in order, by the Presidency, the High Council of Kirtland, the High Council of Zion, the Twelve, the Seventies, and the Bishoprics of Zion and Kirtland (*History of the Church* 2:370).

Organizing the Quorums

The meeting held in the nearly-completed Kirtland Temple on January 15, 1836, was for the specific purpose of organizing the quorums of the Priesthood. Elder Don Carlos Smith, brother of the Prophet, was chosen "to be ordained to the High Priesthood, also to officiate as President, to preside over that body in Kirtland." Presidencies were also chosen for the quorums of elders, priests, teachers and deacons. The First Presidency, consisting of Joseph and Hyrum Smith and Sidney Rigdon, ordained the presidents of the high priests and elders, while Bishop Newel K. Whitney ordained the presidents of the priests, teachers, and deacons quorums. This separation of the two orders of priesthood was further emphasized when it was decided "that the presidency of the High Council [i.e., the First

---

2 *History of the Church* 2:369. The term "Presidency of the Church" also appears in the record from two days earlier (*History of the Church* 2:364). About a week later, Joseph Smith signed a marriage certificate as "Presiding Elder of said Church" (*History of the Church* 2:377).

Presidency] hold the keys of the House of the Lord, except the keys of one vestry, which is to be held by the Bishopric of the Aaronic Priesthood" (*History of the Church* 2:370-371).

William Cowdery, not one of the bishops, was made "President over the Priests of the Aaronic Priesthood in Kirtland" at the meeting. The practice of having priests preside over the priests quorums was based on scriptural precedent (D&C 107:61). For August of 1835, the History makes two mentions of the "acting president of the Priests." (*History of the Church* 2:244, 246). At the same time, we read that John Corrill was the "acting Bishop" in Missouri (*History of the Church* 2:244, 246). He was, in fact, second counselor to Bishop Edward Partridge (*History of the Church* 2:436), but later became a bishop.

Anointing in the Temple

Part of the preparation for the Temple dedication was the anointing of members of the Priesthood. The ordinances were begun on January 21, 1836, when the "Presidency" (meaning the presidencies of Kirtland and Zion) met in the Temple and anointed and blessed Joseph Smith Sr. "to be our Patriarch, to anoint our heads." He, in turn, anointed the Presidency (*History of the Church* 2:379-80). Afterward, Warren Parrish, the Prophet's scribe, and the Bishoprics of Kirtland and Zion were anointed by Joseph Smith Sr. (*History of the Church* 2:381-2). Then the High Councils of Kirtland and Zion were assembled and "President Hyrum Smith anointed the head of the President of the Councilors in Kirtland, and President David Whitmer the head of the President of the Councilors of Zion. The President of each quorum then anointed the heads of his colleagues" (*History of the Church* 2:382).

From this, it is clear that each high council had its own president, in addition to the Church presidencies in Kirtland and Zion. In the early days of the Church, the High Council often acted independently of the Stake Presidency and sometimes had its own president.

The following day, the Presidency met in the Temple with the Twelve and the Presidency of the Seventy, the two High Councils also being present. Joseph noted that "We then laid our hands upon Elder Thomas B. Marsh, who is President of the Twelve, and ordained him to the authority of anointing his brethren." After he had done this, the Twelve "proceeded to anoint and bless the Presidency of the Seventy, and seal upon their heads power and authority to anoint their brethren." "Brother Don C. Smith was also anointed and blessed to preside over the High Priests' quorum" (*History of the Church* 2:382-3).

Six days later, Joseph Smith and his counselors met again in the Temple and "consecrated and anointed the counselors of the presidents of the High Priests' quorum," then went to another room, to do the same for the elders quorum presidency. Each of these presidencies was then left to anoint the members of their respective quorums (*History of the Church* 2:386).

The quorums were again assembled on February 6 for an anointing and sealing of blessings, with the high priests and elders in one room, the Twelve and Seventy in another and the bishops in a third (*History of the Church* 2:391).

Authorization for Ordinations

In view of the organization of the priesthood quorums, it became important that the Church lay down rules for the ordination of men to the priesthood. On January 30, 1836,

> At a conference of the Presidency of the Church,[3] it was resolved that no one be ordained to an office in the Church at Kirtland, without the voice of the several quorums, when assembled for Church business.
>
> Resolve—That Alva Beaman, president of the Elders, be directed to give to the Presidents of the Church a list of the names of the several Elders, comprising his quorum, and all other Elders in Kirtland, not belonging to any quorum now established. (*History of the Church* 2:388)

Two weeks later, on February 12, the resolution was put to "the several quorums" assembled in the Temple:

---

3 Again, we presume, from earlier examples, that this means the presidencies of both Kirtland and Zion.

First. Resolved—That no one be ordained to any office in the Church in this stake of Zion, at Kirtland, without the unanimous voice of the several bodies that constitute this quorum, who are appointed to do Church business in the name of said Church, viz., the Presidency of the Church; the Twelve Apostles of the Lamb; the twelve High Councilors of Kirtland; the twelve High Councilors of Zion; the Bishop of Kirtland and his counselors; the Bishop of Zion and his counselors; and the seven presidents of Seventies; until otherwise ordered by said quorums.

Second. And further Resolved—That no one be ordained in the branches of said Church abroad, unless they are recommended by the voice of the respective branches of the Church to which they belong, to a general conference appointed by the heads of the Church, and from that conference receive their ordination.

The foregoing resolutions were concurred in by the presidents of the Seventies. (*History of the Church* 2:394-5)

The following day, the Twelve met and amended the second resolution to read as follows:

That none be ordained to any office in the branches in which they belong; but to be recommended to a general conference appointed by those, or under the direction of those, who are designated in the book of Doctrine & Covenants, as having authority to ordain and set in order all the officers of the Church abroad, and from that conference to receive their ordination. (*History of the Church* 2:395)

The amendment had reference to the calling of the Twelve to regulate the affairs of the churches "abroad", i.e., outside the organized stakes. However, the amendment met with little success. It was rejected by the High Council of Kirtland at its meeting on February 17 (*History of the Church* 2:396-7), by the High Council of Zion on February 18 (*History of the Church* 2:397), and by the Presidency on February 22 (*History of the Church* 2:398). Finally, at a meeting of the Presidency and all the quorums on March 3, following discussion, nine of the Twelve repealed their amendment (*History of the Church* 2:402, 405). The other three members of the Twelve met separately with the

Presidency on March 19 and did the same (*History of the Church* 2:408).

The Seventy

At a meeting held March 30, 1836, Joseph Smith explained the role of the Twelve and the Seventy:

> The Seventies are not called to serve tables, or to preside over churches, to settle difficulties, but are to preach the Gospel and build them up, and set others, who do not belong to these quorums, to preside over them, who are High Priests. The Twelve also are not to serve tables, but to bear the keys of the Kingdom to all nations, and unlock the door of the Gospel to them, and call upon the Seventies to follow after them, and assist them. The Twelve are at liberty to go wheresoever they will. (*History of the Church* 2:431-2)[4]

At a meeting held the previous month (February 14), the "quorums" voted "that the Twelve and Seventy see that the calls for preaching in the region round about Kirtland be attended to, and filled by judicious Elders of this Church" (*History of the Church* 2:400). It thus became the responsibility of these two quorums to call elders to missionary service. This evidently meant the calling of other Seventies as well. In the revelation of a year earlier, the Lord had made provision for other seventies to be called when necessary:

> And these seven presidents are to choose other seventy besides the first seventy to whom they belong, and are to preside over them; and also other seventy, until seven times seventy, if the labor in the vineyard of necessity requires it. (D&C 107:95-96)

---

4 The expression "wait on tables" comes from the story found in Acts 6. Some members of the early Christian Church complained that the widows were being neglected and demanded that the twelve apostles take action. Knowing that their duties lay in missionary work and in the spiritual affairs of the Church, "the twelve called the multitude of the disciples unto them, and said, It is not reason that we should leave the word of God, and serve tables" (Acts 6:2). They then proposed that seven worthy men be selected to head up the welfare responsibilities of the early Church.

At a meeting held on May 2, 1835, Joseph Smith had said:

> If the first Seventy are all employed, and there is a call for more laborers, it will be the duty of the seven presidents of the first Seventy to call and ordain other Seventy and send them forth to labor in the vineyard, until, if needs be, they set apart seven times seventy, and even until there are one hundred and forty-four thousand thus set apart for the ministry. (*History of the Church* 2:221)

At that same meeting, the Church passed the following resolutions:

> Voted, that when other Seventy is required, the presidency of the first Seventy shall choose, ordain, and set them apart from among the most experienced Elders of the Church.
>
> Voted, that whenever the labor of other Seventy is required, they are to be set apart and ordained to that office; those who are residing at Kirtland and the regions round about, who can come to Kirtland, to be set apart and ordained by the direction of the Presidency of the Church in Kirtland. (*History of the Church* 2:222)

In accordance with this, on February 3, 1836, in the midst of the organization and anointing of the quorums, the president of the elders' quorum "handed in seventy of his quorum designed for another Seventy if God will" (*History of the Church* 2:391). Four days later, Joseph Smith "met with the Presidency . . . in company with the presidency of the Seventy, to choose other seventy also" (*History of the Church* 2:393).[5]

Dedicating the Temple

The dedication services for the Kirtland Temple began on March 27, 1836 and lasted three days. On the first day, the quorums were arranged in order, beginning with the Presidency. All acknowledged Joseph Smith "as a Prophet and Seer" (*History of the Church* 2:416). President Smith then "called upon the several quorums, and all the

---

5 The term "other seventy" implies that this expression in the King James Version of Luke 10:1 had been misunderstood to refer to a second quorum of seventy in Jesus' day.

congregation of Saints, to acknowledge the Presidency as Prophets and Seers . . . I then called upon the quorums and congregation of the Saints to acknowledge the Twelve Apostles, who were present, as Prophets, Seers, Revelators" (*History of the Church* 2:417).[6] The Seventy were then sustained as apostles and special witnesses (*History of the Church* 2:418).

Following this, the Church sustained "the High Council of Kirtland, in all the authority of the Melchisedek Priesthood," "the Bishops of Kirtland and Zion, and their counselors, in all the authority of the Aaronic Priesthood," and "the High Council of Zion . . . in all the authority of the High Priesthood." Finally, the presidents and counselors of the elders, priests, teachers, and deacons quorums were sustained (*History of the Church* 2:418).

The dedicatory prayer was then read for the first time.

Two days later, "Presidents Joseph Smith, Jun., Frederick G. Williams, Sidney Rigdon, Hyrum Smith, and Oliver Cowdery, met in the most holy place in the Lord's House." These men comprised the First Presidency, with Hyrum Smith being an additional counselor and Oliver Cowdery being the "Assistant President" of the Church. The Spirit told them to "call the other presidents" and the Bishoprics. The "other presidents," who then came into the room, were David Whitmer, William W. Phelps and John Whitmer, the Presidency in Zion (*History of the Church* 2:429-30). The "Presidency" sustained at the meeting of March 27 as "prophets and seers" evidently included all eight.

By March 30, the last day of the dedication ceremonies, Joseph Smith was able to observe "to the quorums, that I had now completed the organization of the Church . . . and that they now were at liberty, after obtaining their licenses, to go forth and build up the Kingdom of God" (*History of the Church* 2:432). It yet remained, however, for him to receive further priesthood keys in the Kirtland Temple.

Restoration of the Keys

At the outset of the dedicatory services for the Kirtland Temple on March 27, 1836, Sidney Rigdon read from Matthew 18:18-20 (*History*

---

6 The sustaining of the Twelve as "Prophets, Seers and Revelators" in the Kirtland temple was later recalled in discourses by Orson Pratt (*Journal of Discourses* 19:114) and John Taylor (*Journal of Discourses* 19:124).

of the Church 2:413-4). The passage has particular significance because it refers to the keys of the priesthood that Jesus promised to Peter (Matthew 16:19) and given to the Savior's three chief apostles atop the mountain shortly thereafter (Matthew 17; see *History of the Church* 3:387). Matthew 18:18, worded in the plural rather than the singular of Matthew 16:19, confirms that all of the apostles had, by then, received these keys. The restoration of the keys of the priesthood is discussed in D&C 27:

> And also with Elias, to whom I have committed the keys of bringing to pass the restoration of all things spoken by the mouth of all the holy prophets since the world began, concerning the last days;
>
> And also John the son of Zacharias, which Zacharias he (Elias) visited and gave promise that he should have a son, and his name should be John, and he should be filled with the spirit of Elias;
>
> Which John I have sent unto you, my servants, Joseph Smith, Jun., and Oliver Cowdery, to ordain you unto the first priesthood which you have received, that you might be called and ordained even as Aaron . . .
>
> And also Elijah, unto whom I have committed the keys of the power of turning the hearts of the fathers to the children, and the hearts of the children to the fathers, that the whole earth may not be smitten with a curse...
>
> And also with Peter, and James, and John, whom I have sent unto you, by whom I have ordained you and confirmed you to be apostles, and especial witnesses of my name, and bear the keys of your ministry and of the same things which I revealed unto them. (D&C 27:6-7, 9, 12)[7]

The keys of the priesthood are the right of presidency. In May 1829, Joseph and Oliver first received priesthood "keys," as noted in the wording of their ordination by the resurrected John the Baptist

---

7 Though this section is dated August 1830, the last half of verse 5 continuing through verse13 were added later, for they were not part of the corresponding Section 28 of the 1833 *Book of Commandments*. BC 28 not only does not contain these verses, but it ends at what corresponds to D&C 27:15, which is worded a little differently.

(JS-H 69; D&C 13). Those keys constituted the presidency of the Aaronic Priesthood. A short time later, they received the keys of the Melchizedek Priesthood from Peter, James and John. The fullness of the keys, however, was not restored until April 3, 1836 when, in the Kirtland Temple, Joseph Smith and Oliver Cowdery received the visit of Jesus Christ, Elias, Elijah and Moses (D&C 110).[8]

Moses and Elijah (referred to in the Greek form as "Elias") had previously appeared with the Savior on the mount of transfiguration (Matthew 17:1-13) where, according to the Prophet Joseph, they conferred the keys of the priesthood on Peter, James and John (*History of the Church* 3:387). The Elias of D&C 110 also appeared in the meridian of time, shortly before the ministry of Christ, to proclaim his authority, as noted in the passage cited above from D&C 27:6-7. The Biblical account (Luke 1:5-17) calls him Gabriel, whom Joseph Smith identified with the Old Testament Noah (*History of the Church* 3:386). It is possible that Noah, who presided at the baptism of the earth (i.e., the Great Flood),[9] is the angel who ordained John to the Priesthood (D&C 84:27-28). Further, he may be the individual who told John what sign to look for in the Messiah (John 1:33).

In the Kirtland Temple, Elias (evidently Gabriel) restored the "dispensation of the gospel of Abraham" (D&C 110:12). Noah, of course, was still alive when Abraham was born. The "gospel" or "good news" given to Abraham was that in him all nations would be blessed (Galatians 3:8; Genesis 22:18). The authority of Elias, there-

---

8 John Taylor, speaking in 1877, indicated that the keys restored at that time were soon thereafter given to the Twelve and the Seventys, as they received their endowments (presumably washings and anointings): "We read in the history of the Church that at a certain time there was a revelation given in the Temple which was built at Kirtland, Ohio; when Joseph Smith and Oliver Cowdery were seated in it, several important personages appeared and gave certain keys, powers and privileges . . . the keys of this dispensation [brought back by Moses] were given to Joseph Smith, and conferred by him on the Twelve, the Seventies and others, and they received this as a part of their ministry, their endowments" (*Journal of Discourses* 19:144). The idea that all of the prophets who held keys from the beginning of the world ultimately appeared to Joseph Smith to restore their authority has often been expressed. One of the first statements to this effect was made by President Heber C. Kimball on July 5, 1857: "All the prophets from the days of Adam and from the creation of the world have conferred their priesthood and keys of this dispensation, and brother Brigham holds them in connection with the old Prophets and Apostles" (*Journal of Discourses* 5:7).

9 See 1 Peter 3:20-21; *Journal of Discourses* 8:83.

fore, is to bring blessings to all the nations of the earth. This becomes more significant when we realize that Elias, as Noah, is the ancestor of all those who live on the earth today. The keys he restored, therefore, are very broad in their application, and may include the right to govern all of Noah's inhabitants.

The keys restored by Moses were more restricted. They deal specifically with the tribes of Israel. Moses was the first prophet to unite Israel after the Egyptian captivity and to lead them to the promised land. He therefore restored to Joseph Smith the "keys of the gathering of Israel from the four parts of the earth, and the leading of the ten tribes from the land of the north" (D&C 110:11). This was in conformity with the prophecy of Jeremiah, who saw the formal end of the nation of Israel when the kingdom of Judah was taken captive by the Babylonians in 586 B.C.

> Therefore, behold, the days come, saith the Lord, that it shall no more be said, The Lord liveth, that brought up the children of Israel out of the land of Egypt:
>
> But, the Lord liveth, that brought up the children of Israel from the land of the north, and from all the lands whither he had driven them; and I will bring them again into their land that I gave unto their fathers. (Jeremiah 16:14-15)

The third messenger to restore keys on April 3, 1836, was Elijah, who came to "turn the heart of the fathers to the children, and the heart of the children to their fathers" (Malachi 4:5-6; see D&C 110:13-16). When Moroni quoted this prophecy to Joseph Smith on the night of his first visit, he used wording that varies from the version in Malachi: "Behold, I will reveal unto you the priesthood, by the hand of Elijah the Prophet" (D&C 2:1; *Joseph Smith-History* 38).

Elijah restored the priesthood that seals a man to his wife and a couple to their children. It is the family or patriarchal authority of which the Lord spoke in D&C 131:1-4:

> In the celestial glory there are three heavens or degrees;
>
> And in order to obtain the highest, a man must enter into this order of the priesthood (meaning the new and everlasting covenant of marriage);
>
> And if he does not, he cannot obtain it.

He may enter into the other, but that is the end of his kingdom; he cannot have an increase."

The patriarchal order of the priesthood is the one spoken of in D&C 107:39-52, the keys of which were preserved and held by the senior patriarch or family head. It is one of three orders of the priesthood discussed by Joseph Smith in a discourse delivered on August 27, 1843. Using Hebrews chapter 7 as his text, he explained:

There are three grand orders of Priesthood referred to here.

1st. The King of Shiloam (Salem) had power and authority over that of Abraham, holding the key and power of endless life . . .

What was the power of Melchizedek? 'Twas not the Priesthood of Aaron, which administers in outward ordinances, and the offering of sacrifices. Those holding the fulness of the Melchizedek Priesthood are kings and priests of the Most High God, holding the keys of power and blessings. In fact, that Priesthood is a perfect law of theocracy, and stands as God to give laws to the people, administering endless lives to the sons and daughters of Adam . . .

"Without father, without mother, without descent, having neither beginning of days nor end of life, but made like unto the Son of God, abideth a priest continually." The Melchizedek Priesthood holds the right from the eternal God, and not by descent from father and mother.

The 2nd Priesthood is Patriarchal Authority. Go to and finish the temple, and God will fill it with power, and you will then receive more knowledge concerning this priesthood.

The 3rd is what is called the Levitical Priesthood, consisting of Priests to administer in outward ordinances, made without an oath; but the Priesthood of Melchizedek is by an oath and covenant.

The Holy Ghost is God's messenger to administer in all these Priesthoods. (*History of the Church* 5:554-555)

On a later occasion, Joseph Smith spoke thus of the three orders of the priesthood:

The spirit of Elias is first, Elijah second, and Messiah last. Elias is a forerunner to prepare the way, and the spirit and power of Elijah is to come after, holding the keys of power, building the Temple to the capstone, placing the seals of the Melchizedek Priesthood upon the house of Israel, and making all things ready; then Messiah comes to his Temple, which is last of all.

Messiah is above the spirit and power of Elijah, for he made the world, and was that spiritual rock unto Moses in the wilderness. Elijah was to come and prepare the way and build up the kingdom before the coming of the great day of the Lord, although the spirit of Elias might begin it. (*History of the Church* 6:254)

Joseph said that the Melchizedek Priesthood "is the highest and holiest Priesthood, and is after the order of the Son of God"(*History of the Church* 4:207). The holders of the offices of Elias, Elijah and Messiah are bearers of the Melchizedek Priesthood, but each has keys pertaining to a different order of the Priesthood. The office of Messiah presides over the Melchizedek Priesthood; the office of Elijah presides over the Patriarchal Priesthood; and the office of Elias presides over the Aaronic Priesthood.

The title Elias is the Greek rendition of the Old Testament name Elijah. At the mount of transfiguration, Jesus along with Peter, James and John, were visited by Elijah. Afterward, Jesus implied that John the Baptist was Elias, but he stated that there was yet an Elias to come. In this sense, the term was used as the title of any forerunner to restoration of priesthood authority on the earth.[10]

The individual charged with the oversight of the restoration of all the keys was the last living apostle on the earth, John the Revelator, who has never died (D&C 7). He received the commission "to gather the tribes of Israel; behold, this is Elias, who, as it is written, must come and restore all things" (D&C 77:14; see also verse 9). He must therefore be the Elias of whom Jesus spoke when he said that he "truly shall first come and restore all things" (Matthew 17:11). He along with Peter and John, gave priesthood keys to Joseph Smith, after John the Baptist, another Elias or forerunner of Christ, had come.

---

10 For a discussion of this topic, see James E. Talmage, *Jesus the Christ*, chapter 23.

Chapter 8

THE CHURCH IN ZION

*What is meant by the command in Isaiah, 52d chapter,
1st verse, which saith: Put on thy strength, O Zion—and
what people had Isaiah reference to? He had reference
to those whom God should call in the last days, who
should hold the power of priesthood to bring again Zion,
and the redemption of Israel; and to put on her strength
is to put on the authority of the priesthood, which she,
Zion, has a right to by lineage; also to return to that
power which she had lost. (D&C 113:7-8)*

On April 3, 1837, the High Council of Zion met. Seven of its
members were in attendance, but they were without the Missouri
Presidency. The council objected to a number of actions that had been
taken by the Presidency without first consulting with the High
Council. These included disfellowshipping a High Council member
without trial, and ordaining Jacob Whitmer (brother of two members
of the Presidency) without High Council approval. After discussion,
the High Council set a meeting for April 5 and invited Presidents
William W. Phelps and John Whitmer to join them, along with Bishop
Edward Partridge and his two counselors and two members of the
Quorum of the Twelve, Thomas B. Marsh and David W. Patten. On
April 5, President Phelps, with President Whitmer, asked that the
apostles and bishopric be excluded, but the High Council and others
refused, forcing President Phelps to back down. The meeting recon-
vened on April 6 and 7.[1]

Similar meetings were held during the months that followed. For
example, minutes inserted into the Far West Record show that, on an
unknown date, the Presidency convened a meeting comprising "the
high council, two of the Apostles and about 10 of the Seventies and

---

1 Donald Q. Cannon and Lyndon W. Cook, *Far West Record* (Salt Lake City: Deseret,
1983), 103; see *History of the Church* 2:483f.

the Bishop and one of his councilors together with a numerous body of members."[2] In the attendance list for the meeting of May 22, 1837, though Presidents W. W. Phelps and John Whitmer were present, the members of the High Council are called "Presiding Counsillors."[3] This is perhaps because of the unresolved difference of opinion between the Presidency and the High Council.

A week later, charges were filed by five brethren against David Whitmer, President in Zion, Frederick G. Williams of the First Presidency, Luke Johnson and Parley P. Pratt of the Quorum of the Twelve, and Warren Parrish. The High Council in Kirtland was assembled under the presidency of Sidney Rigdon to investigate the matter. Presidents Frederick G. Williams and David Whitmer argued that the council had no authority to try them because of their positions, and claimed that they "ought to be tried before the Bishop's court" (as provided in D&C 107:82).

A disagreement over jurisdiction arose, and by majority vote it was decided to discharge the presidents. After an adjournment, the council met under the presidency of Sidney Rigdon, Oliver Cowdery and Frederick G. Williams, who declined to pass judgment on Parley P. Pratt. The council was broken up and "dispersed in confusion" (*History of the Church* 2:484-6).

The calling of a high council without the presidency was not unique to the Missouri situation. On September 9, 1837, "the High Council of Kirtland met in the Lord's House and organized by electing Jared Carter, president, and Phinehas Richards, clerk." The council, listing these two among the twelve, then proceeded to hold a Church court (*History of the Church* 2:511). When Jared Carter moved to Far West, the High Council chose Samuel H. Smith as president in his stead (*History of the Church* 2:518). He presided at the meeting of October 18, 1837 (*History of the Church* 2:519). Joseph Smith, who had been named as president of the Kirtland High Council when it was consti- tuted four years before (D&C 102), did not object to these proceedings. Nor were there objections raised when John Murdock was named "President of the High Council" of Zion when, under the direction of Bishop Edward Partridge, David Whitmer and Oliver Cowdery were

2 Donald Q. Cannon and Lyndon W. Cook, *Far West Record*, 106.
3 *Ibid.*, 112.

tried for their membership.[4] It would appear that, just as high priests could be called to substitute for absent high council members, it was possible to appoint substitutes for the presidency when they were absent or otherwise unable to preside.

Regulating the Seventy

During the conference session held in the Kirtland Temple on April 6, 1837, a problem arose with respect to the position of the Seventy. Joseph Smith's history records the events of that day:

> Another subject of vital importance to the Church, was the establishing of the grades of the different quorums. It was ascertained that all but one or two of the presidents of the Seventies were High Priests, and when they had ordained and set apart any from the quorums of Elders, into the quorum of Seventies, they had conferred upon them the High Priesthood, also. This was declared to be wrong, and not according to the order of heaven. New Presidents of the Seventies were accordingly ordained to fill the places of such of them as were High Priests, and the ex-officio presidents, and such of the Seventies as had been legally ordained to be High Priests, were directed to unite with the High Priests' quorum. (*History of the Church* 2:476)

There are two factors that make this passage difficult for today's LDS Church members to understand. The first is that we currently use the term "high priesthood" to refer to apostles, seventies, high priests, and elders, while in Joseph Smith's day, it referred only to those holding the office of high priest. The second is that today's Seventies tend to have been ordained high priests prior to their call as Seventies.

One must note that the problem in 1837 had to do with the *presidents* of the Seventy. It was not so much that they had been ordained high priests, but that they had not been "chosen out of the number of the Seventy," as required by D&C 107:93. I.e., they had not been ordained as seventies and were therefore not actually members of that quorum.

Further explanations were forthcoming at the meeting:

---

4 *Ibid.*, 162.

President Joseph Smith, Jun., addressed the assembly and said, the Melchizedek High Priesthood was no other than the Priesthood of the Son of God; that there are certain ordinances which belong to the Priesthood, from which flow certain results; and the Presidents or Presidency are over the Church; and revelations of the mind and will of God to the Church, are to come through the Presidency. This is the order of heaven, and the power and privilege of this Priesthood. It is also the privilege of any officer in this Church to obtain revelations, so far as relates to his particular calling and duty in the Church. All are bound by the principles of virtue and happiness, but one great privilege of the Priesthood is to obtain revelations of the mind and will of God. It is also the privilege of the Melchizedek Priesthood, to reprove, rebuke, and admonish, as well as to receive revelation . . .

A High Priest, is a member of the same Melchizedek Priesthood with the Presidency, but not of the same power or authority in the Church. The Seventies are also members of the same Priesthood,[5] are a sort of traveling council or Priesthood, and may preside over a church or churches, until a High Priest can be had. The Seventies are to be taken from the quorum of Elders, and are not to be High Priests. They are subject to the direction and dictation of the Twelve, who have the keys of the ministry." (*History of the Church* 2:477)

In his footnote in *History of the Church* 2:476, B. H. Roberts noted regarding these Presidents of Seventy, "That is, they ordained them High Priests. Since they were Elders, however, they already possessed the High Priesthood, and hence it was only necessary to ordain them to the office of Seventy in that Priesthood; but the brethren who had immediate charge of ordaining Seventies (the first presidents of Seventies) seemed to have thought it necessary to ordain them High Priests in order for them to hold the High Priesthood, hence the correction made by the Prophet."

This interpretation employs the later LDS usage of the term "High Priesthood" to interpret what was said in Joseph Smith's day. But Joseph Smith and his contemporaries, "High Priesthood" meant only

---

5 Here, we omit the parenthetical insert added by B. H. Roberts.

the office of High Priest. Elders and Seventies did not hold the "High Priesthood," as Joseph used that term.[6] Nevertheless, it is interesting that the Prophet, for the first time, suggested that high priests, elders, and seventies, hold the same priesthood.

It may well have been that some felt the Seventy should be ordained to the office of High Priest, perhaps because they were authorized under D&C 107 (and several statements by Joseph Smith) to "set in order the churches," which would include the calling and ordination of high priests.[7]

At the conference held in Kirtland on September 3, 1837, new presidents of the Seventy were sustained to replace those who had been ordained high priests, and it was "voted that the old presidents of the Seventies be referred to the quorum of High Priests" (*History of the Church* 2:510).

Apostasy in the Church

There were, however, far more serious problems that arose during the conference of September 3, 1837. The congregation refused to accept Frederick G. Williams as Second Counselor in the First Presidency. "President Smith then introduced Oliver Cowdery, Joseph Smith, Sen., Hyrum Smith, and John Smith for assistant counselors. These last four, together with the first three, are to be considered the heads of the Church." This was carried unanimously. But three members of the Twelve—Luke S. Johnson, Lyman E. Johnson, and John F. Boynton—"were rejected and disfellowshipped" (*History of the Church* 2:509). The latter three had sought the life of Joseph Smith. They had actually drawn knives on him in the Temple. The trouble

---

6 Indeed, the official history as originally published in *Millennial Star* 15:849 under the date of April 6, 1836, reads: "such of the Seventies as had been legally ordained to the High Priesthood, were directed to unite with the High Priests." Roberts changed this to read as follows in *History of the Church* 2:476: "such of the Seventies as had been legally ordained to be High Priests, were directed to unite with the High Priests' Quorum."

7 John Whitmer, who was Church Historian at this time, described events of February 1835 in these words: "About the same time there were seventy high priests chosen, who were called to be under the direction of the Twelve, and assist them according to their needs; and if seventy were not enough, call seventy more, until seventy times seventy" (John Whitmer's History manuscript, 51). The passage is included in a footnote to *History of the Church* 2:221, where B. H. Roberts notes that these men were not high priests. Most were elders. He refers us to Joseph Young, "History of the Organization of the Seventies," 4-5.

they stirred up in Kirtland ultimately made it necessary for Joseph to move to Missouri.

The problems with the Missouri Presidency did not escape the notice of President Joseph Smith. The day after the conference, he wrote, "Verily thus saith the Lord unto you my servant Joseph—my servants John Whitmer and William W. Phelps have done those things which are not pleasing in my sight, therefore if they repent not they shall be removed out of their places. Amen" (*History of the Church* 2:511).

The problems worsened at a "general assembly" (conference) of the Church held at Far West the following November 7 and attended by Joseph Smith and Sidney Rigdon of the First Presidency. Elder Thomas B. Marsh, President of the Twelve, was chosen Moderator, while the business of sustaining the authorities of the Church was presented by Sidney Rigdon of the First Presidency. When it came time to sustain the Presidency in Zion, there was considerable disagreement. The minutes reflect the feelings of those present:

> David Whitmer was then nominated as the first President of this branch[8] of the Church, and was objected to by Elder Marsh. Bishop Partridge said he should vote for prest. [*sic*] Whitmer . . . Pres't. Joseph Smith jr. [*sic*] then nominated John Whitmer for an assistant President, who was objected, and Elder Marsh spake in opposition to him . . . Wm. W. Phelps was nominated for an assistant President, for this Church, by Pres't Joseph Smith jr. . . . passed unanimous."[9]

The members of the High Council were then sustained, but only one of the "branch" (stake) presidency was approved by the conference.

Moving to Missouri

During the latter part of 1837, it became obvious that Joseph Smith would have to move to Missouri, both to remove himself from the danger in Kirtland and to set the Church in Zion in order.

---

8 In the early days of the Church, the terms "branch" and "stake" were used interchangeably. Cf. D&C 107:39.

9 Donald Q. Cannon and Lyndon W. Cook, *Far West Record*, 122-123; see *History of the Church* 2:522-3.

Even before the restoration of the Priesthood keys in the Kirtland Temple, the feasibility of the leadership of the Church moving to Zion had been discussed. At a meeting held on March 13, 1836, two weeks prior to the Temple dedication, the First Presidency and some of the Twelve met and "felt the necessity of the Presidency removing to that place" in the spring for her "redemption" (*History of the Church* 2:407).

The influx of members of the Church into Missouri made it necessary to consider the establishment of additional stakes in that area. This became a topic of discussion among the Church leaders in Kirtland at a meeting held on September 17, 1837:

It appeared manifest to the conference that the places appointed for the gathering of the Saints were at this time crowded to overflowing, and it was necessary that there be more stakes of Zion appointed in order that the poor might have a place to gather to, "wherefore it was moved, seconded and voted unanimously that President Joseph Smith, Jun., and Sidney Rigdon be requested by this conference to go and appoint other stakes, or places of gathering."[10]

Things became critical for the Church in Kirtland during the closing days of 1837. A number of people had apostatized, including some members of the Twelve, and there were some who sought to slay the Prophet Joseph. In consequence of increasing mob violence, Joseph Smith and Sidney Rigdon fled the city on January 12, 1838, and went their separate ways to Missouri (*History of the Church* 3:1). Brigham Young had already left. He arrived at Far West on December 22. Joseph arrived there on February 14 (*History of the Church* 3:8), while Sidney did not arrive until April 4.

On the day of the Prophet's departure from Kirtland, he inquired about the status of stakes and received the following revelation:

In the presence of Joseph Smith Jr., Sidney Rigdon, Vinson Knight and G. W. Robinson at the French Farm, the following inquiry was made of the Lord.

A question was asked of the Lord concerning the trying of the First Presidency of the Church of Latter-day Saints for transgression according to the item of law found in third Section of

---

10 *History of the Church* 2:514. This was also noted in the memorial issued by the Kirtland Bishopric the following day.

the Book of Covenants 37th verse; Whether the decision of such a council of one Stake shall be conclusive for Zion and all the Stakes—

Answer: Thus saith the Lord the time has now come when a decision of such an council would not answer for Zion and all her Stakes—

What will answer for Zion and all her Stakes?

Answer: Thus saith the Lord, let the First Presidency of my Church be held in full fellowship in Zion and all her stakes until they shall be found transgressors by such an high council—as is named in the 3rd Section 37th Verse of the Book of Covenants, in Zion by 3 witnesses standing against each member of said Presidency and said witnesses shall be of long and faithful standing and such also as cannot be impeached by other witnesses, before said council and when a decision is had by such an council in Zion it shall only be for Zion it shall not answer for her Stakes but if said decision be acknowledged by the Council of her Stakes then it shall answer for her Stakes but if it is not acknowledged by the Stakes then such Stakes may have the privilege of hearing for themselves. Or if said decision shall be acknowledged by a majority of her Stakes then it shall answer for all her Stakes. And again the Presidency of said Church may be tried by the voice of the whole body of the Church of Zion, and the voice of a majority of all her Stakes. And again except a majority is had by the voice of the Church of Zion, and a majority of all her Stakes, the charges will be considered not sustained, and in order to sustain such charge or charges before said Church of Zion or her Stakes such witnesses must be had as is named above, that is three witnesses to each president—who are of long and faithful standing that cannot be impeached by other witnesses before the Church of Zion or her Stakes. And all this saith the Lord, because of wicked and aspiring men, let all your doings be in meekness and in humility before me even so Amen.[11]

The importance of this revelation in dealing with leadership problems in Missouri was soon to become apparent.

---

11 Revelation to Joseph Smith at Kirtland, January 12, 1838, Joseph Smith Collection, in LDS Church Historian's Office.

The Missouri Presidency

At general assemblies of the Church held February 5-9, 1838 in four different places in Missouri, the Presidency in Zion were rejected. At the first of these meetings, held in Far West on February 5, Bishop Partridge spoke out against the proceedings, saying that they were "hasty and illegal." He felt that the Presidency should be tried "before the common council," as would be done in the case of the First Presidency (D&C 107:82).

As is evident from the minutes, this was the opinion of the bishops, Partridge, Corrill, and Billings. This is not surprising when one considers that the bishop is the presiding officer at the "common council."[12] On the other hand, the High Council believed that it had the authority to try the presidents.

> Elder John Corrill then spake against the High Council in regard to their proceedings, and labored hard to show that the meeting was illegal, and that the Presidency ought to be had before a proper tribunal, which he considered to be a Bishop and twelve High Priests . . . Titus Billings said that he could not vote until they had a hearing in the common council. Elder Marsh said that the meeting was according to the directions of Br Joseph. he, [sic] therefore, considered it legal.

Church members present tended to agree and voted to reject the presidency.[13]

Despite the objections by the bishops, the Missouri Church membership, following the lead of Joseph Smith and the Twelve, evidently believed that the common council was for trial of a member of the First Presidency but not of stake presidencies. It is likely, based on subsequent evidence, that David Whitmer felt he could not be tried by the High Council because he had been ordained by Joseph Smith as his successor and therefore was a President of the Church. Oliver Cowdery seems to have had the same impression as David Whitmer,

---

12 A letter written by Oliver Cowdery on April 12, 1838 was addressed to "Rev. Edward Partridge, Bishop of the Church of Latter-day Saints." (HC 3:18 fn)

13 Donald Q. Cannon and Lyndon W. Cook, *Far West Record*, 138-140; see *History of the Church* 3:3-8, 11.

his fellow witness, for he too was an Assistant President of the Church and its Second Elder. Both men were, for all intents and purposes, on their way to apostasy and excommunication from the Church.

At a meeting of the High Council, the Bishop and his Council. February 10, 1838, it was moved, seconded and carried, that Oliver Cowdery, William H. Phelps and John Whitmer stand no longer as Chairman & Clerk, to sign and record liceces [*sic*; read "licenses"]. Also, voted that Thomas B. Marsh, and David W. Patten be Presidents, *pro. tempor.* of the Church of Latter Day Saints in Missouri, or until Presidents Joseph Smith Jr. and Sidney Rigdon arrives in the Land of Zion.[14]

Thus, in the absence of the First Presidency, the High Council accepted the two ranking apostles as their Presidency in Missouri. On March 10, 1838, a meeting of the High Council convened under "Thos B. Marsh and David W. Patten Presidents." A letter was read from "David Whitmer, W. W. Phelps, John Whitmer: Presidents of the Church of Christ in Mo.," addressed to "T. B. Marsh, one of the travelling Councillors" with the notation, "Attest: Oliver Cowdery, Clerk of the High Council of the Church of Christ in Mo."[15] Addressing the two apostles by the titles given them as members of the traveling high council was evidently intended to stress the fact that on May 2, 1835 Joseph Smith had said "that the Twelve will have no right to go into Zion, or any of its stakes, and there undertake to regulate the affairs thereof, where there is a standing high council" (*History of the Church* 2:220).

Technically speaking, however, the Twelve did not usurp the functions of the high council. Rather, the high council itself asked two members of the Twelve to serve as their presidents in the matter at hand. The Twelve could act as a traveling high council only when all of them were present, which was not the case.

In consequence of the discussion that followed the reading of this letter from the Missouri presidency, W. W. Phelps and John Whitmer were cut off from the church, while the cases of David Whitmer and Oliver Cowdery were held over for further investigation.[16]

---

14 Donald Q. Cannon and Lyndon W. Cook, *Far West Record*, 141.

15 *Ibid.*, 145.

16 *Ibid.*, 149.

It is probable that the council hesitated to excommunicate these two brethren because of their special calling as Witnesses of the Book of Mormon and as Assistant Presidents of the Church (being also two of the first three ordained apostles in this dispensation). Action was therefore delayed until the arrival of Joseph Smith a few days later.

On March 15, 1838, "The High Council of Zion, together with the Bishoprick [*sic*] met in Far West, on March the 15th 1838, agreeable to appointment and was organized as follows. President Joseph Smith jr took the charge of the Council." Minutes indicate that the High Council of this date was not identical in composition to the one that had met five days earlier (e.g., Brigham Young, a member of the Twelve who had arrived from Kirtland, was added to the High Council).

During the course of the meeting, "President Joseph Smith jr gave a history of the ordination of David Whitmer, which took place in July 1834, to be a leader, or a prophet to this Church, which (ordination) was on condition that he (J. Smith jr) did not live to God himself." This seems to have allayed the apprehension of the council at cutting off David Whitmer. At the morning session, "President J. Smith Jr. approved of the proceedings of the High Council, after hearing the minutes of the former Councils."[17]

With the dissolution of the Missouri Presidency, it was the First Presidency and Quorum of the Twelve who took charge of the High Council of Zion at subsequent meetings. Thus, on March 17, 1838, Thomas B. Marsh is listed as its President,[18] while at the meeting held on March 14, we read that the "Council was organized as follows: Presidents Joseph Smith jr. David W. Patten and Thomas B. Marsh" being the Presidency.[19]

On the anniversary of the Church's restoration, celebrated April 6, 1838, Joseph Smith presided at a meeting of the Missouri Saints in Far West. It was decided that "a clerk will be appointed for a High Council and to keep the Church records of this Stake. And three Presidents will be appointed to preside over this Church of Zion." Meanwhile, "Thomas B. Marsh was appointed President *Pro tempore* of the Church in Zion, and Brygum [*sic*] Young and David W. Patten

---

17 *Ibid.*, 151.
18 *Ibid.*, 152.
19 *Ibid.*, 153.

his assistant Presidents."[20] The minutes for the session held the following day indicate that Joseph Smith, Sidney Rigdon, David W. Patten, and Brigham Young took the stand (*History of the Church* 3:14).

Four days later (April 11, 1838), Elder Seymour Brunson leveled charges against Oliver Cowdery before the High Council in Far West. The indictment was addressed "to the Bishop and Council of the Church of Jesus Christ of Latter-day Saints," who thus comprised the "common council" necessary for trying the Presidency of the Church (*History of the Church* 3:16). The next day, "The High Council and Bishoprick of Zion, met according to appointment in Far West, April 12, 1838, Edward Partridge presiding." It was "voted unanimously that John Murdock be a President of the High Council." Cowdery's letter to Bishop Partridge was then read, in which the Church's Assistant President asked to withdraw from the Church over disagreements with a number of practices. Pursuant to his request, the council excommunicated him.[21]

The following day, charges were made against David Whitmer before the Council in Far West. In a letter addressed to John Murdock of the High Council, Whitmer refused to attend, believing that the High Council had no authority to try him, since he was a President of the Church. The letter was read and the council complied with Brother Whitmer's wishes to withdraw his Church membership and he was also excommunicated.[22] In attendance were Joseph Smith, with Thomas B. Marsh, David W. Patten and Brigham Young presiding.[23] At the same time, they excommunicated Lyman E. Johnson of the Quorum of the Twelve (*History of the Church* 3:20).

On July 8, 1838, Joseph Smith received a revelation at Far West, indicating what the Lord now expected of W. W. Phelps of the Missouri Presidency and Frederick G. Williams of the First Presidency:

20 *Ibid.*, 157-8; see *History of the Church* 3:14.

21 Donald Q. Cannon and Lyndon W. Cook, *Far West Record*, 162; see *History of the Church* 3:16-18.

22 For a discussion of David Whitmer's reaction to his excommunication and of subsequent events concerning him, see the appendix to this volume.

23 Donald Q. Cannon and Lyndon W. Cook, *Far West Record*, 178 (for those in attendance, see page 171). See also *History of the Church* 3:19-20.

Verily, thus saith the Lord,

In consequence of their transgressions their former standing has been taken away from them,

And now, if they will be saved, let them be ordained as Elders in my Church to preach my Gospel, and travel abroad from land to land and from place to place, to gather mine elect unto me, saith the Lord, and let this be their labors from henceforth. Amen. (*History of the Church* 3:46)

Presidency of the Church

The conflicts with the Missouri Presidency may have given rise to a new emphasis on the status of the First Presidency, even before they left Kirtland. Initially, Joseph Smith was sustained as "President of the High Priesthood" (i.e., President of the High Priests), with the proviso that this position also governed the Church. With the establishment of a second presidency in Missouri, it was time to stress the latter role. Hence, at the conference held in Kirtland on September 3, 1837, the Prophet was sustained "as the President of the whole Church." "President Smith presented Sidney Rigdon and Frederick G. Williams as his counselors, and to constitute with himself the three first Presidents of the Church."[24] "President Smith then introduced Oliver Cowdery, Joseph Smith, Sen., Hyrum Smith, and John Smith for assistant counselors. These last four, together with the first three, are to be considered the heads of the Church" (*History of the Church* 2:509).

The following day, the Prophet addressed a letter "Joseph Smith, Jun., President of the Church of Christ of the Latter-day Saints in all the world, to John Corrill and the whole Church in Zion" (*History of the Church* 2:508), in which he included the minutes of the conference. Thereafter, the stress was on the "Presidency of the Church" rather than the "Presidency of the High Priesthood" (e.g., *History of the Church* 3:147; D&C 117:13).

---

24 All were sustained, but there were some votes against Williams, who soon found objections among the Missouri saints as well.

The Bishopric in Zion

On June 25, 1833, the First Presidency, in a letter addressed to William W. Phelps and other Church leaders in Missouri, recommended that Isaac Morley and John Corrill, counselors to Bishop Edward Partridge, be ordained as bishops. Bishop Partridge's counselors were to be replaced by Parley P. Pratt and Titus Billings (*History of the Church* 1:363). These men, in fact, played a very important role in the work of the bishopric in Missouri, though the proposed ordinations did not take place at once.

On May 22, 1837, the Presidency in Zion (W. W. Phelps and John Whitmer being present) nominated John Corrill "for an agent to the Church and Keeper of the Lord's Store House." The action was unanimously approved by the high council and congregation.[25] On June 11, the high council at Far West approved the opening of a leather store under the direction of Lyman Wight, Simeon Carter and Elias Higbee, and agreed "that John Corrill, Isaac Morley and Calvin Bebee engage in the mercantile business if they choose" (*History of the Church* 2:491). Mercantile activities were the means by which the bishops, their counselors and bishops' agents were able to make a living while administering the law of consecration and stewardship.

On August 1, 1837, John Corrill was finally replaced as counselor to Bishop Partridge by Titus Billings. This was more than four years after the original recommendation from the First Presidency (*History of the Church* 2:504). At the November 7 meeting in Far West, Corrill's position as "Keeper of the Lord's Storehouse" was reaffirmed, as were the positions of Bishop Partridge and his counselors, Isaac Morley and Titus Billings. Morley, however, was also sustained as "Patriarch of this Branch of the Church" and "ordained to the office of Patriarch under the hands of Pres'ts. Joseph Smith, jr. Sidney Rigdon and Hyrum Smith."[26] He had not yet been made bishop, for at the conference of October 5 of the following year, it was voted "That Brs Isaac Morley, John Buchanan and James Allred be ordained or not to the Bishopric, by the First Presidency, as they see proper."[27]

25 Donald Q. Cannon and Lyndon W. Cook, *Far West Record*, 113.
26 *Ibid.*, 124.
27 *Ibid.*, 209.

Meanwhile, in Kirtland, at a conference held in the Temple on September 17, 1837, "Bishop Newel K. Whitney said the time had arrived when it became necessary for him to travel, and necessarily he must have an agent to act in his absence agreeable to the provisions made in the revelations. He nominated William Marks [a member of the high council], who was elected agent to the Bishop by unanimous vote" (*History of the Church* 2:513). The following day, Bishop Whitney and his counselors issued a "memorial" addressed "to the Churches abroad," which was read at Far West on November 10, 1837.[28]

From this, we learn that bishops were not wholly confined to geographic areas. Bishop Whitney was able to address instructions to Church members in Missouri and elsewhere and to travel away from Kirtland in the performance of his duties.

The term "Bishop and his council" or "Bishop's council" was in common use during 1837-1838.[29] The term "Bishoprick," referring to the Bishop and his counselors, appears to have been employed first in the high council minutes of February 24, 1838.[30] As a "council," the bishopric was mainly an ecclesiastical tribunal. Still, the principal role of the bishopric was in the care of the Church's needy members.[31] In this connection, we note the following resolutions, adopted at the high council meeting of April 21, 1838, attended by Joseph Smith:

> 8th Resolved that the Council, the Bishop and his Council use their influence to cause the people to consecrate to the Lord, for the support of the poor and needy.
>
> 9th Resolved that the Bishop be authorized to obtain or build a sufficient storehouse or houses to receive all the consecrations of the people, to be paid out for the avails of the town plot.[32]

---

28 *Ibid.*, 125; *History of the Church* 2:515-8.

29 See, e.g., Donald Q. Cannon and Lyndon W. Cook, *Far West Record*, 112 (22 May 1837), 182 (21 April 1838).

30 *Ibid.*, 141. In D&C 114:2, dated to April 17 of the same year, the term "bishopric" refers to any calling in the Church. Since the term, originating in the Greek, means "overseership," this makes perfect sense. In Acts 1:20, it denotes the office formerly held by the fallen apostle Judas Iscariot.

31 E.g., at the conference held on October 6, 1838, "Bishop E. Partridge made a Report of the temporal affairs of the Church." Donald Q. Cannon and Lyndon W. Cook, *Far West Record*, 211.

32 *Ibid.*, 182.

The law of consecration and stewardship failed due to the persecutions in Missouri and the unwillingness of many Church members to live the law as given. As a consequence, the Lord revealed an alternate plan. Only surplus properties would be given to the bishop of the Church in Zion. After that the members would pay a tithe of their annual increase. The plan was detailed in a revelation of July 8, 1838 (D&C 119). Ten days later, another revelation indicated that the tithes thus received would be disposed of by a council composed of the First Presidency of the Church, the Bishop and his council and the High Council (D&C 120).[33]

It was during the Missouri period that bishops came to be recognized as the heads of the Aaronic Priesthood. At a meeting held in Far West on August 1, 1837, it was "Resolved unanimously that every President of High Priests and Elders be ordained by some higher authority, and [that] the president of any quorum when Counsellors are needed may ordain his Counsellors himself and the Bishop shall take charge of the Lesser Priesthood."[34] At the conference held on April 8 of the following year, "Bishop Partridge represented the lesser Priesthood, and his council."[35]

Priesthood Regulations in Zion

At a meeting held on February 24, 1838, the High Council of Zion passed a number of resolutions relative to the government of the Church within the stake. We list some of them here:

1. "No High Priest, Elder or Priest (except the Presidency, High Council and Bishoprick) has any right or authority to preside over or take charge of any Branch, Society or neighborhood within the bounds of this Stake: but that the teachers, assisted by the deacons, be considered the standing ministry to preside each over his respective branch of the Stake agreeable to the covenants."[36]

---

33 This is essentially the pattern followed today. The Church's Committee on the Disposition of the Tithes comprises the First Presidency, the Twelve (who are, in effect, the high council over the entire Church), and the Presiding Bishopric. In Joseph Smith's day, there was no Presiding Bishopric.

34 Donald Q. Cannon and Lyndon W. Cook, *Far West Record*, 117.

35 *Ibid.*, 161; *History of the Church* 3:15.

36 Donald Q. Cannon and Lyndon W. Cook, *Far West Record*, 142.

2. "We recommend to all High Priests, Elders and Priests who are in good standing & friends to Joseph Smith jr, the Prophet that they do not take the lead of nor appoint meetings in any branch or neighborhood of Saints within the bounds of this Stake without the invitation or consent of the Presiding officer of that branch. We also, consider that the teacher, who is the presiding officer, has a right to object to any official character, who may come among them to officiate, who is not in good standing or a friend to the true cause of Christ. And also, that the teacher report, to the High Council, such as are unruly or teach corrupt doctrine among them."[37]

3. "Resolved, that each branch of this Stake send one or more teachers once in three months to the Quarterly conference of this Stake, with a written account of the true situation of his Branch, agreeable to the Covenants."[38]

Evidently, the Stake in Zion was allowing the teachers to appoint and conduct branch meetings, pursuant to their calling to "see that the church meet together often" (D&C 20:55). However, they were ignoring the verse that follows, which states that the teacher is "is to take the lead of meetings in the absence of the elder or priest" (D&C 20:56). Quarterly conferences, however, were under the direction of the stake presidency, which at that time consisted of the three senior members of the Quorum of the Twelve.

On April 7, 1838, "the general authorities of the Church met, to hold the first quarterly Conference of the Church of Latter Day Saints of Zion, at Far West." Presidents Joseph Smith, Sidney Rigdon, Thomas B. Marsh, David W. Patten and Brigham Young took the stand, after which the High Council and the quorums "were organized by their Presidents."[39]

---

37 *Ibid.*, 142.

38 *Ibid.*, 143. The "Covenants" are the revelations given to Joseph Smith, as contained in the "Doctrine & Covenants," where the "Doctrine" originally comprised the "Lectures on Faith" for the School of the Prophets. Note that these resolutions are the first occurrence of the word "stake" in the Far West Record. This resolution marks the beginning of the practice of holding quarterly stake conferences, which continued until the latter part of the twentieth century.

39 *Ibid.*, 159. Under the date of May 28, 1837, *History of the Church* 2:482 reads: "About this time the Presidency of the Church at Far West called a general meeting of the Church, at which were present the High Council, two of the Twelve Apostles, ten of the Seventies, the Bishop, and one counselor." One man was disfellowshipped by the council.

A similar order prevailed at a meeting held on July 6. On that occasion, Sidney Rigdon spoke of what later came to be called "ward/block/home teaching":

> The foundation of the happiness of the Church rests upon the heads of the Teachers and Deacons, whose duty it is to go from house to house and see that each family in the Church is kept in order, and that the children are taught the principles of righteousness; and also that the time had come when it was required at the hands of the Deacons, Teachers & Priests to render an account of their stewardship, the standing of the various branches to which they belonged, &c.[40]

At the same meeting, "the Bishop, Edward Partridge represented the Lesser Priesthood, also gave an account of the temporal affairs of the Church."[41]

New Stakes

In a revelation given on January 12, 1838 (the day Joseph Smith and Sidney Rigdon left Kirtland), it was commanded that only the First Presidency should have the right to organize new stakes.[42] A subsequent revelation given on April 26 designated Far West as a stake and indicated that other stakes would be revealed to Joseph Smith, who held the keys of the kingdom and the ministry (D&C 115:17-19).

On May 5, Joseph Smith and Sidney Rigdon, in company with Thomas B. Marsh, David W. Patten, Edward Partridge, and others left

---

40 Donald Q. Cannon and Lyndon W. Cook, *Far West Record*, 198-9.

41 *Ibid.*, 200.

42 The revelation consisted of questions put to the Lord, followed by their answers. It reads, in part:

  Can any branch of the Church of Latter-day Saints be considered a Stake of Zion until they have acknowledged the authority of the First Presidency, by a vote of said Church, thus saith the Lord, Verily I say unto you nay. How then?

  Answer: No Stake shall be appointed except by the First Presidency and this Presidency be acknowledged by the voice of the Lord, otherwise it shall not be counted as a Stake of Zion, and again except it be dedicated by this Presidency it cannot be acknowledged as a Stake of Zion, for unto this end, have I appointed them, in laying the foundation of and establishing my Kingdom. (Revelation to Joseph Smith, Kirtland, Ohio, January 12, 1838, in Joseph Smith Collection, LDS Church Historian's Office)

Far West "for the purpose of visiting the north country, and laying off a stake of Zion" (*History of the Church* 3:34). They arrived in the small settlement of Spring Hill, in Daviess County, which Joseph renamed Adam-ondi-Ahman, identifying the site as the spot where Adam blessed his posterity prior to his death (*History of the Church* 3:35). On June 28, 1838, Adam-ondi-Ahman was named a "Stake of Zion," with John Smith (Joseph's uncle) as President and Reynolds Cahoon and Lyman Wight as counselors. Vinson Knight was chosen "acting Bishop *pro tempore*" and a High Council was designated (*History of the Church* 3:38-39).

By 1838, the stake was the primary church unit, over the bishop, high council, elders, priests, teachers, deacons and possibly the seventies living in the stake area (who, however, were under the direction of the first seven presidents of the Seventy). At this time, each of the stakes of the Church had (1) a presidency, (2) a high council and (3) a single bishopric. There were also patriarchs, as we learn from Joseph Smith's historical entry for Far West under the date of July 4, 1838, where he mentions "the Patriarchs of the Church . . . presidents of the stakes" (*History of the Church* 3:41). The "Patriarch at Far West" was Isaac Morley (*History of the Church* 3:86).

It should be noted that stakes in the early Church were not large ecclesiastical units with several congregations (wards), as today. Rather, a stake could be either a congregation in and of itself or a collection of smaller "branches." On March 28, 1835, the Lord had commanded that "evangelical ministers" or patriarchs should be ordained "in all large branches of the church" (D&C 107:39). The term "branch," as used in this passage, refers to a stake and not to a small congregation, as we use the term today. The terms "stake" and "branch" were used interchangeably for the next few decades. Thus, on January 21, 1836, when asked by a visitor how many members the Church had, Joseph Smith said "that we had between fifteen hundred and two thousand in this branch," referring to the Kirtland Stake (*History of the Church* 2:379). The Far West "stake" is called a "branch" in the *Far West Record* under the date of November 7, 1837.

The existence of a single presidency and a single bishopric in each stake reflects the two areas of activity of the priesthood on the earth, spiritual and temporal. In an article published in the *Messenger and Advocate* in June 1835, the prophet Joseph wrote that "according to the order of the kingdom . . . the Elders in Zion or in her immediate region, have no authority or right to meddle with her spiritual affairs, to regulate her concerns, or hold councils for the expulsion of members, in her unorganized condition. The High Council has been expressly organized to administer in all her spiritual affairs; and the Bishop and his council are set over her temporal matters; so that the Elders' acts are null and void" (*History of the Church* 2:228).

This, of course, explains why the minutes of the High Council at Far West reflect the attendance of the "Bishop and his Council" at many of the meetings.

In a later section, we will return to the subject of stakes and their organization in the early Church, and learn more about how the two priesthoods operate together.

The Kirtland Camp

In the spring of 1836, just three days after the Kirtland Temple was dedicated, in the midst of performing washings and anointings, the prophet Joseph declared that "the Seventies are at liberty to go to Zion if they please, or go wheresoever they will, and preach the gospel" (*History of the Church* 2:432). In point of fact, the Seventy were the last of the leading authorities of the Church to leave Kirtland for Missouri. During the early months of 1838, in the absence of the First Presidency and the Quorum of the Twelve (some of whom had gone to Zion, while others left the Church), the Saints in Kirtland looked to the Seventy for guidance.

In 1838,

at a meeting of the Seventies in the House of the Lord in Kirtland, on the sixth day of March, the moving of the Saints from Kirtland to the land of Missouri, in accordance with the commandments and revelations of God, was spoken of and also the practicability of the quorum of the Seventies locating in as compact a body as possible in some stake of Zion in the west, where they could meet together when they were not laboring in the vineyard of the Lord. (*History of the Church* 3:87)

The following day, the Seventys made a formal decision to go up to Zion as a body (*History of the Church* 3:88-89).

The discussion continued on March 17, when the members in Kirtland met with the Seventy in the Temple. Following speeches by some of the presidents, "President Hyrum Smith came in" and spoke, saying "that he knew by the Spirit of God" that the plan of the Seventy "was according to the will of the Lord" (*History of the Church* 3:94). He urged the people to go to Missouri. By the end of the meeting, some eighty family heads had subscribed their names to the constitution of what came to be known as the "Kirtland Camp" (*History of the Church* 3:95).

The main body of the camp left Kirtland on July 6, 1838. By then, they numbered 105 families with 529 people (*History of the Church* 3:100-101). The journal of the camp reflects the same kinds of hardships encountered three years previously by Zion's Camp, which also went to Missouri from Kirtland. The wisdom of the Lord in requiring that the Seventy be chosen from among those who participated in Zion's Camp was thus manifest. These same men, as leaders of the Kirtland Camp, had gained the experience they needed to make the trip with their families.

On October 2, 1838, the members of the Kirtland Camp arrived at Far West, Missouri, and were greeted by the First Presidency. Two days later, they were brought to Adam-ondi-Ahman to settle (*History of the Church* 3:147-148).

The Council of the Seventy

The record of the Kirtland Camp left many insights into the organization of the First Quorum of Seventy. We learn, for example, that the seven presidents of the quorum constituted what was called "the Council of the Seventies," while the presidents themselves were termed "Councilors." Five of the "councilors" met with Hyrum Smith on March 13, 1838 to draw up a constitution for the Kirtland Camp. At the afternoon meeting of the entire quorum, "it was resolved that two of the quorum should be appointed to act as members of the Council, *pro tem,* in the place of Daniel S. Miles and Levi Hancock—who were then in the west—till the camp should arrive at Far West. This to be in accordance with the first article of the Constitution, which recognized the whole seven as councilors of the camp." Two "assistant councilors" were also chosen (*History of the Church* 3:89-90).

Throughout the travels of the Kirtland Camp, the seven presidents were called "the councilors," while they as a body constituted "the Council" or "the Council of the Seventies."[43] In an historical entry made a few months later, we read of "Elder Joseph Young, First President of the Seventies" (*History of the Church* 3:182). What distinguished this Council of the Seventy from the rest of the first quorum is that they presided over all seventies, including those in other quorums (D&C 107:93-97).

Expulsion from Missouri

The year 1838 saw some of the worst times for the Church. Expelled from Jackson County by the mobs in 1833, the Saints now found Far West threatened. To make matters worse, Missouri governor Lilburn W. Boggs, sided with the mobs and ordered the militia to intervene. Joseph Smith and other Church leaders were arrested. As the year drew to a close, events such as the Haun's Mill Massacre and the Battle of Crooked River (at which Apostle David W. Patten was shot and killed) were etched in the annals of Mormon history. Through the courageous intervention of a state militia officer who was also their lawyer, Joseph Smith and his fellow prisoners narrowly escaped being summarily shot, without trial.

Weaker members of the Church, unable to endure further persecution, began to renounce the faith. Even some of the hardier members left the Church, often with little provocation. As winter approached, Latter-day Saints could be seen making the trek into the adjoining areas of Iowa and Illinois. On January 16, 1839, Brigham Young, now President of the Twelve by virtue of his seniority in age, led that quorum in organizing a committee to conduct the removal of the Saints from Missouri. They assisted in finding shelter for the larger groups in and around Quincy, Hancock County, Illinois (*History of the*

---

43 *History of the Church* 3:87-90, 95-6, 102, 105, 107, 110, 114-5, 117, 119-132, 135, 137, 143-4, 147.

Church 3:261). During the months of February through March of 1839, most of the Saints moved to Illinois.

On March 17, 1839, in the midst of the exodus from Missouri, when the stakes and their high councils had been disrupted by persecution, death, apostasy and flight, the Twelve Apostles, as the Traveling High Council, took charge of trying various members for their conduct. Four prominent members of the Church, including a counselor in the First Presidency (Frederick G. Williams) and the President of the Quorum of the Twelve (Thomas B. Marsh) were excommunicated at a conference conducted by Brigham Young on that date (*History of the Church* 3:283-284). Williams returned to the Church in April of the following year, but Marsh did not rejoin the Church until 1857.

From his prison cell in the Missouri city bearing the ironic name of Liberty, Joseph Smith continued to send instructions to the Church and encourage its members to keep their faith in God and in the restored Church. Finally, on April 16, 1839, Joseph, Hyrum, and others managed to escape from their captors and made plans to settle the Church in a new location. The area of Montrose, Iowa, was seriously considered, as was the town of Commerce, Illinois.

On May 9, Joseph left Quincy for Commerce, where he took up residence in a log house. The town was situated on a beautiful bend in the Mississippi River, but was plagued with marshy areas and mosquitoes. Until the marshes were drained, the Saints suffered innumerable diseases and much hardship. But from these humble beginnings arose the city of Nauvoo, a name that comes from the Hebrew word for "beautiful." It was destined to become a center of commerce and industry, seat of a university and the largest militia in the United States. It was, in its day, the largest city in the state of Illinois. Over the next few years, Nauvoo became a refuge for Joseph Smith's battered flock.

The Mission to England

Six months prior to Joseph Smith's departure from Kirtland, on June 1, 1837, Elder Heber C. Kimball of the Quorum of the Twelve was called to open and preside over a mission in England, assisted by Orson Hyde, another of the Twelve (*History of the Church* 2:489-490; 4:313). The work in the British Isles went well, and on April 1 of the following year, Elder Kimball appointed three others to preside over the mission, in order that he might prepare for his return to the United States.

"Brother Joseph Fielding was chosen President over the whole Church in England, and Willard Richards and William Clayton were chosen his Counselors, and were ordained to the High Priesthood and to the Presidency" (*History of the Church* 3:20). In a subsequent communication, they are called "the Presidency of the Church in England," thus paralleling the title "Presidency of the Church in Missouri" accorded to the first stake presidency ordained in Zion in 1834 (*History of the Church* 3:342).

In a revelation given on July 23, 1837 (D&C 112), the position of the Twelve was further clarified. While Joseph Smith held keys over the Twelve (verse 15), Thomas B. Marsh held the keys of the kingdom as pertaining to the Twelve, to send them where the First Presidency (Joseph Smith, Sidney Rigdon, and Hyrum Smith) were unable to go (verses 16-17). Nevertheless, it was the First Presidency who would decide to send the Twelve abroad (verses 19, 21). The revelation designates the First Presidency as counselors and leaders to the Twelve, though both quorums hold the power and keys of the priesthood (verses 20, 30-32). Throughout the revelation, the Lord made it clear that the Twelve were to preach "abroad" (D&C 112:1, 4, 12, 16-17, 19, 21, 28-29).

On April 17, 1838, the Lord instructed David W. Patten and twelve others to go on a mission the following spring (D&C 114:1). On July 8, Joseph Smith received a commandment that the Twelve should leave on missions to England the following April. At the same time, provisions were made to fill vacancies in the Quorum of the Twelve resulting from the apostasy in Kirtland. The newly-named Apostles were John Taylor, John E. Page, Wilford Woodruff and Willard Richards, the latter then being in England (D&C 118:1-6; *History of the Church* 3:47). During the months that followed, these men were duly sustained, though their ordinations had to wait for a few months.[44]

---

44 John Taylor and John E. Page were ordained apostles under the hands of Brigham Young and Heber C. Kimball during a high council meeting held at Far West on December 19, 1838.

Meanwhile, Thomas B. Marsh, President of the Twelve, aposta-tized and left for Richmond on October 24 (*History of the Church* 3:166-7). He did not return to the Church until 1857, when he came to Utah. The following day, David W. Patten, the second Apostle in seniority, was shot and killed by a Missouri mob at the Battle of Crooked River (*History of the Church* 3:170-1). This made Brigham Young President of the Twelve, and he is so called in the minutes of a high council meeting held at Far West on December 13 (*History of the Church* 3:224-5).

Soon after the Prophet's arrival in Illinois, the Twelve and others gathered on the temple site at Far West, pursuant to the revelation con-tained in D&C 118. On April 26, 1839, having ordained Wilford Woodruff and George A. Smith to fill some of the vacancies in the quorum, the Twelve began preparing for their journey to England (*History of the Church* 3:336-39).

Their actions were sustained by the members of the Church at a general conference held in Quincy, Illinois, on May 4, 1839 (*History of the Church* 3:345). On July 2, Joseph Smith met with the Twelve and some of the Seventy, who were about to leave on missions. "The Presidency proceeded to bless two of the Twelve, who had lately been ordained into the quorum, namely, Wilford Woodruff and George A. Smith" (*History of the Church* 3:383).

A number of the Twelve, led by President Brigham Young, went to the British Isles, where they held their first council at the house of Willard Richards in Preston on April 14, 1840. On that occasion, Brigham Young ordained Willard Richards to the apostleship (*History of the Church* 4:114). Brigham Young was sustained as President of the Twelve and of the British Mission.[45] Pursuant to the Lord's instructions in D&C 107:3, it was decided to send for twenty of the Seventy to assist in the missionary work (*History of the Church* 4:115-116).

Joseph Smith instructed the Twelve when they first left for England not to preach the gathering of Zion to their new converts.[46]

---

45 By seniority, Brigham Young automatically became the leader of the Twelve. The History, under the date of February 14, 1839, speaks of "Elder Brigham Young (on whom devolved the presidency of the Twelve by age, Thomas B. Marsh having apostatized" (*History of the Church* 3:261). It is possible, however, that he was first sustained in this position at the meeting in Preston, England. He is thereafter frequently called "President of the Twelve Apostles" (e.g., *History of the Church* 4:470).

46 John Taylor, in a discourse delivered June 18, 1883 (*Journal of Discourses* 24:199).

In consequence of this, branches of the Church were organized in the British Isles. At the general conference of the Church held in Preston, England, on April 15, 1840, some 32 branches (called "churches") were represented. "Elder Willard Richards having been previously ordained into the quorum of the Twelve, according to previous revelation, it was moved by Elder Young, and seconded by Elder Taylor, that Elder Hyrum Clark be appointed as a counselor to Elder Fielding, in place of Elder Richards; carried unanimously" (*History of the Church* 4:116-118).

At the same meeting, Elder Kimball brought up "the importance and propriety of ordaining a Patriarch to bestow patriarchal blessings on the fatherless, &c.," and noted that it was the responsibility of the Twelve to make such appointments, pursuant to the instructions in D&C 107:39 (*History of the Church* 4:118). Accordingly, at a meeting of the Twelve held the following day, it was decided "that Elder Peter Melling be ordained an evangelical minister [patriarch] in Preston" (*History of the Church* 4:119). On April 17, the Twelve "ordained Peter Melling, Patriarch." He was the first to hold this office outside the United States (*History of the Church* 4:120).

The next couple of years saw tremendous growth of the Church in England. In consequence of this growth, the mission was subdivided into "conferences," each comprising a collection of "churches" or "branches." For example, the Froome's Hill Conference was organized at a meeting held on April 21, 1840. Nineteen ordained priests were charged with the care of different "churches." (In the minutes, one of these, which served four towns, was also termed a "branch".) One to five of these "churches" were grouped together into "divisions," with each division placed in the charge of an elder, who is termed a "president." Each division, as well as the conference itself, had a clerk in addition to the presiding officer. In an addendum to the minutes made by Wilford Woodruff, who presided at the meeting that organized the Froome's Hill Conference, there is mention of "the different branches in this region . . . each individual church." Elder Thomas Kington was appointed "the Presiding Elder over this conference" (*History of the Church* 4:138-140).

The minutes describing the organization of other conferences provide us with additional information about the various officers appointed to govern the Church in England. For example, the Bran Green and

Gadfield Elm Conference, organized on June 14, 1840, comprised fourteen "churches," each appointed to the care of a priest. Two of the men are, however, termed "Priest, Assistant," implying that they were not ordained priests but, rather, teachers who presided in the absence of a priest.

The various churches were grouped into two larger units, each having an elder as "President," plus a clerk. The conference itself also had a clerk and Elder Thomas Kington, who had already been appointed to preside in Froome's Hill, was named as Presiding Elder here, too (*History of the Church* 4:134-5).

On July 6, 1840, "a General Conference" was held in Manchester, England, with seven of the apostles present, including Parley P. Pratt, who was chosen President of the Conference. "Three persons were then ordained to the high Priesthood . . . also [seven others] were ordained Elders; seven individuals were ordained to the lesser Priesthood."[47]

The minutes of the general conference held in England on October 6, 1840, call the Twelve by the title "the Traveling High Council," and the British Mission was conducted very much like a stake (*History of the Church* 4:214-217). For example, it was "moved by Willard Richards, seconded by Elder Thomas Smith, and carried unanimously, that all ordinations be confined to or under the regulation of the Traveling High Council" (*History of the Church* 4:216). That is, the Twelve were, in effect, the high council for the British Mission.

Interestingly, when the priesthood of the officers attending the conference was recorded, the Twelve were included as "high priests" (*History of the Church* 4:216), though at least two of them—Brigham Young and Heber C. Kimball—had never been ordained to that office, being elders at the time of their call to the apostleship. As apostles, they were authorized to serve in all offices of the Church and consequently could be considered members of the high council (as often happened in Missouri), a position held by high priests.

At a conference of the Church held in Manchester, England, on April 6, 1841, nine of the Quorum of the Twelve were present. They proceeded to organize the mission into fifteen conferences, each hav-

47 Parley P. Pratt (Jr.), ed., *Autobiography of Parley Parker Pratt* (Salt Lake City, 1873; 3rd ed. Deseret, 1938), 308.

ing branches within its geographical boundaries. A second patriarch, John Albertson, was sustained and ordained by the Twelve. Meanwhile, Peter Melling, England's first patriarch, was called as President of the Preston Conference, though he continued to give patriarchal blessings.

Information gleaned from the minutes of this "general conference," indicates that it was customary for the presidents of the various regional conferences to be ordained to the office of high priest (*History of the Church* 4:333-334). Parley P. Pratt wrote that "Eleven persons were chosen and ordained to the High Priesthood during this Conference, and twelve persons were ordained Elders . . . Several new Conferences were also organized, and Presidents were appointed for each Conference in the kingdom."[48]

The rapid growth of the Church in England provided thousands of new members to replace those who fell away during the Ohio and Missouri persecutions. It was natural that Church leaders should wish that as many as possible of these faithful British Saints immigrate to the United States and settle in the Nauvoo region. On February 6, 1841, the Twelve organized, in the port city of Liverpool, the first group of English Saints to go to America. The group was organized with a President, six counselors and a clerk/historian (*History of the Church* 4:297). This no doubt followed the organizational pattern of the highly successful Kirtland Camp, led to Missouri in 1838 by the Presidents of the Seventy (that quorum being specially designed for ease of government while traveling in their missionary labors). These English saints sailed for America five days later (*History of the Church* 4:296-297).

A second group of 130 left from the same port under the presidency of seven of the Twelve (including Brigham Young), on April 20. Parley P. Pratt was left to preside in England (*History of the Church* 4:352). A group comprising about 200 Saints sailed from Liverpool on September 20, 1841, under the presidency of Joseph Fielding, while another group, led by Patriarch Peter Melling, left for American on November 5 (*History of the Church* 4:441). Over the next couple of years, many more followed, as did the rest of the Twelve.

---

48 *Ibid.*, 314-15.

In his farewell message in the October 1842, issue of the *Millennial Star*, Parley P. Pratt wrote, "I recommend and appoint Elder Thomas Ward as my successor in the office of the General Presidency of the Church in Europe." Elder Pratt had been appointed to this position at the conference of April 15, 1841, as the other members of the Twelve were preparing to leave England to return home.[49] Now he, too, would return to the United States.

The missionary efforts of the Twelve in England contributed to the upbuilding of Nauvoo after a time of apostasy in Ohio and Missouri. From the ranks of the energetic new converts across the sea came a number of leaders for the growing Church. In future years, these English saints, loyal to the apostles who converted them, would literally save the Church from attempted takeovers following the death of Joseph Smith.

---

49 *Ibid.*, 324.

Chapter 9

THE NAUVOO ERA

And let all those who come from the east, and the west,
and the north, and the south, that have desires to dwell
therein, take up their inheritance in the same, as well as
in the city of Nashville, or in the city of Nauvoo, and in
all the stakes which I have appointed, saith the Lord.
(D&C 125:4)

Soon after Joseph Smith's arrival in Illinois, a general conference was held (May 4-6, 1839) near Quincy, in which it was "resolved . . . that Bishop Vinson Knight be appointed, or received into the Church in full bishopric," and that the choice of George A. Smith as one of the Twelve be ratified. The conference also determined that the Saints in the eastern part of the country might move to Kirtland, if they wish, "and again settle that place as a stake of Zion" (*History of the Church* 3:345).

On the third day of the conference, it was resolved "that Elder [William] Marks be hereby appointed to preside over the Church at Commerce, Illinois," and "that Bishop [Newel K.] Whitney also go to Commerce, and there act in unison with the other Bishops of the Church" (*History of the Church* 3:347). On the twenty-fourth of the same month, the Prophet wrote a letter to Bishop Whitney, in which he asked that he settle in Commerce as soon as possible (*History of the Church* 3:363). Bishops Whitney and Knight both arrived at Commerce on June 17 (*History of the Church* 3:377), but Bishop Knight soon returned to Quincy (*History of the Church* 3:378).

The sad financial state of the Church and of its members following the exodus from Missouri was what necessitated early involvement of the bishops in the area where most of the Saints had settled. Work was commenced immediately to procure additional plots of land for settlement. On July 2, 1839, Joseph Smith met with Sidney Rigdon, Hyrum Smith, Bishops Whitney and Knight and others regarding a purchase made by Bishop Knight where the town of Zarahemla was to be built (*History of the Church* 3:382).

On October 5-7, 1839, a general conference was held at
Commerce to determine how best to organize the Church and to assist
in the settlement of refugees in the Mississippi River area where the
states of Illinois and Iowa met. Two stakes were organized at that
time, one in Commerce and one in Iowa.

> The Presidency [of the Church] . . . wanted to know the
> views of the brethren, whether they wished to appoint this a
> stake of Zion or not . . . It was then unanimously agreed upon,
> that it should be appointed a stake and a place of gathering for
> the Saints . . .
>
> William Marks to be President; Bishop Whitney to be Bishop
> of middle ward; Bishop Partridge to be Bishop of upper ward;
> Bishop Knight to be Bishop of lower ward [and twelve] to be the
> High Council [including Newel Knight] . . .
>
> It was then voted that a stake of the Church be established on
> the west side of the river, in Iowa Territory; over which Elder John
> Smith was appointed President; Alanson Ripley, Bishop; [and
> twelve high councillors] . . .
>
> Don C. Smith was elected to be continued as President of the
> High Priesthood [High Priest's quorum]. Orson Hyde to stand in
> his former office [as an Apostle], and William Smith to be contin-
> ued in his standing [in the Quorum of the Twelve]. (*History of the
> Church* 4:12)

In the earlier published version of the history (*Millennial Star*
17:359), the word "branch" was used instead of "stake." At this stage,
there was still no real distinction between "branches" and "stakes."
The typical stake still had a single presidency, a high council,[1] and a
single bishopric. Because of its size, the Commerce (later renamed
Nauvoo) stake was an exception, being divided into three "wards"
(*History of the Church*).

The wards of Commerce were not akin to our modern LDS wards.
The bishop was neither the presiding officer nor did the various wards
hold meetings. These matters were in the hands of the stake president
and high council, while the bishops occupied themselves with caring

---

1 Under the date of November 7, 1839, we read of "the President of the High Council
of Iowa" (History of the Church 4:42).

for the material needs of the members and settling refugees from Missouri.[2] The wards were political units within the city of Nauvoo.

On the day the two stakes were organized, counselors to the presidents had not yet been selected. On October 19, "the high council appointed for the Stake of the Church in Iowa, met at Asahel Smith's, Nashville, and organized; John Smith, President; Elias Smith, Clerk; Reynolds Cahoon and Lyman Wight were chosen Counselors to President John Smith, and approved by the Council" (*History of the Church* 4:16). The stake clerk was also a member of the high council. On November 3, the Iowa presidency and high council met and Alanson Ripley was ordained bishop by the presidency. "Elder Daniel Avery was instructed to call the Elders together and organize the Elder's Quorum" (*History of the Church* 4:42).

It is interesting that the high council chose counselors for the stake president, along with a bishop and clerk. The ordination of the bishop was in complete accord with D&C 107:17, which calls for the choice of a bishop from among the high priests, "provided he is called and set apart and ordained unto this power by the hands of the Presidency of the Melchizedek Priesthood."

It is significant that the revelation does not specify that it must be done by the "First" Presidency. This is further illustrated by the fact that, after Alanson Ripley moved to Nauvoo, "Elias Smith was appointed Bishop by the High Council of Iowa" on July12, 1840, and ordained to that office six days later (*History of the Church* 4:154, 161). After Lyman Wight was called to the Twelve, the Iowa high council met on April 24, 1841 and appointed two new counselors to President John Smith (*History of the Church* 4:352).

The Nauvoo High Council

Commerce was soon renamed Nauvoo and became the headquarters of the Church. The new name, a Hebrew word meaning "beautiful," first appears in official Church records in the minutes of the high

---

2 This role was to change in later years, as the Church membership failed to live the full law of consecration and stewardship. At a meeting of the High Council of Iowa on March 6, 1840, Joseph Smith suspended the law (History of the Church 4:93-94). It was revived for a time in Utah, under Brigham Young, who set up the "United Order," in which certain communities of the Saints could participate in the law of consecration. Ultimately, that, too, came to an end.

council meeting held there on October 20, 1839 (*History of the Church* 4:16).

During the Nauvoo era, the high council of the stake in which resided the First Presidency continued to play a more important role than other high councils that were established. This practice began in Kirtland, where the Church's first high council was under the direct leadership of the First Presidency. But Joseph Smith's plan to establish Church headquarters in Missouri led to the declaration in D&C 107:37 that "The high council in Zion form a quorum equal in authority in the affairs of the church, in all their decisions, to the councils of the Twelve at the stakes of Zion." With the removal of the Saints from Missouri, the Nauvoo high council took over the position of leading high council of the Church and in later years it fell to the high council of the Salt Lake Stake.

During 1839 and 1840, when the Twelve Apostles were in England, we find Joseph Smith sitting in judgment with the high council (e.g., *History of the Church* 4:250). On December 7, 1839, "the High Council of Nauvoo issued an Epistle to the Saints west of Kirtland not to return thither." The memorandum was published in the *Times and Seasons* 29 (see *History of the Church* 4:44-45). The brethren wrote, "We warn you, in the name of the Lord, not to remove back there, unless you are counseled to do so by the First Presidency, and the High Council of Nauvoo." The declaration concludes by noting that it was "Done by order and vote of the First Presidency and High Council for the Church of Jesus Christ of Latter-day Saints, at Nauvoo, December 8, 1839" (*History of the Church* 4:45 note).[3]

The ambiguity in the position of the Nauvoo High Council became a topic of discussion at the general conference of April 6, 1840.

> A letter was read from presidents of the Seventies, wishing for an explanation of the steps, which the High Council had taken, in removing Elder F. G. Bishop from the quorum of the Seventies to that of the High Priests, without any other ordination than he had

---

3 Interestingly, Joseph Smith, Sidney Rigdon, and Elias Higbee were not present at Nauvoo at the time. They were in Washington, DC, appealing for redress of the Missouri wrongs.

when in the Seventies, and wished to know whether those ordained into the Seventies at the same time F. G. Bishop was, had a right to the High Priesthood or not. After observations on the case by different individuals, the president [Joseph Smith, according to the minutes] gave a statement of the authority of the Seventies, and stated that they were Elders and not High Priests, and consequently Brother F. G. Bishop had no claim to that office. It was then unanimously resolved that Elder F. G. Bishop be placed back again into the quorum of the Seventies. (*History of the Church* 4:105.)

The question of the role of the Seventies and High Priests was to plague the Church for the next four decades (especially after seventies were assigned to stakes), despite efforts of some Presidents of the Church to make it clear that neither office was superior to the other. The essential difference in the office of high priest is that they are the "standing" ministers of the Melchizedek Priesthood, while the elders and seventies, not being called specifically to preside, are the ones generally called to serve as missionaries.

New Stakes Are Organized

The organization of new stakes was inevitable as the Church grew. Some of the circumstances behind the organization of these units, however, are of particular interest. Note, for example, the following minutes:

At a meeting of the Saints of Crooked Creek Branch, on the 2nd of July, 1840, to take into consideration the propriety of having a Stake of Zion appointed or located somewhere in the bounds of this branch . . . Resolved: That it be our wishes that a Stake of Zion be appointed or located within the bounds of this Branch, provided it should meet the minds of the First Presidency of this Church . . . there are one hundred and twelve members belonging to this Branch. (*History of the Church* 4:144)

Modern Latter-day Saints, upon reading this, might believe such a request couldn't possibly be approved with so few members.

However, history records differently. In the minutes of the Nauvoo High Council of the following day, we read:

> The resolutions of the Crooked Creek Branch of the 2nd inst., were taken into consideration by President Joseph Smith, Jun., and it was thought proper to establish a Stake on Crooked Creek, agreeably to the request of said Branch, and a letter was written to the brethren to that effect. (*History of the Church* 4:145)

Again, at this stage of the Church's history, there was little if any difference between the terms "branch" and "stake." During the October 1839 General Conference, "It was voted that a branch of the Church be established . . . in Iowa Territory" (*Millennial Star* 17:359). When the history was republished, the word "branch" was changed to read "stake" (*History of the Church* 4:12). When the high council in Iowa met on October 19 to approve the counselors chosen by President John Smith, the minutes speak of "the branch of the Church in Iowa" (*Millennial Star* 17:372), though the history later changed the word to "stake" (*History of the Church* 4:16). In a similar vein, we read of the "Freedom Branch" in *Millennial Star* 18:216, while the corresponding passage in *History of the Church* 4:233 changed the text to "Freedom Stake."

At the Nauvoo conference of October 3, 1840, Joseph Smith suggested that members from the east might gather at Kirtland, "and also that it was necessary that someone should be appointed from this conference to preside over that stake. On motion, Resolved: That Elder Almon W. Babbitt be appointed to preside over the church in Kirtland, and that he choose his own counselors" (*History of the Church* 4:204).

Four days later, during the same conference, a special meeting was held to discuss the organization of new stakes:

> An opportunity was given to the brethren who had any remarks to make on suitable locations for stakes of Zion. Elder H. W. Miller stated that it was the desire of a number of the brethren residing in Adams county, to have a stake appointed at Mount Ephraim in that county . . .
>
> On motion, Resolved: That a stake be appointed at Mount Ephraim, in Adams county.

There being several applications for the appointment of stakes, it was Resolved: That a committee be appointed to organize stakes between this place and Kirtland, and Hyrum Smith, Lyman Wight, and Almon W. Babbitt compose said committee. (*History of the Church* 4:204-205)

The first stake organized by the special committee was at Lima, where, with Hyrum Smith presiding, a presidency and "Bishop's Court" of three each, along with a clerk, were chosen on October 22, 1840.[4] The committee organized another stake at Quincy on the twenty-fifth of that month, choosing a full compliment of presidency and bishopric. Two days later, presidencies and bishoprics were also chosen for the Mount Hope Stake in Columbus, and the Freedom Stake near Payson, both in Adams County, Illinois (*History of the Church* 4:233). On November 1, the Geneva Stake was organized in Morgan County, Illinois, with a presidency and "Bishop's Court" (*History of the Church* 4:236). In none of these instances is there mention of a high council.

At a conference held at Philadelphia on April 6, 1841, with Hyrum Smith presiding, many branches were represented. The branch at Philadelphia was organized at that time by choosing a presidency and a bishopric (*History of the Church* 4:331). Exactly a week later, Elder George W. Harris of Nauvoo presided over a conference in New York City. Present at the Philadelphia conference, he had been assigned by Hyrum Smith "to organize more perfectly the branch in New York." A presidency and bishopric were chosen by the conference and ordained by Elder Harris (*History of the Church* 4:344).

The stake was essentially a gathering-place, a site where members of the Church could settle, receive land inheritances, and begin working. The importance of this gathering to cities where stakes would be appointed was stressed in a revelation given to the prophet Joseph in March 1841. Known to us as D&C 125, the revelation concerns the gathering and appointment of stakes in the territory of Iowa. The small size of these stakes or branches is illustrated by the fact that they

---

4 The bishop of the stake was ordained the following day by Hyrum Smith (*History of the Church* 4:233).

comprised about 750 members according to statistics given at the Iowa conference of August 7, 1841 (*History of the Church* 4:399).

To twentieth-century Latter-day Saints, a stake is essentially a conglomerate of wards, each of which is headed by a bishop. But this was not the case for the fledgling Church during the Nauvoo era or during the early years in Utah. The clear-cut division of responsibilities in the Church at that time placed the stake or branch presidency in the position of leadership over the Melchizedek Priesthood and the Saints in general, while the bishops, working with the Aaronic Priesthood, administered the law of consecration and stewardship.

In the early days of the Church, a "branch" was, it appears, any organized unit of the Church, while a "stake" had both a presidency and a single bishopric. Thus, a Stake was a branch of the Church, but a Branch wasn't necessarily a "Stake of Zion." We read of "Brother William Allred, Bishop of the stake at Pleasant Vale, and also Brother Henry W. Miller, president of the stake at Freedom" (*History of the Church* 4:311, under date of March 20, 1841). A notation of February 7, 1840, calls the Montrose Stake a "branch of the Church" (*History of the Church* 4:80).

On June 11, 1843, Elder Heber C. Kimball presided at a conference held in Lima, Iowa, where the branch was organized. Isaac Morley, an ordained patriarch, was chosen as president, with two counselors. Also appointed were a bishop and counselors and a high council with a "clerk of the branch" (*History of the Church* 5:427-8).

Reorganizing in Nauvoo

The peace and prosperity afforded by the settlement of the Latter-day Saints in Nauvoo made it possible to consolidate the Church once again. One of the first steps was taken on January 19, 1841, when the revelation known to us as D&C 124 was recorded. Several of the Church's most prominent leaders had died, including Apostle David W. Patten (in Missouri), Bishop Edward Partridge,[5] and Patriarch Joseph Smith Sr.[6] (D&C 124:19). The Lord reaffirmed George Miller's position as bishop[7] (verses 20-21), after which he

---

5 Nauvoo, May 27, 1840 (*History of the Church* 4:132).
6 Nauvoo, September 14, 1840.
7 He was ordained a few days later, on January 24, 1841.

gave instructions for the construction of a number of buildings. The Lord then discussed the organization of the Church in these terms:

> Verily I say unto you, I now give unto you the officers belonging to my Priesthood, that ye may hold the keys thereof, even the Priesthood which is after the order of Melchizedek, which is after the order of mine Only Begotten Son.
>
> First, I give unto you Hyrum Smith to be a patriarch unto you, to hold the sealing blessings of my church, even the Holy Spirit of promise, whereby ye are sealed up unto the day of redemption . . .
>
> I give unto you my servant Joseph to be a presiding elder over all my church, to be a translator, a revelator, a seer, and a prophet.
>
> I give unto him for counselors my servant Sidney Rigdon and my servant William Law, that these may constitute a quorum and First Presidency, to receive the oracles for the whole church.
>
> I give unto you my servant Brigham Young to be a president over the Twelve traveling council; which Twelve hold the keys to open up the authority of my kingdom upon the four corners of the earth, and to send my word to every creature. (D&C 124:123-128)

The other ten remaining members of the Twelve are then named (verse 129), following which the names of the "high council, for the corner-stone of Zion" are listed (verses 131-2). We then have, in succession, the presidency of the high priests quorum (verses 133-136), of the elders quorum (verse 137) and of the seventies quorum (verses 138-140). At this point, the Lord says, "I give unto you Vinson Knight, Samuel H. Smith, and Shadrach Roundy, if he will receive it, to preside over the bishopric; a knowledge of said bishopric is given unto you in the book of Doctrine and Covenants" (D&C 124:141). This new bishopric became a presidency over the other bishops.[8]

When these authorities were sustained in conference, it was done by having each quorum stand and vote separately, thus setting a practice

---

8 For additional perspectives on the office of bishop and its development in the Church, including the calling of Vinson Knight to preside over the other bishops, see the appendix.

followed in later years whenever the First Presidency was reorganized.[9] The revelation calling these officers indicated that the "Twelve hold the keys to open up the authority of my kingdom upon the four corners of the earth, and after that to send my word to every creature" (D&C 124:128). From this time on, the Twelve stood next to the First Presidency in directing the affairs of the Church. Speaking on October 5, 1877, Elder Orson Pratt noted that this revelation set a precedent, in that all previous instructions to the "traveling high council" had been that they were to set in order the Church only outside the organized stakes (*Journal of Discourses* 19:114).

The Patriarch of the Church

Joseph Smith Sr. was ordained patriarch in December of 1833 in Kirtland. It was his right by descent, as we learn from subsequent statements made by Brigham Young and others, because he was of the lineage of Joseph, son of Jacob (Israel). At a conference of the Twelve held in Nauvoo on June 27, 1839, Joseph Smith explained:

> An evangelist is a patriarch, even the oldest man of the blood of Joseph or of the seed of Abraham. Wherever the Church of Christ is established in the earth there should be a patriarch for the benefit of the posterity of the Saints, as it was with Jacob in giving his patriarchal blessing unto his sons. (*History of the Church* 3:381)

The Lord seems to have kept a close watch on the Smith line over the centuries. Joseph Smith Jr. once wrote,

> My grandfather Asael Smith, long ago predicted that there would be a prophet raised up in his family, and my grandmother was fully satisfied that it was fulfilled in me. My grandfather Asael . . . after having received the Book of Mormon . . . declared that I was the very Prophet that he had long known would come in his family. (*History of the Church* 2:443)

---

9 John Taylor noted this on October 14, 1877, after the death of Brigham Young, in explanation of the pattern just followed at the conference. He further noted that this was the procedure which had been followed earlier at Far West (*Journal of Discourses* 19:139-140).

These words were written on May 17, 1836, just a week after Joseph Smith Sr. and his brother John met with the church at Ogdensburg, on the Saint Lawrence River, to give patriarchal blessings (*History of the Church* 2:441). The following month, the prophet Joseph said, "My father and Uncle John Smith started on a mission to visit the branches of the Church in the Eastern States, to set them in order, and confer on the brethren their patriarchal blessings" (*History of the Church* 2:446). After more than three months and 2,400 miles in four states, they returned to Kirtland, having "conferred blessings upon many hundreds" (*History of the Church* 2:467).

The Prophet Joseph felt keenly the importance of having patriarchs. This was one of the principal topics he brought up at the general conference of the Church held in Commerce (Nauvoo) in October of 1839 (*History of the Church* 4:13). The minutes of the conference are such that it is unclear whether he proposed to set up a patriarch for the entire Church or one specifically to serve the Nauvoo Stake. But the next September 14, when his father died, Joseph recorded that he had been "Patriarch of the whole Church of Jesus Christ of Latter-day Saints" (*History of the Church* 4:189).

Hyrum Smith, as the eldest surviving son of Joseph Sr., succeeded him as Patriarch. In his dying blessing, the elder Smith said to Hyrum, "I now seal upon your head the patriarchal power, and you shall bless the people. This is my dying blessing upon your head in the name of Jesus. Amen."[10] In his account of the death of his father, written "to the Traveling High Council and Elders of the Church of Jesus Christ of Latter-day Saints in Great Britain," written October 19, 1840, Joseph Jr. noted, "Brother Hyrum succeeds him as Patriarch of the Church according to his last directions and benedictions" (*History of the Church* 4:229).[11]

Hyrum Smith's calling was foreshadowed as early as April of 1830, when the Lord told him, "thy calling is to exhortation, and to

---

10 Preston Nibley, ed., *History of Joseph Smith by His Mother Lucy Mack Smith* (Salt Lake City: Bookcraft, 1958), 309.

11 Joseph may have ordained his elder brother to his new position. In a discourse delivered on July 5, 1857, President Heber C. Kimball noted, "Joseph Smith the Prophet ordained his father a Patriarch, and he ordained Hyrum" (*Journal of Discourses* 5:7). Unfortunately, we don't know whether "he" refers to "Joseph Smith the Prophet" or "his father."

strengthen the church continually. Wherefore thy duty is unto the church forever, and this because of thy family" (D&C 23:3).

On January 24, 1841, five days after recording the revelation found in D&C 124, Joseph Smith wrote:

> Hyrum Smith, who received the office of Patriarch in the Church, in place of Joseph Smith, Sen., deceased, has by revelation been appointed a Prophet and Revelator. William Law has by revelation been appointed one of the First Presidency, in place of Hyrum Smith, Patriarch. George Miller has been appointed by revelation, Bishop in place of Edward Partridge, deceased. (*History of the Church* 4:286)

It is interesting that Hyrum, who succeeded his father, was made "a prophet and a revelator" and that the revelation calling him to his new position indicated that he held the "keys" (D&C 124:91-96). It is perhaps in this light that we must see his role as patriarch for the entire Church. Joseph Jr said of his father, Joseph Smith Sr., that in 1833 he "was ordained Patriarch and President of the High Priesthood" (*History of the Church* 4:190). B. H. Roberts, in compiling the *History of the Church*, believed that this meant the elder Smith was made president of the high priests in Kirtland, not of the High Priesthood in general, since this was a position held by his son Joseph Jr. (see *History of the Church* 4:190-191).

It seems likely that Joseph Sr. was brought into the First Presidency, as was Hyrum. Roberts' explanation is based on a dual meaning of the term "high priesthood," one referring to those holding the office of high priest and the other referring to the totality of the offices known to us as apostle, high priest, seventy and elder. There is abundant evidence that, for several decades at least, the term referred only to the office of high priest. But we have no record of any presidency over the high priests at Kirtland other than the First Presidency itself.

Having succeeded his father, Hyrum Smith's position in the Church became significantly more important than that of the other patriarchs. In various official letters, he signed as "Patriarch for the whole Church" (e.g., *History of the Church* 4:444.). At times, we find him, as "Patriarch of the Church," presiding at conferences. For example, Hyrum led the stake conference held at Ramus on December 4-5 1841, though four members of the Twelve (including President Brigham Young) were in attendance (*History of the Church* 4:467).

Statements made by Brigham Young after the death of Joseph and Hyrum make it clear that Hyrum Smith had been ordained as Joseph's successor in the Presidency.[12] Elder Orson Pratt, in the October 1877 General Conference, speaking of the 1841 reorganization in Nauvoo, said, "And Oliver Cowdery, although never one of the Twelve, had his place filled up; and the keys and the glories and the promises conferred upon and made to Oliver Cowdery were taken from him and bestowed upon brother Hyrum Smith" (*Journal of Discourses* 19:117).

Hyrum's position as a president of the Church is confirmed in a number of statements in the History.[13] Concerning the general conference of April 6, 1842, we read that "the First Presidency did not attend . . . President William Law, General Bennett, president *pro tem,* and President Hyrum Smith all spoke" (*History of the Church* 4:583). In a journal entry dated November 28 of the same year, we read of "Counselor William Law" and "President Hyrum Smith," though it was Law who was a member of the First Presidency (*History of the Church* 5:197). An announcement made in the *Times and Seasons* on October 1, 1843, was signed "Joseph Smith, Hyrum Smith, Presidents of the Church of Jesus Christ of Latter-day Saints," but it was not signed by Joseph's counselors, Sidney Rigdon and William Law even though the announcement spoke of a decision by "the First Presidency" (*History of the Church* 6:41). On January 15, 1841, a Proclamation was signed at Nauvoo by Joseph Smith, Sidney Rigdon, and Hyrum Smith, as "Presidents of the Church" (*History of the Church* 4:273).

---

12 See Chapters 10 and 11.

13 The terms "President" and "Patriarch" are used alternately for Hyrum Smith. E.g., in the minutes of the general conference held on Sunday, October 8, 1843, he was called "President Hyrum Smith" (*Millennial Star* 22:216), but the later version (History of the Church 6:49) changed this to read "Patriarch Hyrum Smith." Under the date of October 23, 1843, the history records, "This morning President Hyrum Smith, Patriarch of the Church of Jesus Christ of Latter-day Saints, entered upon the duties of his office [on the temple committee]" (*Millennial Star* 22:279). The words "Patriarch of the Church of Jesus Christ of Latter-day Saints" were deleted in the later version (*History of the Church* 6:61).

The First Presidency in Nauvoo

The position of the First Presidency as prophets, seers and revelators was affirmed by the Lord in the revelation of January 1841, reorganizing the priesthood in Nauvoo (D&C 124:125).[14] On June 1 of that year, Joseph Smith wrote that "Elder Sidney Rigdon has been ordained a Prophet, Seer, and Revelator" (*History of the Church* 4:364).[15]

At a special conference of the Church held in Nauvoo on January 30, 1841, "pursuant to public notice," Joseph Smith "was unanimously elected sole Trustee-in-Trust for the Church of Jesus Christ of Latter-day Saints" (*History of the Church* 4:286). This position was held by Bishop Edward Partridge until his death in Nauvoo on May 27, 1840.[16] In an official declaration of his election as trustee, delivered to the Recorder of Hancock County, Illinois, on February 1, 1841, Joseph wrote that he was "to hold my office during my life (my successors [as trustee] to be the First Presidency of said Church)" (*History of the Church* 4:287).[17]

The reorganization of the First Presidency in Nauvoo was necessitated by several factors. Initially, Sidney Rigdon and Jesse Gause were counselors to Joseph Smith. Gause was replaced by Frederick G. Williams in March 1833, but Williams was excommunicated in Missouri in November 1837 and replaced by Hyrum Smith. When Hyrum became Patriarch and Assistant President in January 1841, William Law was named second counselor to Joseph.[18] Sidney

---

14 On July 29, 1843, Brigham Young, while teaching the elders in Nauvoo, said, "The first principle of our cause and work is to understand that there is a prophet in the Church, and that he is the head of the Church of Jesus Christ on Earth. Who called Joseph Smith to be a prophet? Did the people or God? God, and not the people called him" (*History of the Church* 5:521). On February 8, 1843, Joseph Smith indicated that a prophet was a prophet only when acting as such (*History of the Church* 5:265). On January 1, 1843, he explained the office of a prophet (History of the Church 5:215, see also 231-232).

15 This statement, inserted in the midst of other events for that day, is given without explanation. There is no indication that a meeting was held.

16 This is undoubtedly why later generations considered Edward Partridge to be the Church's "Presiding Bishop," though during his lifetime he was never sustained as such, and even presided over one of the three original wards at Nauvoo.

17 Sidney Rigdon, of course, felt that this justified him to be trustee when Joseph died. But since the Quorum of the Twelve became the First Presidency upon the death of the Prophet, it was they who were sustained as the new trustees, until they passed that role to the bishops.

18 See the wording of the re-sustaining of the First Presidency at the general conference of April 6, 1843, in *History of the Church* 5:328-329.

Rigdon remained Joseph's first counselor to the very end, but William Law apostatized and was released on April 18, 1844. Meanwhile, Joseph called others as additional counselors.

At the General Conference held in Nauvoo April 7-11, 1841, John Cook Bennett played a prominent role (*History of the Church* 4:338-340). He "was present, with the First Presidency, as Assistant President, until President Rigdon's health should be restored" (*History of the Church* 4:341). At the meeting of April 8, Bennett was called to be an "Assistant President" with the First Presidency.

Bennett had not yet become a Latter-day Saint when, in 1839, he helped convince the Illinois Legislature to allow the refugees from Missouri to establish the city of Nauvoo (then Commerce). He was rewarded for his kindness by being elected the first mayor of the city, and ultimately joined the Church and became one of its leaders. On May 25, 1842, the First Presidency, the Twelve and the Bishops withdrew fellowship from Bennett, removing him as a counselor to the First Presidency (*History of the Church* 5:18). He was later excommunicated for sexual immorality and in retaliation wrote a book "exposing" the Mormons.

It was in Nauvoo that the First Presidency first became regularly involved in hearing appeals from the decisions of the High Council. Several examples are given in the History (e.g., see *History of the Church* 4:514; 5:371).

The High Priests' Quorum

During the reorganization of January 1841, Joseph Smith's brother Don Carlos was confirmed as President of the High Priests' Quorum (D&C 124:133-136). At the general conference of October 1839, held at Commerce, he was "elected to be continued as President of the High Priesthood" (*History of the Church* 4:12). At that conference, the Commerce and Iowa Stakes were organized, and though there were two stakes, there was but one high priests quorum.

When Don Carlos died the next fall, Bishop George Miller was chosen to replace him as president of the high priests quorum (*History of the Church* 4:424). Up to that time, there appears to have been a single quorum of high priests, located at Nauvoo. There may, however, have been plans for other such quorums. On August 31, 1842, "the

High Priests' Quorum met in council, and instructed their clerk to publish in the *Times & Seasons* that it is the duty of the High Priests to have their names enrolled on the records of the quorums when they arrive at Nauvoo" (*History of the Church* 5:84).

It was not until April 28, 1844 that a conference of Elders assembled in Lima, Iowa, under President Isaac Morley, and organized a (second?) quorum of high priests with thirty-one members (*History of the Church* 6:346).

The Aaronic Priesthood in Nauvoo

It is from events in Nauvoo that we first learn details of the organization of the Aaronic Priesthood in the Church. In the revelation of January 1841, the Lord called "Vinson Knight, Samuel H. Smith, and Shadrach Roundy, if he will receive it, to preside over the bishopric; a knowledge of said bishopric is given unto you in the book of Doctrine and Covenants" (D&C 124:141). These men presided over the other bishops in the Church.

In addition to the three named, there was a separate presidency for the priests, with a president (Samuel Rolfe) and counselors (verse 142). The same verse that calls for the priests' presidency also speaks of presidents and counselors for the teachers and deacons quorums and for "the stake" (of Nauvoo), but does not name any individuals to these offices. The presidencies of the teachers and deacons quorums were named at a meeting held two months later:

> The Lesser Priesthood was organized in the City of Nauvoo, March 21, 1841, by Bishops Whitney, Miller, Higbee, and Knight. Samuel Rolf was chosen president of the Priests' quorum, and Stephen Markham and Hezekiah Peck, his counselors. (*History of the Church* 4:312)

When the priests quorum was reorganized on January 1, 1844, a president and two counselors were again designated (*History of the Church* 6:175). Clearly, neither the Church nor the Lord (as evidenced in D&C 124) viewed the bishop's role as that of "president" over the priests quorum, though the bishops presided over the Aaronic Priesthood in general. Indeed, on the date the priests quorum was organized, the bishops met with the lesser priesthood, meaning that quorum specifically (*History of the Church* 6:170).

The teachers quorum was not organized until May 2 (*History of the Church* 4:354). Neither this quorum nor the priests quorum were under the supervision of the stake presidency. The stake officers were essentially responsible for the Melchizedek Priesthood. The number of individuals in Nauvoo who were priests and teachers appears to be quite small. On October 7, 1842, the teachers had to organize their quorum again (the previous quorum evidently no longer existed). They chose a presidency and scribe for a quorum totaling only fifteen members (*History of the Church* 5:169).

The principal duty of what we term today the Aaronic Priesthood (which originally referred only to the priests) appears to have been to visit the house of members and teach them their duties (today known as "home teaching"). In response to a question asked of Brigham Young at a conference held in New York City on August 27, 1843 concerning such teaching, he said, "any officer from a high priest to a deacon may visit the Church or members, and be set apart for this purpose, if the Church will receive it" (*History of the Church* 5:551).

Gathering to Nauvoo

The revelation of January 19, 1841 designated the Nauvoo Stake as a "cornerstone of Zion" (D&C 124:2). Only four days earlier, the First Presidency issued a proclamation to the Saints, asking that they gather in as soon as practicable to the Nauvoo area (*History of the Church* 4:266-267, 269).[19] In order to more fully encourage this gathering, another declaration was issued under the signature of Joseph Smith on May 14, 1841:

> The First Presidency of the Church of Jesus Christ of Latter-day Saints, anxious to promote the prosperity of said Church, feel it their duty to call upon the Saints who reside out of the county [of Hancock, Illinois], to make preparations to come in without delay. This is important, and should be attended to by all who feel an interest in the prosperity of this cor-

---

19 The letter was signed "Joseph Smith, Sidney Rigdon, Hyrum Smith, Presidents of the Church."

ner-stone of Zion. Here the Temple must be raised, the University built, and other edifices erected which are necessary for the great work of the last days, and which can only be done by a concentration of energy and enterprise. Let it, therefore, be understood, that all the stakes, excepting those in this county, and in Lee county, Iowa, are discontinued, and the Saints instructed to settle in this county as soon as circumstances will permit. (*History of the Church* 4:362)

At a special conference held in Nauvoo on August 16, 1841, Joseph Smith announced that the First Presidency had approved a decision of the Twelve concerning the settling places of the English immigrants. The conference approved the building up of Nauvoo, Zarahemla, Warren, Nashville, and Ramus (*History of the Church* 4:404). On August 26, the Twelve issued an epistle in which they reminded the Saints not to gather outside "Hancock county, Illinois, and Zarahemla in Lee county, Iowa, opposite Nauvoo" (*History of the Church* 4:410).

By December, it was decided to gather the Saints further from outlying areas of Hancock county to Nauvoo. On December 4, Hyrum Smith presided over a conference at Ramus, in company with four members of the Twelve (including President Brigham Young).

It was unanimously resolved by the conference that the organization of the Church at Ramus as a Stake be discontinued and that John Lawson be presiding Elder over the branch at Ramus, and Joseph Johnson, clerk; and that William Wightman, the Bishop, transfer all the Church property in Ramus to the sole Trustee in Trust, Joseph Smith, President of the whole Church" (*History of the Church* 4:467-8).

On December 13, Isaac Decker, presiding Elder at Warsaw, was instructed that "the First Presidency decided that the Saints should remove from Warsaw to Nauvoo immediately" (*History of the Church* 4:471-2). Finally, on January 1, 1842, a conference was held at Zarahemla, Iowa, "at which that stake was discontinued; a branch was organized in place thereof, and John Smith appointed president" (*History of the Church* 4:493).

The Kirtland Stake

At the time these stakes were discontinued, the Kirtland Stake presented a problem. At a general conference held in Nauvoo on October 3, 1840, it was decided "that Elder Almon W. Babbitt be appointed to preside over the church in Kirtland and that he choose his own counselors" (*History of the Church* 4:204). In a letter written by Joseph and Hyrum Smith to the Saints in Kirtland just sixteen days later, the decision of the conference was explained. The Prophet stated "that Elder Almon W. Babbitt should be appointed to preside over the stake of Kirtland, and that he be privileged to choose his own counselors" (*History of the Church* 4:225-6).

By the time of the reorganization of the Church in Nauvoo, when the revelation in D&C 124 was received, there were already problems in Kirtland. Mentioning Almon Babbitt by name, the Lord informed the prophet Joseph that it was his intention to build up Kirtland, but that he would scourge it (D&C 124:84-86). The prophetic nature of this utterance is evident from subsequent events.

It was not until May 22, 1841 that Elder Babbitt held a conference at Kirtland and chose his counselors, along with a bishopric and presidents for the high priests and elders quorums (*History of the Church* 4:362). By then, the First Presidency was already advising the Saints to gather in Nauvoo. At the general conference held on October 2, 1841, Almon W. Babbitt was disfellowshipped for trying to convince the Saints to remain in Kirtland (*History of the Church* 4:424). On the same day, Babbitt held a conference in Kirtland. This prompted a letter from Hyrum Smith,[20] in which he said concerning "the organization of that branch of the Church, it is not according to the Spirit and will of God," and instructed the Saints to remove from Kirtland (*History of the Church* 4:443-4).

Still, there was resistance in Kirtland to the wishes of the First Presidency. On November 16, Almon W. Babbitt's counselors (signing as "acting presidents"), along with the bishop and his counselors, wrote to Presidents Joseph Smith and Brigham Young, inquiring as to the status of their former stake president. In a reply dated December 15, 1841,

---

20 It was signed "Hyrum Smith, Patriarch for the whole Church."

the prophet informed these brethren that Babbitt would have to "offer satisfaction" if he wished to have his membership reconsidered.

Concerning the Kirtland Stake, he wrote:

> You are doubtless all well aware that all the stakes, except those in Hancock county, Illinois, and Lee county, Iowa, were discontinued some time since by the First Presidency, as published in the *Times & Seasons;* but as it appears that there are many in Kirtland who desire to remain there, and build up that place, and as you have made great exertions according to your letter, to establish a printing press, and take care of the poor, &c., since that period, you may as well continue operations according to your designs, and go on with your printing, and do what you can in righteousness to build up Kirtland, but do not suffer yourselves to harbor the idea that Kirtland will rise on the ruins of Nauvoo. It is the privilege of brethren emigrating from any quarter to come to this place, and it is not right to attempt to persuade those who desire it, to stop short. (*History of the Church* 4:476)

Almon W. Babbitt returned to the Church, and on March 13, 1843, he was selected as presiding elder in Ramus, Illinois (*History of the Church* 5:303). Less than a month later, on April 6, "a conference was also held in the House of the Lord at Kirtland, at which was passed a resolution for the removal of all Saints in that place to Nauvoo" (*History of the Church* 5:352). Thus ended a brief period of rebellion in the place that had formerly been headquarters for the restored Church.

The Nauvoo Stake

With Nauvoo becoming the central gathering place for the Church, the headquarters stake became a very important entity. During the years 1841-42, the city's wards appear to have been transferred to the control of the stake presidency and high council. On March 1, 1841, at the suggestion of Joseph Smith, the Nauvoo high council re-divided the city into four wards, with Newel K. Whitney, George Miller, Isaac Higbee[21] and Vinson Knight as bishops (*History of the Church*

---

21 Higbee was bishop of the Second Ward. The wards assigned to the other bishops are not known. See the footnote on the history of the Nauvoo wards in *History of the Church* 5:120.

4:305-306). The bishops continued to handle financial and welfare matters and did not preside over priesthood quorums. Meetings were conducted on a stake level.

On March 29, 1841, "William Marks, president of the stake at Nauvoo, made choice of Charles C. Rich and Austin Cowles as his counselors" (*History of the Church* 4:323). Nearly a year later (January 18, 1842), in a listing of the members of the Nauvoo high council, we find William Marks named as "President," while the entire high council, along with Cowles and Rich (whose names appear last in the list) are termed "Counselors" (*History of the Church* 4:505).

The Nauvoo High Council occupied a position of higher authority in the Church than do today's stake high councils. It was, in effect, the "supreme high council," subservient only to the First Presidency and Quorum of the Twelve. Indeed, the Prophet Joseph and other leaders frequently met with the high council during its deliberations and occasionally presided over its meetings.[22]

On January 21, 1842, "the presidents of the different quorums met with the high council at Brother Hyrum's office, to receive instructions, according to appointment of the council on the 18th." President Joseph Young of the First Quorum of Seventy explained to the high council why the Seventies had granted licenses in place of the high council. He noted that they had gotten permission from Joseph Smith to do so because these licenses could not be obtained from the Church clerk. This explanation satisfied the high council (*History of the Church* 4:501).

The overall authority of the Nauvoo High Council is demonstrated by "An Epistle of the High Council of the Church of Jesus Christ of Latter-day Saints in Nauvoo, to the Saints scattered abroad," which was signed on May 22, 1842, by the Nauvoo Presidency and High Council (*History of the Church* 5:15-17). Moreover, the Nauvoo High Council sat as a court of appeal for the entire Church.[23]

Though the typical stakes of the time had a single presidency and a single bishopric, with a high council and patriarch, Nauvoo, by

22 Examples of Joseph Smith meeting with the Nauvoo High Council are found in *History of the Church* 5:14, 280. Hyrum Smith presided over a meeting of the same council on an appeal from a bishop's court on March 25, 1843 (*History of the Church* 5:311-312).

23 Donald Q. Cannon and Lyndon W. Cook, *Far West Record* (Salt Lake City: Deseret, 1983), 229, note 6. For examples of appeals made from outside the bounds of the Nauvoo Stake, see *ibid.*, 227-9 and *History of the Church* 5:312.

1843, was divided into four wards, each with a bishopric. In a further development, on December 7, 1843, "the German brethren met at the assembly room at six p.m., and chose Bishop Daniel Garn as their Presiding Elder, and organized to have preaching in their native language" (*History of the Church* 6:103). Meanwhile, with the continuing growth of the city of Nauvoo, it was decided that the stake should be re-divided into ten wards, with a bishop appointed over each (*History of the Church* 5:119-20, 199-200).

The Position of the Twelve

During the Kirtland period, it was difficult for some Latter-day Saints to understand the position of the Twelve Apostles in the Church. The authority of the high priests and of the high council overshadowed the work of the "Traveling High Council." Joseph Smith tried to correct some of the misconceptions, but was not entirely successful, except in the Missouri settlements. All this was to change when the Twelve returned from Great Britain with large numbers of their own converts, loyal to the Apostles.

When the Twelve returned to Nauvoo with this loyal following, it became possible for them to remain at the headquarters of the Church and take their proper place in the hierarchy of the Church, as outlined in the revelation known to us as D&C 107. In another revelation, given to the prophet Joseph on July 9, 1841, the Lord informed Brigham Young, President of the Twelve, that he would no longer be required to travel in his capacity as an Apostle. Instead, he was commanded "to send my word abroad" and to remain at home, "henceforth and forever"(D&C 126).

The position of the Twelve and their leadership role in the Church was consolidated at a special conference held in Nauvoo on August 16, 1841. President Joseph Smith was absent from the morning session due to the passing of his two-year-old son the previous day. In consequence, "Elder Brigham Young [President of the Twelve], was unanimously appointed to preside over the conference" (*History of the Church* 4:402). Of the afternoon session we read:

> President Joseph Smith now arriving, proceeded to state to the conference at length, the object of their present meeting, and, in addition to what President Young had stated in the morning,

said that the time had come when the Twelve should be called upon to stand in their place next to the First Presidency, and attend to the settling of immigrants and the business of the Church at the stakes, and assist to bear off the kingdom victoriously to the nations . . . Moved, seconded and carried, that the conference approve of the instructions of President Smith in relation to the Twelve, and that they proceed accordingly to attend the duties of their office. (*History of the Church* 4:403)

In an epistle prepared by the Apostles on November 15, 1841, it was noted:

Since our arrival in this place [Nauvoo] there has been one special and one general conference of the Church, and the Twelve have been called to tarry at home for a season, and stand in their lot next to the First Presidency, and assist in counseling the brethren, and in settling of immigrants, &c. (*History of the Church* 4:449)

After that time, we find the Twelve more and more involved in presiding functions in the Church. Most notably, they are found to be organizing the Seventy and sending them as missionaries to various parts of the country and abroad. Thus, at a meeting held on May 23, 1843, Brigham Young and three other Apostles ordained some Seventies and set them apart to teach the gospel in the Society Islands (Tahiti) of the South Pacific, with Noah Rogers being appointed president of the new mission. In his instructions to these brethren, Brigham Young said, "We commit the keys of opening the gospel to the Society Islands to you," whereupon the other members of the Twelve replied, "Aye" (*History of the Church* 5:404-405).

Revelations for the Twelve, however, continued to come through the Prophet Joseph Smith from time to time. In December 1841, he received a revelation regarding Amos Fuller: "Verily thus saith the Lord unto my servants the Twelve; let them appoint unto my servant A. Fuller a mission to preach my gospel unto the children of men, as it shall be manifested unto them by my Holy Spirit. Amen."[24]

---

24 Joseph Smith Collection in LDS Church Historian's Office.

In a discourse delivered during a New York City conference held on August 17, 1843,

> Elder [Brigham] Young said that if elders or high priests are so situated that they cannot get word from the Prophet or the Twelve Apostles, they may get a revelation concerning themselves. The Twelve may get a revelation in any part of the world concerning the building up of the kingdom, as they have to establish it in all parts of the world. So any person can ask the Lord for a witness concerning himself, and get an answer, but not to lead the Church; that belongs to the head of the Church. (*History of the Church* 5:551)

On May 14, 1842, Joseph Smith recorded that he had granted the petition of about seventy members of the Church in Philadelphia "for the organization of a branch of the Church in the north part of the city." But, because the Twelve were specifically designated by the Lord to govern the Church outside the organized Stakes, he made sure that his actions "were sanctioned by the Twelve" (*History of the Church* 5:8). Because Joseph held keys over all the earth, he obviously did not need the permission of the Twelve to act as he did. His deference to the Quorum was probably an effort to both sustain them in their calling and teach the members that all things were being done in order.

The Cases of Orson Pratt & Amasa Lyman

During the summer of 1842, Elder Orson Pratt of the Quorum of the Twelve was cut off from the Church by his own quorum. On August 20, "the Twelve met in council, and ordained Amasa Lyman to be one of the Twelve Apostles" in his stead (*History of the Church* 5:120).

Elder Pratt was not guilty of any great sin and the loss of his Church membership was the cause of much sadness and repentance on his part. At the beginning of 1843, he approached the Prophet Joseph to ask to be re-baptized. Joseph declared that the Quorum's action was illegal because a majority had not been present to act on the matter. On January 20, Joseph and Hyrum met with eight members of the Twelve. Joseph wrote:

This council was called to consider the case of Orson Pratt who had previously been cut off from the Church for disobedience,[25] and Amasa Lyman had been ordained an Apostle in his place. I told the quorum: you may receive Orson back into the quorum of the Twelve and I can take Amasa into the First Presidency.[26] President Young said there were but three present when Amasa was ordained,[27] the rest of the Twelve being either on a mission or sick. I told them that was legal when no more could be had. (*History of the Church* 5:255)

That afternoon, Joseph Smith baptized Orson and his wife in the Mississippi River "and confirmed them in the Church, ordaining Orson Pratt to his former office in the quorum of the Twelve" (*History of the Church* 5:256).[28] When Amasa Lyman visited Joseph on February 4, the Prophet told him "that I had restored Orson Pratt to the quorum of the Twelve Apostles, and that I had concluded to make Brother Amasa a counselor to the First Presidency" (*History of the Church* 5:256).[29] Elder Lyman served in that position until the death of Joseph.

Problems with Sidney Rigdon

Sidney Rigdon had long been a problem for the Prophet Joseph. As early as November 19, 1833, Joseph recorded in his diary:

---

25 The earlier published version of the history (*Millennial Star* 20:423) indicates that Elder Pratt had been "cut off from the Quorum of the Twelve for neglect of duty." This was reworded in *History of the Church*.

26 The earlier published version of the history (*Millennial Star* 20:423) read, "I told the council that as there was not a quorum present when Orson Pratt's case came up before them, that he was still a member—that he had not been cut off legally, and I would find some other place for Amasa Lyman, to which the council agreed."

27 The earlier published version of the history (*Millennial Star* 20:423) did not contain any of these words after "ordained."

28 The earlier published version (*Millennial Star* 20:423) indicates that he ordained "Orson Pratt to his former office and standing in the quorum of the Twelve." This, however, was changed because, as subsequent events showed, had Elder Pratt been considered the senior apostle at the time of Brigham Young's death, he and not John Taylor would have become President of the Church. It was not deemed appropriate by President Young that one who had apostatized, even for a short time, should lead the Church.

29 The earlier published version of the history (*Millennial Star* 20:518), reads, "I had restored Orson Pratt to his former standing in the quorum of the Twelve Apostles." The reason for the change is explained in the note preceding this one.

Brother <Sidney> is a man whom I love but is not capa[b]le of that pure and steadfast love for those who are his benefactors as should possess the breast of a President of the Chu[r]ch of Christ, this with some other little things such as a selfish and indipendance [*sic*] of mind which to[o] often destroys the confidence of those who would lay down their lives for him.[30]

During the Nauvoo era, Joseph Smith had several occasions to suspect that Sidney Rigdon was plotting against him.[31] At a meeting held on August 13, 1843, Joseph called for a vote of the congregation and it was unanimously approved "that Sidney Rigdon be disfellowshipped and his license demanded" (*History of the Church* 5:532).

On October 7, 1843, at a general conference held in Nauvoo, Joseph Smith "stated his dissatisfaction with Elder Rigdon as a Counselor." President Rigdon denied various accusations that had been made against him. The following day, he and others spoke in his defense. "On motion by President William Marks and seconded by Patriarch Hyrum Smith, conference voted that Elder Sidney Rigdon be permitted to retain his station as Counselor in the First Presidency" (*History of the Church*.6:49). A note in the manuscript history adds that "President Joseph Smith arose and said, 'I have thrown him off my shoulders, and you have again put him on me. You may carry him, but I will not'" (*History of the Church* 6:48-49).[32]

With Rigdon's rejection and with the apostasy of Joseph's second counselor, William Law,[33] Joseph and Hyrum signed at least one

---

30 Dean C. Jessee, ed., *The Personal Writings of Joseph Smith* (Salt Lake City: Deseret, 1984), 21. Some corrections and errors in the handwritten account from Joseph's diary have been ignored.

31 E.g., see *History of the Church* 5:6, 46, 553-4, 556; 6:46.

32 The significance of Marks' actions in sustaining Rigdon as Joseph's counselor became clear during the discussions of August 1844, following Joseph Smith's death, when Marks opposed the Twelve and supported Rigdon's attempts to take over the Church. At the trial of Sidney Rigdon held on September 8, 1844, Elder Heber C. Kimball reminded those present that Joseph had rejected him a year earlier. Years later, William Marks cast his lot with Joseph Smith's son, Joseph Smith III, when he ordained him as President of the Reorganized Church of Jesus Christ of Latter Day Saints.

33 On April 18, 1844, a council comprising six of the Twelve, five of the City Council (one of them William Marks) and two of the High Council, plus 19 others (including W. W. Phelps, Newel K. Whitney, John Smith, Levi W. Hancock and Joseph Young) cut off several people from the Church, including the Law brothers, William and Wilson (*History of the Church* 6:341).

document as the "Presiding Elders of the whole Church of Jesus Christ of Latter-day Saints" (*History of the Church* 6:264).[34] Nevertheless, Rigdon was present as a member of the First Presidency and spoke to the Church (*History of the Church* 6:287). In disfavor with Joseph, he soon thereafter went to Philadelphia, where he remained until after the prophet's death.

The Nauvoo Temple

The cornerstones for the temple in Nauvoo were laid at the general conference held on April 6, 1841. Immediately after performing the ceremony, President Smith spoke of the priesthood symbolism thereof:

> If the strict order of the Priesthood were carried out in the building of Temples, the first stone would be laid at the south-east corner by the First Presidency of the Church. The south-west corner should be laid next. The third, or north-west corner next; and the fourth, or north-east corner last. The First Presidency should lay the south-east corner stone and dictate who are the proper persons to lay the other corner stones.
>
> If a Temple is built at a distance, and the First Presidency are not present, then the Quorum of the Twelve Apostles are the persons to dictate the order for that Temple; and in the absence of the Twelve Apostles, then the Presidency of the Stake will lay the south-east corner stone; the Melchisedec Priesthood laying the corner stones on the east side of the Temple, and the Lesser Priesthood those on the west side. (*History of the Church* 4:331)

The procedure was followed when the Saints moved to Utah and on April 6, 1853, laid the cornerstones of the Salt Lake Temple.

Joseph Smith saw the temple as a place where the fullness of the Priesthood could be conferred upon men, for it was in the temple that men and women were endowed with power from on high and could be sealed to their kindred dead. He declared,

---

34 It is interesting that the title "presiding elder" was used in the Church long after the organization of the First Presidency. A letter written at Commerce on May 13, 1839 starts out "Joseph Smith, Jun., Sidney Rigdon, and Hyrum Smith, presiding Elders of the Church of Jesus Christ of Latter-day Saints" (Joseph Smith Collection, LDS Church Historian's Office).

The spirit, power, and calling of Elijah is, that ye have power to hold the key of the revelation, ordinances, oracles, powers and endowments of the fullness of the Melchizedek Priesthood and of the kingdom of God on the earth; and to receive, obtain, and perform all the ordinances belonging to the kingdom of God, even unto the turning of the hearts of the fathers unto the children, and the hearts of the children unto the fathers, even those who are in heaven . . . I wish you to understand this subject, for it is important; and if you will receive it, this is the spirit of Elijah, that we redeem our dead, and connect ourselves with our fathers which are in heaven, and seal up our dead to come forth in the first resurrection; and here we want the power of Elijah to seal those who dwell on earth to those who dwell in heaven. This is the power of Elijah and the keys of the kingdom of Jehovah. (*History of the Church* 6:251)

In the revelation instructing Joseph Smith to reorganize the Church in Nauvoo, the Lord also commanded him to build a temple, saying,

For there is not a place found on earth that he may come to and restore again that which was lost unto you, or which he hath taken away, even the fulness of the priesthood. For a baptismal font there is not upon the earth, that they, my saints, may be baptized for those who are dead—For this ordinance belongeth to my house, and cannot be acceptable to me, only in the days of your poverty, wherein ye are not able to build a house unto me. But I command you, all ye my saints, to build a house unto me. (D&C 124:28-31; *see also* D&C 127:8; 128:17)

Speaking at a meeting held in Philadelphia on August 6, 1843, Brigham Young said that,

if any in the Church had the fullness of the Melchisedec Priesthood, he did not know it. For any person to have the fullness of that priesthood, he must be a king and priest. A person may have a portion of that priesthood, the same as governors or judges of England have power from the king to transact business; but that does not make them kings of England. A person may be anointed king and priest long before he receives his kingdom. (*History of the Church* 5:527)

In accordance with these principles, on May 4, 1842, Joseph Smith administered the first endowments to a select group of people in the room over the store he owned and operated,

> instructing them in the principles and order of the Priesthood, attending to washings, anointings, endowments and the communication of keys pertaining to the Aaronic Priesthood, and so on to the highest order of the Melchisedek Priesthood, setting forth the order pertaining to the Ancient of Days, and all those plans and principles by which any one is enabled to secure the fullness of those blessings which have been prepared for the Church of the First Born, and come up and abide in the presence of the Eloheim in the eternal worlds. In this council was instituted the ancient order of things for the first time in these last days. And the communications I made to this council were of things spiritual, and to be received only by the spiritual minded: and there was nothing made known to these men but what will be made known to all the Saints of the last days, so soon as they are prepared to receive, and a proper place is prepared to communicate them, even to the weakest of the Saints; therefore let the Saints be diligent in building the Temple, and all houses which they have been, or shall hereafter be, commanded of God to build; and wait their time with patience in all meekness, faith, perseverance unto the end, knowing assuredly that all these things referred to in this council are always governed by the principle of revelation. (*History of the Church* 5:1-2)

Significantly, those in attendance included Hyrum Smith, who was assistant president and patriarch to the Church, the leading bishops (Newel K. Whitney and George Miller), and the three apostles who would constitute the First Presidency after Joseph Smith died (Brigham Young, Heber C. Kimball, and Willard Richards).

Over the next two years, Joseph also blessed the rest of the Twelve and others with the endowment and sealed a number of people in eternal marriage. Unlike other aspects of the priesthood, those available through temple ordinances were available to men and women alike, for they would share in the blessings of eternal patriarchal priesthood. (See the discussion in chapter 7, *The Keys of the Priesthood.*)

The Relief Society

It seems less than coincidental that the prophet Joseph Smith organized the Relief Society on March 17, 1842, just two months before giving the first endowments. On that occasion, he told the sisters, "I will organize the sisters under the priesthood after a pattern of the priesthood."[35]

Four decades later, President John Taylor spoke of the event:

> I was in Nauvoo at the time the Relief Society was organized by the Prophet Joseph Smith, and I was present on the occasion . . . Emma Smith . . . was elected to preside over the Relief Society, and she was ordained to expound the Scriptures. In compliance with Brother Joseph's request I set her apart, and also ordained Sister Whitney, wife of Bishop Newel K. Whitney, and Sister Cleveland, wife of Judge Cleveland, to be her counselors. Some of the sisters have thought that these sisters mentioned were, in this ordination, ordained to the priesthood . . . it is not the calling of these sisters to hold the Priesthood, only in connection with their husbands, they being one with their husbands. Sister Emma was elected to expound the Scriptures, and to preside over the Relief Society; then Sisters Whitney and Cleveland were ordained to the same office; and I think Sister Eliza R. Snow to be secretary. (*Journal of Discourses* 21:367-8)

The Relief Society has since become the largest women's organization in the world, and one of the most powerful forces for good on the face of the earth.

---

35 "Story of the Organization of the Relief Society," *Relief Society Magazine* 6 (March 1919): 127-42.

Chapter 10

JOSEPH AND HYRUM

Joseph Smith, the Prophet and Seer of the Lord, has done more, save Jesus only, for the salvation of men in this world, than any other man that ever lived in it. In the short space of twenty years, he has brought forth the Book of Mormon, which he translated by the gift and power of God, and has been the means of publishing it on two continents; has sent the fulness of the everlasting gospel, which it contained, to the four quarters of the earth; has brought forth the revelations and command-ments which compose this book of Doctrine and Covenants, and many other wise documents and instruc-tions for the benefit of the children of men; gathered many thousands of the Latter-day Saints, founded a great city, and left a fame and name that cannot be slain. He lived great, and he died great in the eyes of God and his people; and like most of the Lord's anointed in ancient time, has sealed his mission and his works with his own blood; and so has his brother Hyrum. In life they were not divided, and in death they were not separated! (D&C 135:3)

For a time, Nauvoo proved to be a refuge to the Saints. But during the years 1843 and 1844, the Missouri mobocracy followed the Saints to Illinois. Joseph found himself betrayed even by his closest associates in the Church leadership. At the conference of April 6, 1843, he asked the congregation "if they were satisfied with the First Presidency, so far as he was concerned as an individual to preside over the whole Church, or would they have another? He was unanimously sustained as "President of the whole Church" (*History of the Church* 5:328).

Still, some opposition continued. On Sunday, July 16, 1843, Joseph addressed the membership in meeting at Nauvoo:

The same spirit that crucified Jesus is in the breast of some
who profess to be Saints in Nauvoo. I have secret enemies in the
city intermingling with the Saints, etc. Said I would not prophecy any more, and proposed Hyrum to hold the office of prophet
to the Church, as it was his birthright. I am going to have a reformation, and the Saints must regard Hyrum, for he has the authority, that I might be a Priest of the Most High God. (*History of the
Church* 5:510.)[1]

The next day, Joseph recorded that he was "at home with my
brother Hyrum, conversing on the Priesthood" (*History of the Church*
5:510). Viewed from outside, this meeting might be construed as a
planning session to turn the Presidency over to Hyrum when Joseph
retired. But remarks made by the Prophet the following Sunday make
it clear that this was not his intention:

Last Monday certain brethren came to me and said they
could hardly consent to receive Hyrum as a prophet, and for me
to resign. But I told them, "I only said it to try your faith; and it
is strange, brethren, that you have been in the Church so long,
and not yet understood the Melchizedek Priesthood." (*History of
the Church* 5:517-8)

Hyrum had long held Joseph's respect, both for his wisdom and
because he was his elder brother. It was Hyrum who reconciled
Joseph and their brother William after a violent disagreement. The
reverence in which Hyrum's advice was held by Joseph is reflected in
an entry dated June 17, 1834, during Zion's Camp, in which Joseph
declared, "My brother Hyrum said he knew, in the name of the Lord,
that it was best to go on to the prairie; and as he was my elder brother, I thought it best to heed his counsel, though some were murmur-
ing in the camp" (*History of the Church* 2:100).

Hyrum's position as Assistant President made him, in effect, the
second presiding authority of the Church. This is shown by a certificate signed by Joseph and Hyrum on March 13, 1844 in which they

---

1 See Willard Richards' account of the discourse in a letter to Brigham Young two days
later (*History of the Church* 5:512).

use the title "Presiding Elders of the whole Church of Jesus Christ of Latter-day Saints" (*History of the Church* 6:264).

Developments in Nauvoo

During the prophet's last several months in Nauvoo, there were few changes in the organization of the Church. Still, there were developments that suggested the Church's role in the world and the organizational structure by which it would accomplish its purposes were still evolving.

A very important development took place at the general conference session held on April 4, 1844. It was the Prophet's last conference, and he gave some important instructions concerning the course the Church should take after his death.

> I have received instructions from the Lord that from henceforth wherever the Elders of Israel shall build up churches and branches unto the Lord throughout the States, there shall be a stake of Zion. In the great cities, as Boston, New York, and Chicago, there shall be stakes. It is a glorious proclamation, and I reserved it to the last and designed it to be understood that this work shall commence after the washings, anointings and endowments have been performed here. (*History of the Church* 6:319)

This vision of the future, "reserved . . . to the last," constituted the prophet's last instructions regarding the organization of the Church. It remains today the principal guiding force in the building up of the Church in the world.

The Martyrdom

In the midst of troubles in Nauvoo and the surrounding region, Hyrum Smith drafted a letter on June 17, 1844, calling for the Twelve to return home from their missions (*History of the Church* 6:486-487). Joseph asked him not to mail it "at present" (*History of the Church* 6:494). Three days later, the Prophet wrote letters to the absent members of the Twelve, asking that they "come home immediately" (*History of the Church* 6:519). On that same day, he advised Hyrum to take his family by steamboat to Cincinnati for safety, but his elder brother refused.

Joseph expressed the wish that "I could get Hyrum out of the way, so that he may live to avenge my blood" (*History of the Church* 6:520).

Joseph's foreknowledge of what would soon happen is evidenced from this and other events that took place during the last week of his life. On June 22, he "told Stephen Markham that if I and Hyrum were ever taken again we should be massacred, or I was not a prophet of God. I want Hyrum to live to avenge my blood, but he is determined not to leave me" (*History of the Church* 6:546). In a footnote to this entry, B. H. Roberts drew attention to the fact that Edward Tullidge, in his biography of Joseph Smith, quoted him differently, saying, "I want Hyrum to live to lead the Church, but he is determined not to leave me."

On June 27, 1844, Joseph and Hyrum Smith were shot and killed by a mob in Carthage, Illinois. With them at the time were two members of the Quorum of the Twelve, John Taylor and Willard Richards, both of whom survived the attack, though Taylor was severely wounded.

On June 30, "a few of the brethren met in council, and agreed to send Brother George J. Adams to bear the news of the massacre to the Twelve." Willard Richards wrote a letter for Adams to deliver to Brigham Young (*History of the Church* 7:147). When Adams failed to meet his obligation, Jedediah M. Grant was sent to inform President Young and the Twelve (*History of the Church* 7:158-9).

At least one member of the Twelve did not need to be informed. Parley P. Pratt recorded:

A day or two previous to this circumstance I had been constrained by the Spirit to start prematurely for home, without knowing why or wherefore . . . My brother William Pratt, being then on a mission in the same State (New York), happened, providentially, to take passage on the same boat. As we conversed together on deck, a strange and solemn awe came over me, as if the powers of hell were let loose . . . I . . . exclaimed—"Brother William, this is a dark hour; the powers of darkness seem to triumph, and the spirit of murder is abroad in the land; and it controls the hearts of the American people, and a vast majority of them sanction the killing of the innocent . . . this is a dark day, and the hour of triumph for the powers of darkness.

O, how sensible I am of the spirit of murder which seems to pervade the whole land." This was June 27, 1844, in the afternoon, and as near as I can judge, it was the same hour that the Carthage mob were shedding the blood of Joseph and Hyrum Smith, and John Taylor, near one thousand miles distant.[2]

Elder Pratt arrived in Wisconsin, at a spot 50-60 miles from Chicago, where the news of the martyrdom was learned from new passengers. He then went on to Chicago, then Peoria, and from thence walked 105 miles over a period of 2-3 days to Nauvoo. During this time, he realized that "my President and the older members of the now presiding council" were absent, and that the people at Nauvoo would look to him for advice. He asked the Lord, "show me what these things mean, and what I shall say to Thy people?"

In response, he received the following:

The Spirit said unto me: "Lift up your head and rejoice; for behold! it is well with my servants Joseph and Hyrum. My servant Joseph still holds the keys of my kingdom in this dispensation, and he shall stand in due time on the earth, in the flesh, and fulfil that to which he is appointed. Go and say unto my people in Nauvoo, that they shall continue to pursue their daily duties and take care of themselves, and make no movement in Church government to reorganize or alter anything until the return of the remainder of the Quorum of the Twelve."[3]

Pratt received this revelation on July 7 or 8. Meanwhile, on July 1, William W. Phelps, Willard Richards, and John Taylor issued a letter to the Saints in outlying areas, informing them of the martyrdom of "President Joseph Smith, our 'Prophet and Seer,' and President Hyrum Smith, our 'Patriarch'" (*History of the Church* 7:152).[4]

---

2 Parley P. Pratt (Jr.), ed., *Autobiography of Parley Parker Pratt* (Salt Lake City, 1873; 3rd ed. Salt Lake City: Deseret, 1938), 331.

3 *Ibid.*, 334, 368-71.

4 The significance of the title "President" for Hyrum Smith was mentioned in the previous chapter and will be discussed below.

The Twelve Care for the Church

Most of the Twelve were away from Nauvoo when maneuvers began for position in the now-leaderless Church. On July 11, 1844,

> [Stake] President Marks consulted with William Clayton about calling a meeting of the presidents of various quorums to appoint a trustee-in-trust in behalf of the Church of Jesus Christ of Latter-day Saints. A council was held at 3 p.m.; but as Dr. Willard Richards and Bishop Whitney considered it premature, the council was adjourned till Sunday evening, the 14th. (*History of the Church* 7:183)

Arriving in Nauvoo, Parley P. Pratt found John Taylor and Willard Richards conducting the labors on the Temple building. The three of them were the only members of the Quorum of the Twelve present. At a meeting held on July 14, Elder Pratt told his brethren of the revelation he had received and spoke in favor of delaying any decisions in the matter of leadership. Willard Richards "proposed that the church postpone electing a trustee until the Twelve returned, and called a special conference." That evening, several members of the high council met "to investigate the subject of choosing trustees, but decided to wait until the Twelve arrived" (*History of the Church* 7:184). There seems to have been no question of summoning Joseph Smith's First Counselor, Sidney Rigdon, to assist in deciding how to govern the Church. With few exceptions, the Saints looked to the Twelve as their leaders after the death of the Prophet.

Not only was there concern that no decisions be made until the rest of the Twelve returned to Nauvoo, the records indicate it was the Apostles remaining in Nauvoo who took charge of affairs in the absence of their President, Brigham Young. For example, when Illinois Governor Ford wrote to the LDS leaders in Nauvoo during July 1844, he addressed those letters to Willard Richards and William W. Phelps, who replied in kind (e.g., *History of the Church* 7:200-201). On July 15, Elders Parley P. Pratt, Willard Richards and W. W. Phelps, assembling with the bishops and other brethren, organized a company of fishermen, appointing a president with two counselors.

On July 18, Brigham Young sent a letter to Nauvoo addressed "To the Elders and Saints Scattered Abroad." The letter appointed a meeting in council for "the presidents of the different quorums, high priests, high council, seventies and bishops," as soon as the Twelve should arrive in Nauvoo. It was signed in the name of "Brigham Young, President, Wilford Woodruff, Clerk."

On July 29, "Elders Richards and Smith met at Elder Richards' and ordained two elders who were about leaving the city. Brother Richards signed their licenses: 'TWELVE APOSTLES, President. Willard Richards, Clerk'" (*History of the Church* 7:212-213).

On July 30, "Elders Willard Richards and George A. Smith met in council with Elder Taylor at his house. Bishop George Miller and Alexander Badlam wanted them to call together the Council of Fifty and organize the church. They were told that the Council of Fifty was not a church organization . . . and that the organization of the church belonged to the priesthood alone" (*History of the Church* 7:213).[5]

Choosing a Trustee

Meanwhile, Sidney Rigdon, who had long served as First Counselor to Joseph Smith, made plans to claim the "guardianship" of the Church. Ironically, on the day before he died, the Prophet said, "Poor Rigdon, I am glad he is gone to Pittsburgh out of the way; were he to preside he would lead the Church to destruction in less than five years" (*History of the Church* 6:592-3). Joseph had rejected Rigdon as a counselor at the conference held the preceding October.[6]

Elder Rigdon arrived at Nauvoo from Pittsburgh on August 3, 1844. Elders Parley P. Pratt, Willard Richards, and George A. Smith "invited President Rigdon to meet in council" the next morning, "which he agreed to" (*History of the Church* 7:223). The Apostles found themselves waiting for an hour until they received a message

---

5 The Council of Fifty was an organization set up by the Prophet Joseph Smith as a nucleus for the world government to be established by Christ during his millennial reign. It comprised both members of the Church and righteous non-members and was political rather than religious in nature. The Council continued to have influence in the early Utah period, but was ultimately disbanded.

6 See the discussion in Chapter 9.

that Rigdon was "engaged with a lawyer," evidently determining his legal position (*History of the Church* 7:224). He held a closed meeting with William Marks, stake president, and others, to lay plans for the appointment of a trustee-in-trust and "guardian" for the Church. Only four of the Twelve were in the city, and Rigdon evidently felt it was necessary to make the change before the rest could return.

At 10:00 that morning, Rigdon preached at a meeting held in Nauvoo. Claiming that his mission had been foreseen by the prophets of old, "he related a vision which he said the Lord had shown him concerning the situation of the church, and said there must be a guardian appointed to build the church up to Joseph, as he had begun it" (*History of the Church* 7:224-5).

At a second meeting held in the afternoon, "Elder William Marks, president of the stake, gave public notice (at the request of Elder Rigdon), that there would be a special meeting of the church at the stand, on Thursday, the 8th inst., for the purpose of choosing a guardian, (President and Trustee)." When Elder Thomas Grover proposed a waiting period in which the members could examine Rigdon's revelation, President Marks stated that the meeting originally slated for Tuesday had already been put off until Thursday.[7] After the meeting,

> Elder Rich called upon William Clayton, and said he was dissatisfied with the hurried movement of Elder Rigdon. He considered, inasmuch as the Twelve had been sent for and were soon expected home, the notice for meeting was premature, and it seemed to him a plot laid to take advantage of the situation of the saints (*History of the Church* 7:225).

Elder Rich's apprehension was, of course, completely justified.

The next day, Apostles Parley P. Pratt, Willard Richards, John Taylor, George Albert Smith and Amasa Lyman, in company with Bishop Whitney, met with Sidney Rigdon at the home of John Taylor. He spoke of the necessity of appointing "a guardian" for the Church,

---

7 As it turned out, Rigdon wanted the meeting on the sixth, but Marks had mistakenly announced it for the eighth. This was fortuitous, for Brigham Young and most of the Twelve returned to Nauvoo on the evening of the sixth.

but indicated that he did not feel the choice would be made at the Thursday meeting.[8]

At a meeting of a few people at the home of Emma Smith, William Marks tried to appoint a trustee. Parley P. Pratt was there, and said that it was "not the business of the local authorities of any one stake of the Church, and that, therefore it could not be done till the remainder of the quorum returned." The council ended without a decision.[9]

On August 6, Elders Pratt, Richards, Taylor, and Smith met to discuss the seriousness of Rigdon's actions in trying to take over the Church.[10] Brigham Young arrived that evening with the rest of the Twelve and the Quorum held a council the next morning, August 7 (*History of the Church* 7:228). A second meeting was held on the afternoon of August 7, attended by the Twelve, the high council and the high priests. After opening prayer by President William Marks, "President Brigham Young called upon President Rigdon to make a statement to the church concerning his message to the saints, and the vision and revelation he had received" (*History of the Church* 7:229). Rigdon explained the vision he claimed to have had in Pittsburgh on the day Joseph died, saying that since no one could succeed the Prophet, he, as spokesman to Joseph (see D&C 100:9-11; 124:103-104), would speak for him and should be the "guardian" of the Church.

Upon hearing this, President Young stated,

> I do not care who leads the church, even though it were Anna Lee; but one thing I must know, and that is what God says about it. I have the keys and the means of obtaining the mind of God on the subject.
>
> I know there are those in our midst who will seek the lives of the Twelve as they did the lives of Joseph and Hyrum. We shall ordain others and give the fulness of the priesthood, so that if we are killed the fulness of the priesthood may remain.

---

8 *History of the Church* 7:226-7; Parley P. Pratt (Jr.), ed., *Autobiography of Parley Parker Pratt*, 334-5

9 *Ibid.*, 335.

10 It seems Rigdon's attempt to fill Joseph Smith's shoes was not unique. Writing years later, David Whitmer reported that some members of the Church approached him about assuming the position to which Joseph Smith had ordained him (i.e., his successor in the Presidency) in July 1834. See David Whitmer, "An Address to All Believers in Christ" (Richmond, Missouri, 1887), 55.

Joseph conferred upon our heads all the keys and powers
belonging to the Apostleship which he himself held before he
was taken away, and no man or set of men can get between
Joseph and the Twelve in this world or the world to come.

How often has Joseph said to the Twelve, "I have laid the foundation and you must build thereon, for upon your shoulders the
kingdom rests." . . . I want to see this people, with the various quorums of the priesthood, assembled together in special conference
on Thursday next at 10 a.m. (*History of the Church* 7:230)

The members of the Church assembled at the appointed hour at the
request of President Marks "to choose a guardian, or President and
Trustee." After Sidney Rigdon had spoken for about an hour and a half,
Brigham Young asked that the brethren reassemble at 2 p.m. At the afternoon meeting, seven of the Twelve presided[11] and organized the quorums at the stand "according to order" (*History of the Church* 7:231).
This was evidently done in order to show the people that the Twelve, as
the highest remaining quorum in the Church, stood at its head.

Brigham Young then spoke of the calling of the "Apostles whom
God has called by revelation through the Prophet Joseph, who are
ordained and anointed to bear off the keys of the kingdom of God in
all the world." When he asked if the Church wanted a guardian, the
people replied by shouting "No!"

President Young continued:

If the people want President Rigdon to lead them they may
have him; but I say unto you that the Quorum of the Twelve have
the keys of the kingdom of God in all the world.

The Twelve are appointed by the finger of God. Here is
Brigham, have his knees ever faltered? Have his lips ever quiv-
ered? Here is Heber and the rest of the Twelve, an independent
body who have the keys of the priesthood—the keys of the kingdom of God to deliver to all the world; this is true, so help me God.
They stand next to Joseph, and are as the First Presidency of the
Church . . .

---

11 Four of them had not yet returned (Orson Hyde, John E. Page, William Smith,
Lyman Wight), while John Taylor, wounded in the attack on the Carthage Jail, remained
in bed.

You cannot fill the office of a prophet, seer and revelator: God must do this . . . You must not appoint any man at our head; if you should, the Twelve must ordain him . . . I know where the keys of the kingdom are, and where they will eternally be. You cannot call a man to be a prophet; you cannot take Elder Rigdon and place him above the Twelve; if so, he must be ordained by them . . .

I again repeat, no man can stand at our head, except God reveals it from the heavens . . .

Does this church want it as God organized it? Or do you want to clip the power of the priesthood, and let those who have the keys of the priesthood go and build up the kingdom in all the world . . .

I will ask, who has stood next to Joseph and Hyrum? I have, and I will stand next to him. We have a head, and that head is the Apostleship, the spirit and power of Joseph, and we can now begin to see the necessity of the Apostleship . . .

You cannot appoint a prophet; but if you let the Twelve remain and act in their place, the keys of the kingdom are with them and they can manage the affairs of the church and direct all things aright. (*History of the Church* 7:233-5)

A number of persons present at the time of President Young's discourse testified that when he spoke, it was Joseph Smith's voice they heard. Some declared that they saw him transfigured before them and appear to be the Prophet Joseph.[12] One of the witnesses of this event was Benjamin F. Johnson, who later wrote:

And I do further bear this as a testimony faithful and true, to the Church and to all the world—that at a conference of the whole Church at Nauvoo, subsequent to the Prophet's death, and return of the absent Apostles—that I sat in the assembly near to President Rigdon, closely attentive to his appeal to the conference to recognize and sustain his claim as "Guardian for the Church." And I was perhaps to a degree forgetful of what I knew to be the rights and duties of the Apostleship, and as he closed his address and sat down

---

12 See, for example, the remarks of George Q. Cannon in *Journal of Discourses* 23:363-4. A collection of eyewitnesses accounts was published in *BYU Studies* 36/4 (1996/97).

my back was partly turned to the seat occupied by Apostle Brigham Young and other Apostles. When suddenly and as from heaven I heard the voice of the Prophet Joseph that thrilled my whole being. And quickly turning around I saw in the transfiguration of Brigham Young the tall, straight and portly form of the Prophet Joseph Smith, clothed in a sheen of light, covering him to his feet. And I heard the real and perfect voice of the Prophet even to the whistle; as in years past caused by the loss of a tooth, said to have been broken out by the mob at Hiram. This view or vision although but for seconds was to me as vivid and real as the glare of lightening or the voice of thunder from the heavens. And so deeply was I impressed with what I saw and heard in this transfiguration, that for years I dare not publicly tell what was given me of the Lord to see. But when in later years I did publicly bear this testimony, I found that others could testify to having seen and heard the same. But to what proportion of the congregation who were present I could never know—but I do know that this my testimony is true.[13]

Following President Young's explanation, there were seconding speeches by Amasa Lyman (a counselor to Joseph Smith), William W. Phelps and Parley P. Pratt, all of whom supported the Twelve as the head of the Church (*History of the Church* 7:236-240). President Young then spoke again and put the question, "If the church want the Twelve to stand as the head, the First Presidency of the Church, and at the head of this kingdom in all the world, stand next to Joseph, walk up into their calling, and hold the keys of this kingdom." The vote in favor of this proposition was unanimous (*History of the Church* 7:240). Parley P. Pratt wrote, "President Brigham Young was unanimously chosen and upheld in the Presidency of the whole Church; the keys of which he held by virtue of his apostleship, being the senior and President of the highest quorum of the Church then living in the flesh."[14] The church further sustained the Twelve as trustees, to "teach what will be the duties of the bishops in handling the affairs of the church" (*History of the Church* 7:240-41).

The following day, the Twelve met and "Bishops Newel K. Whitney and George Miller were appointed to settle the affairs of the

---

13 Letter from Patriarch Benjamin F. Johnson to George S. Gibbs, secretary to the First Presidency, October 1903, 53-4, in the LDS Church Historian's Office.

14 Parley P. Pratt (Jr.), ed., *Autobiography of Parley Parker Pratt,* 336.

late Trustee-in-Trust, Joseph Smith, and be prepared to enter upon their duties as Trustees of the Church of Jesus Christ of Latter-day Saints" (*History of the Church* 7:247).[15]

B. H. Roberts pointed out that though the revelation in D&C 107 made it clear that the Twelve were the next quorum in authority after the First Presidency and therefore rightfully succeeded to the leadership of the Church upon the death of the President, there was no reference to this section in the day-long meeting held in Nauvoo (*History of the Church* 7:234-5, note).

The Apostleship and Keys

During the meetings of August 1844, Brigham Young stressed that it was the apostleship that gave Joseph Smith his authority. In a conference discourse of October 6, 1844, he said,

> You have all acknowledged that the Twelve were the Presidents of the whole church when Joseph was not; and now he has stepped behind the veil, he is not here, and the Twelve are the Presidents of the whole church. When did Joseph become a Prophet? I can tell you, when he became an Apostle.[16] Years and years before he had the right of holding the keys of the Aaronic priesthood, he was a Prophet, even before he was baptized. (*History of the Church* 7:287)

Inasmuch as Sidney Rigdon was not an apostle, he had no authority beyond that which Joseph deigned to share with him during his lifetime. Consequently, the keys now rested with the Quorum of the

---

15 Bishop Edward Partridge had been the first Trustee-in-Trust, until his death in 1840, whereupon Joseph Smith was appointed to this position. With the death of the prophet, the charge returned to the bishopric.

16 B. H. Roberts, in a footnote, indicates that he believed Brigham Young's remark to be "a bit confusing," since Joseph Smith was not an apostle before he received the Aaronic Priesthood. But eliminating the comma between the words "you" and "when" may solve this problem. Brigham Young simply said that he knew when Joseph Smith became an Apostle, and this, of course, was when he received the governing keys of the Church. As to his being a prophet, he had that foreordained position in his premortal life and his first prophetic manifestation came in 1820, nine years before he was baptized. Elder Roberts' concern may stem from the same source that prompts most Latter-day Saints to speak of "the Prophet" as if the President of the Church were the only one who ever held that title. Brigham Young made it clear on a number of occasions that the two titles were not synonymous.

Twelve Apostles. When Sidney Rigdon claimed to be following the written word, Brigham Young rejoined, "As to a person not knowing more than the written word, let me tell you that there are keys that the written word never spoke of, nor never will" (*Times and Seasons* 5:667). Of course, he had reference to the power and authority obtainable via the Temple, which Sidney Rigdon never received.

At the meeting of August 25, 1844,

> Elders Orson Hyde and Parley P. Pratt bore testimony that Joseph the Prophet had ordained, anointed and appointed the Twelve to lead the church, and had given them the keys of the kingdom for that purpose . . . Elder William W. Phelps and Reynolds Cahoon bore testimony that Joseph said unto the Twelve "upon you must rest the responsibility of bearing off the kingdom of God in all the world, therefore round up your shoulders and bear it." (*History of the Church* 7:264)

In an 1844 article, Orson Hyde further wrote:

> Before I went east on the 4th of April last, we were in council with Brother Joseph almost every day for weeks. Said Brother Joseph in one of those councils, there is something going to happen; I don't know what it is, but the Lord bids me to hasten and give your endowment before the Temple is finished. He conducted us through every ordinance of the Holy Priesthood, and when he had gone through with all the ordinances he rejoiced very much, and said, now if they kill me you have got all the keys, and all the ordinances and you can confer them upon others, and the hosts of Satan will not be able to tear down the kingdom as fast as you will be able to build it up; and now, said he, on your shoulders will the responsibility of leading this people rest. (*Times and Seasons* 5:651)

A number of other brethren, including some who were not members of the Twelve, were present on the same occasion and bore testimony of Joseph's words.[17]

---

17 For sample testimonies on this matter, see the appendix.

Following the crucial vote in favor of the Twelve at the meeting of August 8, Brigham Young invited William Marks to remain as President of the Nauvoo Stake and asked Sidney Rigdon to build up the Church in Pittsburgh, where he had been living (*History of the Church* 7:240). Under the date of September 3, 1844, Brigham Young recorded, "I had an interview with Brother Sidney Rigdon. He said he had power and authority above the Twelve Apostles and did not consider himself amenable to their counsel." Rigdon refused to surrender his license "and said the church had not been lead by the Lord for a long time" (*History of the Church* 7:267).

Five days later, a high council was organized, with Bishop Newel K. Whitney at its head, for the purpose of trying Sidney Rigdon for his membership. Eight of the Twelve Apostles were also present. The high council's decision to cut Rigdon off was presented by President Young to the congregation and was sustained by all but ten individuals (*History of the Church* 7:268-9).[18]

At the general conference session held on October 7, 1844, Heber C. Kimball reiterated that "President Joseph Smith never rested till he had endowed the Twelve with all the power of the priesthood, because he was about to pass within the veil" (*History of the Church* 7:299). The Twelve were sustained at this conference as the presiding quorum of the Church, and objections were raised to William Marks as stake President.

Sidney Rigdon and William Marks later followed James J. Strang, who laid claim to being Joseph Smith's successor on the basis of a revelation he forged. However, they later left his camp.

Ultimately both participated in the founding of the Reorganized Church of Jesus Christ of Latter-day Saints, with Marks ordaining Joseph Smith III to the presidency in that organization. Of the members of the Twelve at the time of the Prophet's martyrdom, nine went west with Brigham Young.[19]

---

18 Both Joseph Smith and Brigham Young had expressed distrust of Sidney Rigdon.

19 The other three were John E. Page (excommunicated June 27, 1846), William Smith (excommunicated October 12, 1845), and Lyman Wight (excommunicated February 12, 1849 after settling in Texas with a group of Latter-day Saints and refusing to come west).

Chapter 11

THE APOSTOLIC PRESIDENCY

Of the Melchizedek Priesthood, three Presiding High Priests, chosen by the body, appointed and ordained to that office, and upheld by the confidence, faith, and prayer of the church, form a quorum of the Presidency of the Church. The twelve traveling councilors are called to be the Twelve Apostles, or special witnesses of the name of Christ in all the world—thus differing from other officers in the church in the duties of their calling. And they form a quorum, equal in authority and power to the three presidents previously mentioned. (D&C 107:22-24)

A summation of the receipt of the keys of the Priesthood by the Quorum of the Twelve was reported in the *Millennial Star* of March 1845. It noted how, nearly a year earlier, Joseph Smith had called the Twelve together to give them "the same power he had received from heaven," in order to preserve on earth "the fulness of the Priesthood unto them." He then instructed them in the ordinances and government of God. "He after observed that he was laying the foundation, but it would remain for the Twelve to complete the building." He conferred on the Twelve "all the keys, covenants, endowments, and sealing ordinances of the Priesthood," then

> he proceeded to confer on Elder Young, the President of the Twelve, the keys of the sealing power, as conferred in the last days by the spirit and power of Elijah in order to seal the hearts of the fathers to the children, and the hearts of the children to the fathers, lest the whole earth should be smitten with a curse. This last key of the Priesthood is the most sacred of all, and pertains exclusively to the First Presidency of the Church, without whose sanction and approval and authority, no sealing blessing shall be

194

administered pertaining to things of the resurrection and the life to come. (*Millennial Star* 5:12)

By virtue of the keys they received, the Quorum of the Twelve Apostles became the Presidency of the Church when Joseph Smith died. In effect, this made Brigham Young, as President of the Twelve, the President of the Church. At the general conference of October 7, 1844, "Elder W. W. Phelps moved that we uphold Brigham Young the president of the Quorum of the Twelve, as one of the Twelve and the First Presidency of the Church." The proposition was sustained (*History of the Church* 7:294).[1]

Again, at the general conference of April 6, 1845, "Elder Phelps moved that this conference accept the Twelve as the First Presidency and leaders of this church. Carried unanimously." Then each was sustained separately as a member of the Quorum of the Twelve (*History of the Church* 7:392). The Twelve were also sustained as "the Presidents of the whole church" at the next conference, held October 6, 1845 (*History of the Church* 7:458).

Nearly half a century later, President John Taylor noted that when Joseph Smith died, "the Twelve then stepped forward into the position of the First Presidency, and operated for about three years in that capacity. And when President Young left us it was thought proper that the same course should be pursued" (Journal of Discourses 22:38-39).

The Patriarch's Successor

During the speech given by Brigham Young just before the sustaining vote was made on the fateful afternoon of August 8, 1844, he proposed the calling of a new Church patriarch to replace Hyrum Smith, who had been murdered with his brother Joseph.

> We shall have a patriarch, and the right is in the family of
> Joseph Smith, his brothers, his sons, or some one of his relations.

---

1 In a discourse delivered on August 31, 1875, Brigham Young, then President of the Church, said, "I say the rest of the Twelve, because I am the President of the Quorum of the Twelve Apostles on the earth, the only one that the Lord has ever acknowledged. It is true that Thomas B. Marsh was once President, but the Lord never acknowledged any man by revelation as President of that Quorum but myself" (*Journal of Discourses* 18:71). The revelation to which he referred is found in D&C 124:127.

Here is Uncle John, he has been ordained a patriarch. Brother Samuel would have taken the office if he had been alive. It would have been his right; the right is in Uncle John, or one of his brothers. I know it would have belonged to Samuel. But as it is, if you leave it to the Twelve, they will wait until they know who is the man. Will you leave it to the Twelve, and they dictate the matter. (*History of the Church* 7:241-2)

The vote was unanimous in favor of this proposition. The people knew, based on the revelation referred to by President Young (today D&C 107:39) that it was the duty of the Twelve to choose patriarchs.

The previous patriarch to the Church, Hyrum Smith, had been Joseph's designated successor. At the conference held October 6, 1844 in Nauvoo, Brigham Young explained:

There never has a man stood between Joseph and the Twelve, and unless we apostatize there never will. If Hyrum had lived he would not have stood between Joseph and the Twelve, but he would have stood for Joseph.—Did Joseph ordain any man to take his place? He did. Who was it? It was Hyrum, but Hyrum fell a martyr before Joseph did. If Hyrum had lived he would have acted for Joseph, and then when we had gone up, the Twelve would have sat down at Joseph's right hand, and Hyrum on the left hand. The *Bible* says God hath set in the church, first Apostles, then comes Prophets, afterwards, because the keys and power of the Apostleship are greater than that of the Prophets. Sidney Rigdon cannot hold the keys without Joseph.[2]

At a conference session held the following day, Heber C. Kimball referred to Hyrum Smith as "a Prophet and Patriarch in the church" (*History of the Church* 7:294). On the same day, Brigham Young proposed that Asael Smith, brother to Joseph Sr., should be "ordained to the office of patriarch. He went on to show that the right to the office of Patriarch to the whole church belonged to William Smith as a legal right of descent. Uncle Asael [however] ought to receive the office of

---

2 *History of the Church* 7:288; *Times and Seasons*, October 15, 1844, 683.

[a] patriarch in the church." He was ordained at the conference (*History of the Church* 7:301-2).

On August 9, 1844, the day following Sidney Rigdon's defeat in his bid to become the Church's "guardian," the Twelve authorized John Smith, then serving as Patriarch and President at Macedonia, to appoint another president in his stead and move to Nauvoo, if he wished to do so (*History of the Church* 7:247). An uncle to Joseph and Hyrum, they may have thought he would become patriarch to the Church. He had, in fact, been ordained to the office of patriarch the previous January by his nephew Joseph, though still serving as stake president.[3] But his calling as patriarch for the entire Church was delayed for several years. Brigham Young proposed that William Smith, brother to Joseph and Hyrum and a member of the Twelve, be appointed patriarch to the Church. Consequently, "Uncle John" was called to replace William Marks as President of the Nauvoo Stake when the latter was removed at the conference of October 7, 1844 for not sustaining the Twelve.

Calling William Smith to the patriarchate was not an easy matter. He had already been a cause of friction with his brother, the Prophet Joseph, and later with the Twelve. On August 27, 1844, in an attempt to alleviate hard feelings, William wrote to President Brigham Young as follows:

> Will the brethren remember me and my claims in the Smith family. I do not mean I will be president and prophet in Joseph's place, for no man on earth can fill his place. He is our prophet, seer, revelator, priest and king in time and eternity, hence the Twelve come next to him on earth or in heaven. Consequently they must act in Joseph's place on earth as presiding officers, and govern the Church in all things temporally and spiritually, every revelation from Joseph, as the ancient apostles did from Christ, through the President of the Twelve for the instruction and government of the Church. This will constitute a proper head and keep confusion and disorder out of the Church, by the President

---

3 "Uncle John" Smith was a member of the very first High Council in Kirtland and served as stake president in Missouri, Iowa and Illinois before becoming Patriarch to the Church on January 1, 1849.

being supported by the prayers and united faith of the rest of the Twelve and the Church. No foul spirit can mislead our head.

This duty [devolves] then upon you Brother Young its head and revelator, to receive revelation from Joseph for the government of the Church.

This is my opinion and firm conviction and it might as well be plain on this subject as you are the President of the Quorum . . .

The next in Rule is the Patriarch of the Church. This singular personage stands as father to the whole Church. A Patriarch can be a prophet and revelator, not to the Church, to government, but to the Church as his children in Patriarchal blessings upon their heads, in teaching and fatherly care. A patriarch can be an apostle as well as a prophet as in the case of Hyrum. He was appointed prophet and revelator. An apostle is a prophet and begets children by the gospel and strong is his love and he is their spiritual father and patriarch, and all I have to say further is that this office of the Patriarch must continue in the Smith family while they live and are in the faith.

A report is going the rounds in the Eastern papers, that Elder Rigdon will be appointed Patriarch of the Church. This cannot be without my concern and respect. But I must learn first, that the office does not belong to me at present.

You have my sentiments in full on the head and patriarch.[4]

Preparing for Expansion

Only four days after the fateful meeting at which the Twelve were accepted as the Presidency of the Church, steps were taken to prepare the Church for expansion throughout North America. On August 12, 1844, the Twelve, in council, accepted Amasa Lyman as one of their number, then proposed "that the continent of America be organized into districts and high priests appointed to preside over a district" and "that Brigham Young, Heber C. Kimball, and Willard Richards[5] direct the continent and appoint presidents to manage the general affairs of the church" (*History of the Church* 7:248-249).

---

4 The original document, in the Church Historian's office in Salt Lake City, was quoted by Alvin R. Dyer in his book *The Fallacy* (Salt Lake City: Deseret, 1964), 34-35.

5 Significantly, these three were to constitute the reorganized First Presidency in a few short years.

On August 15, the *Times & Seasons* published an epistle of the Twelve addressed to all Latter-day Saints:

> The United States and adjoining provinces will be immediately organized by the Twelve into proper districts, in a similar manner as they have already done in England and Scotland, and high priests will be appointed over each district, to preside over the same, and to call quarterly conferences for the regulation and representation of the branches included in the same . . . Bishops will also be appointed in the larger branches, to attend to the management of the temporal funds, such as tithings and funds for the poor, according to the revelations of God and to be judges in Israel. (*History of the Church* 7:251-2)

At a meeting held August 18, 1844, President Brigham Young declared that

> North and South America is Zion and as soon as the Temple is done and you get your endowments you can go and build up stakes . . . You may go all over North and South America and build up stakes when the time comes. The whole continent of America must be organized into districts and presiding elders appointed over each district: the time has come when all things must be set in order. (*History of the Church* 7:258)

He further announced that "the seventies will be organized and a presidency of seven men will be chosen out of the first quorum to preside over the first ten quorums" (*History of the Church* 7:260). The members of the first quorum chosen to be presidents over the other nine quorums of Seventy nevertheless remained members of the first quorum for purposes of constituting one of the three presiding quorums of the Church (after the First Presidency and Quorum of the Twelve) (*History of the Church* 7:260 fn). On September 1, 1844, the Twelve "proceeded to the Seventies' Hall and instructed the seventies pertaining to the organization of their quorums" (*History of the Church* 7:266).

On September 24, Brigham Young and five other members of the Twelve met with Joseph Young, senior President of the Seventy, to make plans for expanding the Church. They "selected seventy presidents to preside over the seventies and fifty high priests to preside over different sections of the country" (*History of the Church* 7:274). That afternoon, Brigham Young "went to the Seventies' Hall and ordained the sixty-three members of the First Quorum of the Seventy to be presidents over the quorums from the second to the tenth inclusive" (*History of the Church* 7:279).

In preparation for the upcoming general conference, the Twelve issued an epistle to the Saints on October 1, 1844. At the conclusion of the letter, they wrote:

> As the business of the conference is now fast crowding upon our time, we must cut short this communication by informing you that an organization and arrangement is now in progress, by which high priests and presiding officers will be appointed over each district of country, throughout the union, who will have entire charge, under the direction of the Twelve of all spiritual matters, superintending the labors of the elders and the calling of conferences. (*History of the Church*7:283)

At the general conference session held six days later, Brigham Young announced that the following day high priests would be chosen "to go through the states to preside over congressional districts." He also asked that the Elders' quorums and the Seventies be present so the second through the tenth quorums of Seventy might be filled from the ranks of the elders. President Young proposed to "ordain the Presidents of the Seventies and then fill the quorums of seventies from the elders' quorums, and select men from the quorum of high priests to go abroad and preside" (*History of the Church* 7:303).

The following day, at the next session of the conference, "all in the elders quorum under the age of thirty-five" who were "in good standing, and worthy, and will accept it" were chosen to become seventies, along with some priests, teachers, deacons and members who had been recommended (*History of the Church* 7:305). Eighty-five high priests were chosen from the high priests' quorum "to go abroad in all the congressional districts of the United States, to preside over the branches of the church," with the responsibility to "settle down." Later they were to come to the Temple to "get their endowments, and return to their families and build up a stake as large as this" (*History* *of the Church*7:305-307). The assignments were apparently a follow-up to Joseph Smith's last major revelation[6] concerning the spread of the stakes of the Church abroad. Elder Parley P. Pratt, of the Quorum of the Twelve, was subsequently appointed to the presidency over all of the eastern districts (*History of the Church* 7:349).

That afternoon, the Presidents of the Seventy were ordained, and there came "upwards of 400 into the quorums of seventies." Some eleven quorums of seventy were filled and organized, with another forty elders organized as part of the twelfth quorum (*History of the Church* 7:307).

Brigham Young instructed that "if an elder wants to go out preaching let him go into the seventies. You are all apostles to the nations to carry the gospel; and when we [the Twelve] send you to build up the kingdom, we will give you the keys, and power and authority". (*History of the Church* 7:308).

On December 17, 1844,

> The Quorum of the Twelve and others in council assembled at the office of President Brigham Young . . . Moved and seconded that Brother Reuben McBride take the presidency over all the affairs pertaining to the Church of Jesus Christ of Latter-day Saints in Kirtland—both spiritually and temporally—which was carried by a unanimous voice of said council. (*History of the Church* 7:326)

This appears to be the first time that the spiritual and temporal affairs were combined in a single presiding officer. Three decades later, after the Saints moved to Utah, this was precisely what happened in the case of ward bishops.

Other Organizational Changes

A number of other changes in the organization of the Church were made during the general conference held on October 7, 1844. As noted earlier, it was at this conference the Twelve were sustained as the Presidency of the Church. Lyman Wight was sustained to fill a vacancy in the Quorum of the Twelve, while it was proposed "that

---

6 Announced at his last general conference in April 1844.

Elder Amasa Lyman stand in his lot . . . President Young said by way of explanation that Elder Amasa Lyman is one of the Twelve, just in the same relationship as he sustained to the First Presidency [*sic*]. He is one in our midst and a counselor to us" (*History of the Church* 7:295). Elder Lyman was a member of the Twelve for a short time in 1842 before being called as an additional counselor to Joseph Smith in the First Presidency. Here we have the Twelve, like the First Presidency, taking additional counselors.[7]

After reaffirming Bishop George Miller as the president of the high priests' quorum, the conference turned to other business.

> President John Smith moved that William Marks be sustained in his calling as president of this [Nauvoo] stake.
>
> Elder W. W. Phelps objected inasmuch as the high council had dropped him from their quorum.
>
> Elder S. Bent explained and said the reason why the high council dropped Elder Marks, was because he did not acknowledge the authority of the Twelve, but the authority of Elder Rigdon.
>
> President Young said that a president of a stake could be dropped without taking his standing from him in the church. But not so with the First Presidency or the Twelve. A president of a stake is only called for the time being, if you drop him he will fall back into the high priests' quorum. (*History of the Church* 7:296)

Marks was rejected by the conference and John Smith was sustained as stake president. Because he would be moving to Nauvoo, "the Macedonia church" where he presided "must select their own man for a president," said Brigham Young (*History of the Church* 7:296).[8]

Following this, Elder Joseph Young was sustained as "First President over all the quorums of the seventies," after which the other six first presidents were sustained. Newel K. Whitney was sustained "as our first bishop in the Church of Jesus Christ of Latter-day Saints"

---

7 In the minutes of the general conference held on April 6, 1845, Amasa Lyman is listed as one of the Twelve, others having been cut off (*History of the Church* 7:391).

8 John Smith continued for some time as the presiding elder or president at Macedonia, however. Under the date of February 28, 1845, Brigham Young recorded that President Smith held a council at which President Young ordained a bishop and counselor for the Saints at Macedonia (*History of the Church* 7:375).

and George Miller as "second bishop" (*History of the Church* 7:297). Bishop Miller was, at the time, president of the high priests' quorum, an office to which he was re-sustained at the following April and October conferences (*History of the Church* 7:392, 461).

The period of apostolic presidency saw several other changes in the government of the Church. Under the date of December 12, 1844, we read for the first time of a meeting held by the high priests of a single ward in Nauvoo—though they obviously did not constitute a quorum (*History of the Church* 7:325). The following month, on January 26, 1845, the high priests' quorum met under the presidency of George Miller (*History of the Church* 7:364).

At the conference held April 6, 1845, "Patriarch John Smith" (who is also called "Father Smith" in the minutes) was again sustained "as president of this [Nauvoo] Stake" (*History of the Church* 7:392). He is termed "patriarch and president of the stake" in the account (*History of the Church* 7:417).

John Smith was not the only patriarch to simultaneously serve as stake president. On February 14, 1845, "Father [Isaac] Morley," patriarch and president of the stake at Lima, "was counseled to remove his family to Nauvoo and Solomon Hancock was appointed to preside over that branch" (*History of the Church* 7:374). At the same time, "Dr. John M. Bernhisel was appointed a Traveling Bishop to visit the churches" (*History of the Church* 7:374).

Meanwhile, the number of quorums of seventy was fast expanding. On November 24, 1844, "the seven presidents of the thirteenth quorum [of seventies] were ordained" (*History of the Church* 7:317). The fourteenth quorum was organized on December 22 (*History of the Church* 7:327) and the fifteenth and sixteenth on January 12, 1845 (*History of the Church* 7:352). The presidents for the sixteenth and seventeenth quorums were set apart on January 18 (*History of the Church* 7:362), while the seven presidents and thirty members of the nineteenth quorum were set apart on February 9 (*History of the Church* 7:372). We have record of the ordination of presidents for the twenty-seventh quorum on June 1 (*History of the Church* 7:424), and the organization of the twenty-eighth quorum on June 29 (*History of the Church* 7:432), the thirty-first quorum on October 8 (*History of the Church* 7:481), the thirty-first quorum on October 26 (*History of the Church* 7:489), and the thirty-second quorum on December 21

(*History of the Church* 7:549). By the end of 1845, there were thirty-four quorums of seventy.[9]

It was during this period that we read for the first time of "the First Presidency of the Seventy" (*History of the Church* 7:544, 555). At the April 1845 conference, Joseph Young was "sustained as President of the First Presidency of the Seventy" (*History of the Church* 7:392). At the following October conference, he was sustained "as the Senior President of the First Quorum of the Seventy" (*History of the Church* 7:461). Evidently, the title "Senior President" referred to his office in the First Quorum, while the title "President of the First Presidency of the Seventy" had reference to his presidency over all of the Seventies in the Church.

Despite such titles in the Church's hierarchy, there was still one place where equality prevailed—the temple. In a discourse delivered the day after Christmas 1845, President Brigham Young

> remarked that when we began again we should pay no respect to quorums. Every man that comes in, is washed and anointed by good men and it makes no difference. Every man that gets his endowments, whether he is a high priest or seventy may go into any part of the world and build up the kingdom if he has the keys. We have been ordained to the Melchizedek priesthood which is the highest order of the priesthood, and it has many branches or appendages. (*History of the Church* 7:552-3)

The Case of William Smith

Under the date of May 23, 1845, Brigham Young wrote that he was "in council with the Twelve and Bishop Whitney: the improper course of Wm. Smith was the subject of conversation" (*History of the Church* 7:417). The next day,

> the brethren present expressed their feelings towards Elder William Smith to which he responded. The Twelve then laid their hands upon him and ordained him to be a Patriarch to the

---

9 Many of these continued into the Utah period, though their members were widely scattered, some of them living in different stakes.

whole church: there was a warm interchange of good feeling between William Smith and the quorum.[10]

Unfortunately, this spirit was not to last, for William soon turned against his brethren. On June 28,

> Father John Smith [his uncle] and Brother George A. Smith [his cousin] called upon William Smith . . . William evinced a very bitter spirit and declared himself President of the Church, and said he would have his rights: his uncle reasoned with him and endeavored to show him the falsity of his position. (*History of the Church* 7:433)

William's misunderstanding was evidently based on his knowledge that his brother Hyrum had been Joseph's designated successor prior to his death. Had this been because of his position as Patriarch to the Church, William may, indeed, have had a claim on the Presidency. But in fact Hyrum also held the position of "Assistant President," which had previously been held by Oliver Cowdery and David Whitmer at different times.

At the conference of October 6, 1845, the names of the Twelve were presented separately, and William Smith was not sustained as one of them. When his name was presented as "Patriarch of the Church," he was also rejected (*History of the Church* 7:460). He was excommunicated just thirteen days later (*History of the Church* 7:483).

It was William Smith's insistence on his "rights" to the Presidency of the Church that led to his fall. Significantly, his uncle John Smith (patriarch and stake president) and cousin George A. Smith (of the Quorum of the Twelve), did not believe that the right of Presidency was inherent in the Smith family. Both became prominent leaders in the Church in Utah, with "Uncle John" becoming "Patriarch to the Church" and George A. becoming a counselor in the First Presidency.

The Aaronic Priesthood

Under the apostolic presidency, there were several important developments in the government of the Aaronic Priesthood of the

---

10 *History of the Church* 7:418, also History of Brigham Young, Ms. 1845, 84, cited as a note in *History of the Church* 7:301.

Church. The bishops became more involved in the activities of the priests, teachers and deacons. We read of several meetings of the "lesser priesthood" at which Bishop Newel K. Whitney presided (*History of the Church* 7:317, 325, 328).

Other bishops also attended these meetings. For example, at the meeting of November 23, 1844, President Young and Elder Kimball ordained Edward Hunter to the office of bishop, and "set him apart to the care of the [Nauvoo] fifth ward" (*History of the Church* 7:317). At a meeting on January 10, 1845, Bishop Whitney made recommendations to the ward bishops in attendance concerning the institution of small manufacturing (*History of the Church* 7:351). As before, the wards were not congregations, but geographical areas in which the bishops took charge of the temporal welfare of the saints.

At a meeting on March 14, 1845, President Young "proposed that deacons be appointed to take care of the poor, in every neighborhood, with bishops at their head." The following Monday morning was set for the organization of the new system (*History of the Church* 7:381). A further proposal was made by Brigham Young and the Twelve on March 24:

> We ordained bishops who were directed to set apart deacons in their wards to attend to all things needful and especially to watch; being without any city organization [since the revocation of the Nauvoo charter], we deemed it prudent to organize the priesthood more strictly that the peace and good order hitherto sustained by the city might still be preserved. (*History of the Church* 7:388)

Under the date of April 15, 1845, Brigham Young reported that deacons were standing guard "at the corner of every block" at "whatever time of night" (*History of the Church* 7:399). At the general conference of October 6 of the same year, "President Young moved, that there be a quorum of deacons selected, and a president over them, and that the Presiding Bishops see to it, as soon as possible, and make report to this conference before its close; seconded and carried unanimously" (*History of the Church* 7:463).

The term "presiding bishops," used here, had reference to Bishops Newel K. Whitney and George Miller who, as noted earlier, were sustained as the first and second bishops of the Church. After the death of Joseph, these two were sustained as "Trustees-in-Trust" for the Church (e.g., *History of the Church* 7:417). As such, it was they who issued the names of elders appointed as agents to collect donations and tithes for the temple (*History of the Church* 7:369). At the April 1845 conference, they were sustained "as Bishops and Trustees-in-Trust, to the Church of Jesus Christ of Latter-day Saints" (*History of the Church* 7:393). Just eleven days afterward, the History first refers to them by the title of "presiding bishops," when they met with the Twelve (*History of the Church* 7:401).[11] The practice of having the Presiding Bishops meet with the Twelve was common during 1845 (*History of the Church* 7:435, 510, 534, 566). At the conference of October 6, 1845, "Newel K. Whitney [was] sustained as the first Bishop of the Church; and . . . George Miller [was] sustained as his associate" (*History of the Church* 7:462).

Interestingly, the bishops still did not serve as presidents of the priests' quorum, though they presided over the priests, teachers, and deacons. Brigham Young remarked, at the conference session of October 6, 1844, that "the president of the priests has a right to the Urim and Thummim, which gives revelation" (*History of the Church* 7:285). The following day, Steven M. Farnsworth was retained in "his office as president of the priests," while, at the same time, a president was sustained for the teachers and nine men were "sustained as bishops in their several wards" (*History of the Church* 7:298). Though there were at least nine wards with bishops in Nauvoo, there was but one priests' quorum. President Farnsworth, along with two counselors was also "sustained as president of the priests' quorum" at the conference of October 6, 1845 (*History of the Church* 7:463).

The Exodus From Nauvoo

The years 1845-1846 saw a rise in mob attacks on Church members in Illinois. It became clear that the Saints could not remain there much longer. On September 9, 1845, it was decided to investigate the possibility of relocating in the Great Salt Lake Valley—a site previously considered by Joseph Smith (*History of the Church* 7:439).

---

11 The term "Presiding Bishops" is found in other passages as well (*History of the Church* 7:417, 458).

Nearly a month later, on October 5, 1845, as part of the last general conference held in Nauvoo, Brigham Young dedicated the Temple, and began a great rush to accomplish as much work there as possible before leaving (*History of the Church* 7:456f).

At the conference session of October 6, 1845, "Father John Smith" was sustained as president of the Nauvoo Stake, while Samuel Bent was sustained "as president of the high council" (*History of the Church* 7:461). It was John Smith, "president of the stake," who presided at the morning session of general conference the next day, while the afternoon session was led by President Joseph Young of the Seventy (*History of the Church* 7:465-6, 473).

We read that "The Patriarch, John Smith, appointed four bishops to stand at the door, to take a collection for the benefit of the poor" (*History of the Church* 7:469). The presiding authority of the stake president over the ward bishops was beginning to be established, and it is clear that the president of the stake at Church headquarters was accorded honors usually reserved for General Authorities—a practice that continued into the Utah period.

The last formal meeting of the high council in Nauvoo took place on January 17, 1846 (*History of the Church* 7:482). Three days later, the high council drafted a letter to the membership of the Church, that was signed by the Twelve and the High Council, with Samuel Bent, president of the high council, being the first signator (*History of the Church* 7:570-2). The significance of these acts became clear when, during the course of the westward movement, the Nauvoo High Council played an important role in the government of the Church.

Inasamuch as the Twelve would soon absent themselves from Nauvoo, on February 10, 1846, Joseph Young, First President of the Seventy "was appointed to preside over the church during the stay of the saints in Nauvoo and received his letter of appointment from the Quorum of the Twelve" (*History of the Church* 7:584).

Five days later, Brigham Young crossed the Mississippi out of Nauvoo (*History of the Church* 7:585). Many of the Saints spent much of that year trudging through the mud across the state of Iowa, but the final expulsion from Nauvoo did not take place until the end of September 1846 (*History of the Church* 7:614).

Chapter 12

BRIGHAM YOUNG

I give unto you my servant Brigham Young to be a president over the Twelve traveling council; Which Twelve hold the keys to open up the authority of my kingdom upon the four corners of the earth, and after that to send my word to every creature. (D&C 124:127- 8)

Brigham Young and the Pioneer Company arrived in the Great Salt Lake Valley on July 24, 1847. After planting crops and attending to other matters of business concerning the planned settlement, President Young and others returned to Winter Quarters to assist in the westward movement. It was during that trip the First Presidency was again organized.

In a statement to the Camp of Israel's Pioneers, written at Platt River, Nebraska, on May 28, 1847, Brigham Young wrote of "this Camp of Pioneers, who have gone; or who have come out of bondage to find a location for a Stake of Zion."[1] It was at the general conference held on October 3, 1847, in Winter Quarters, that the Salt Lake Stake was organized, with John Smith as President. "Uncle John" had been president in Nauvoo and he retained the same first counselor (Charles C. Rich) as before, with John R. Young called as second counselor. A high council was also sustained. Soon, however, it would be time to reorganize the First Presidency.

In a discourse delivered at the general conference of October 7, 1860, President Young confirmed that he had known from the beginning that the First Presidency would have to be reorganized, and spoke of what happened when he returned to Winter Quarters:

> When I met Sidney Rigdon, east of the Temple in Nauvoo, I knew then what I now know concerning the organization of the church, though I had told no man of it. I revealed it to no living being, until the Pioneers to this valley were returning to Winter

---

[1] Brigham Young Papers, LDS Church Historian's Office.

Quarters. Brother Wilford Woodruff was the first man I ever spoke to about it. Said he, "It is right; I believe it, and think a great deal of it, for it is from the Lord; the Church must be organized." It then went to others, and from them to others; but it was no news to me, for I understood it then as I understand it now. (*Journal of Discourses*, 197-8)

Confirmation of Brigham Young's words comes from the journal of Wilford Woodruff, in which he recorded, under date of October 12, 1847, that President Young had asked his opinion "concerning one of the Twelve Apostles being appointed as the President of the Church with his two counselors." Elder Woodruff expressed his belief that such a move would require a revelation from God (*History of the Church* 7:621 fn).

Brigham Young spent most of the month of November 1847 in planning sessions at Winter Quarters. On November 6, he met "with the council and School of the Seventy" (*History of the Church* 7:618). On the ninth and tenth, the Twelve met with the Presidents of the Seventy, Bishop Whitney and the high council (*History of the Church* 7:618-9). On November 16, "Bishop Whitney was directed to preside over the high priests for the time being" (*History of the Church* 7:619). The Twelve again met with the high council on November 28 and December 3 (*History of the Church* 7:620). From this, we see that the Nauvoo high council continued to play an important role during the period of the Exodus.

On December 5, 1847, ten members of the Quorum of the Twelve met at Orson Hyde's home in Kanesville, Kansas. Brigham Young brought up the question of reorganizing the First Presidency. Orson Hyde moved that Brigham Young be chosen as President of the Church and Brigham selected Heber C. Kimball and Willard Richards as his counselors.[2] All three were unanimously sustained (*History of the Church* 7:621).

---

2 Heber C. Kimball's patriarchal blessing, given by Hyrum Smith on March 9, 1842, foresaw the important position he would occupy in the Church: "You shall be blessed with a fulness and shall be not one whit behind the chiefest; as an apostle you shall stand in the presence of God to judge the people; and as a prophet you shall attain to the honor of the three." Joseph Smith, under the date of May 28, 1843, wrote, "Of the Twelve Apostles chosen in Kirtland, and ordained under the hands of Oliver Cowdery, David Whitmer and myself, there have been but two what have not lifted up their heel against me—namely, Brigham Young and Heber C. Kimball" (*History of the Church* 5:412).

The following day the Twelve "voted that Uncle John Smith be the Patriarch to the whole church" (*History of the Church* 7:622). Both actions were approved at a conference held at Winter Quarters on the twenty-seventh of the same month (*History of the Church* 7:623-4). "Uncle John," who had been sustained as President of the new Salt Lake Stake, wasn't ordained as Patriarch to the Church until January 1, 1949. These acts were ratified at the conference held at Miller's Hollow (renamed Kanesville at this conference) on April 6, 1848, at which "the high council and other authorities in Pottawattomie" were also sustained and William Draper, Sr., became a patriarch (*History of the Church*7:624).

More than a decade later, in a sermon delivered on October 7, 1860, Elder Orson Hyde described events attending the calling of the new First Presidency. It is unclear if he spoke of the events of December 5, 1847, when the Twelve sustained Brigham Young and his new counselors, or if this was a separate event that took place two months later. He may have simply been mistaken about the date.

> In the month of February 1848, the Twelve Apostles met at Hyde Park, Pottawattamie County, Iowa, where a small branch of the church was established . . . We were in prayer and council, communing together; and what took place on that occasion? The voice of God came from on high, and spoke to the council. Every latent feeling was aroused, and every heart melted. What did it say unto us? "Let my servant Brigham step forth and receive the full power of the presiding priesthood in my church and kingdom." This was the voice of the Almighty unto us at Council Bluffs before I removed to what was called Kanesville . . . On the 6th day of April following, at our annual Conference, held in the log tabernacle at Kanesville, the propriety of choosing a man to preside over the Church was investigated. In a very few minutes it was agreed to, and Brigham Young was chosen to fill that place without a dissenting voice; the people not knowing that there had been any revelation touching the matter. (*Journal of Discourses* 8:233-4)

The new First Presidency was also sustained at a general conference held in Manchester, England, on August 14, 1848, with 17,902 people in attendance, making it the largest assembly of saints to ratify the actions of the Twelve (*History of the Church* 7:623). Only 5,000 members were in attendance at the conference session of October 8, 1848 held in Salt Lake City, at which the First Presidency was sustained, along with John Smith as Patriarch to the Church and Newel K. Whitney as Presiding Bishop. A new Presidency and High Council of the Salt Lake Stake were likewise sustained at that time, with Charles C. Rich as president (*History of the Church* 7:623, 628-9). Following the business of the Utah conference, Brigham Young "preached on the holy priesthood, showing the necessity of a First Presidency over the Church; for God had told me we would fall, if we did not organize a First Presidency" (*History of the Church* 7:629).

Succession in the Presidency

The position of the twelve as the senior quorum upon the death of the President of the Church was established in Nauvoo after Joseph Smith's martyrdom. In effect, the Twelve were the Presidency of the Church until a new First Presidency was organized, and Brigham Young, as President of the Twelve, was the President of the Church from the death of Joseph and Hyrum.

The President of the Twelve, when set apart as President of the Church, receives no authority above that which he already possessed as an apostle. "The Twelve, therefore, in the setting apart of the President, do not give him any additional priesthood, but confirm upon him that which he has already received; they set him apart to the office, which is their right to do."[3]

Heber C. Kimball explained that what makes "the President of the Church" different from the other apostles is that he "has all the keys, which he lends to others, giving authority to unlock doors and set in order the kingdom" (*Journal of Discourses* 4:171). So while the keys have been given to all apostles, it is the senior apostle who authorizes their use, a principle already understood in Joseph Smith's day.

Of Joseph, the Lord said, "For I have given him the keys of the mysteries, and the revelations which are sealed, until I shall appoint unto them another in his stead" (D&C 28:7). He also declared that he

---

[3] Joseph Fielding Smith, in *The Improvement Era,* July 1955.

gave Joseph and his counselors "the keys of the kingdom, which belong always unto the Presidency of the High Priesthood" (D&C 81:2). Thus it was that, in 1847, by reorganizing the First Presidency, the Twelve unitedly agreed that Brigham Young should exercise those keys in behalf of the whole Church. Parley P. Pratt explained,

> In the year 1835, in Kirtland, Ohio, they [Joseph Smith & Oliver Cowdery, the first apostles] ordained our President, Brigham Young, also Heber C. Kimball, your servant that is now addressing you, and many others by the word of the Lord. Thus our President and others received the keys of the Apostleship, and we magnified it until Joseph's death, when two of his Quorum of Three went behind the veil, and the third, Sidney Rigdon, who had got in the background, became an apostate. The First President was re-organized, under the authority proceeding from the Almighty through Joseph Smith, in the persons of Brigham Young, Heber C. Kimball, and Willard Richards; and they by virtue of the keys lawfully in their possession, filled up the vacancies occasioned in the Quorum of the Twelve, and also the vacancy made in their own Quorum, by the death of our beloved brother, Willard Richards. (*Journal of Discourses* 5:200)

Wilford Woodruff also explained the principle of apostolic seniority in the succession to the Presidency of the Church. In answer to the question, "Do you know of any reason in case of the death of the President of the Church why the Twelve Apostles should not choose some other person than the President of the Twelve to be the President of the Church?" he replied, "I know several reasons why they should not. First, at the death of the President of the Church the Twelve Apostles become the presiding authority of the Church, and the president of the Twelve is really the President of the Church by virtue of his office as much while presiding over the Twelve Apostles as while presiding over his two counselors."[4]

---

4 Cited in G. Homer Durham, *The Discourses of Wilford Woodruff* (Salt Lake City: Bookcraft, 1946), 91-92, and Mathias F. Cowley, *Wilford Woodruff—His Life and Labors* (Salt Lake City: Bookcraft, 1964), 561. President Woodruff made this declaration in a letter of March 28, 1887.

Apostle and Prophet

Latter-day Saints typically refer to the President of the Church as "the prophet," and some are surprised to learn that Church leaders have said each member should be a prophet in his or her own calling, whether in the family or in the Church. The Bible teaches that " the testimony of Jesus is the spirit of prophecy" (Revelation 19:10). Joseph Smith referred to this passage in reference to the question, "Do you believe Joseph Smith, Jun, to be a Prophet?" He said, "Yes, and every other man who has the testimony of Jesus. For the testimony of Jesus is the spirit of prophecy" (*History of the Church*, 3:28). Joseph cited this passage on a number of other occasions, as well (*History of the Church* 3:389; 4:222; 5:215, 231, 400, 407, 427, 516; 6:77, 290).

On one occasion, he declared that all who claim to be ministers of Christ must be "true and honest witnesses of Jesus Christ, they would acknowledge they have the testimony of Him, and that is the spirit of prophecy; and every man who possesses that spirit is a prophet" (*History of the Church* 5:408). Similarly, in an 1839 discourse, he declared that "No man is a minister of Jesus Christ without being a prophet. No man can be the minister of Jesus Christ, except he has the testimony of Jesus, and this is the spirit of prophecy" (*Journal of Discourses* 6:239).

What distinguishes Joseph Smith and his successors in the Presidency of the Church from others is not the spirit of prophecy, but the apostleship, which must encompass that same spirit as well as the keys of the priesthood. Wilford Woodruff explained that "anybody is a prophet who has the testimony of Jesus Christ, for that is the spirit of prophecy. The Elders of Israel are prophets. A prophet is not so great as an Apostle" (*Journal of Discourses* 13:165).

Brigham Young explained the differences between the titles prophet, apostle, and president. In a conference address delivered April 6, 1853, he said,

> Perhaps it may make some of you stumble, were I to ask you a question Does a man's being a Prophet in this Church prove that he shall be the President of it? I answer, No! A man may be a Prophet, Seer, and Revelator, and it may have nothing to do with his being the President of the Church. Suffice it to say, that Joseph was the President of the Church, as long as he lived; the people

chose to have it so. He always filled that responsible station by the voice of the people. Can you find any revelation appointing him the President of the Church? The keys of the Priesthood were committed to Joseph, to build up the Kingdom of God on the earth, and were not to be taken from him in time or in eternity, but when he was called to preside over the Church, it was by the voice of the people; though he held the keys of the Priesthood, independent of their voice. (*Journal of Discourses* 1:133)

To Brigham Young, being a prophet was secondary to being an apostle and having keys from God. He explained the difference in these words:

Many persons think, if they see a Prophet they see one possessing all the keys of the Kingdom of God on the earth. This is not so; many persons have prophesied without having any Priesthood on them at all . . . To be a prophet is simply to be a foreteller of future events; but an Apostle of the Lord Jesus Christ has the keys of the Holy Priesthood, and the power thereof is sealed upon his head, and by this he is authorized to proclaim the truth to the people, and if they receive it, well; if not, the sin be upon their own heads. (*Journal of Discourses* 13:144)

On another occasion, he explained that Joseph Smith had been a prophet before he became an apostle and possessed the keys.

Joseph Smith was a Prophet, seer and revelator (not by the voice of the people, mind you) before he had power to build up the kingdom of God, or take the first steps toward it. When did he obtain that power? Not until the angel had ordained him to be an Apostle. Joseph Smith, Oliver Cowdery, and David Whitmer were the first Apostles of this dispensation . . . When a man is an Apostle and stands at the head of the kingdom of God on earth, and magnifies his calling, he has the keys of all the power that ever was bestowed upon mortal man for the building up of the kingdom of God on the earth. (*Journal of Discourses* 6:320)[5]

---

5 For other statements by early Church leaders on this topic, see the appendix.

President Young used similar verbiage when he declared that "the calling of an Apostle is to build up the kingdom of God in all the world: it is the Apostle that holds the keys of his power, and nobody else. If an Apostle magnifies his calling, he is the word of the Lord to this people all the time, or else he does not magnify his calling" (*Journal of Discourses* 6:282).

Brigham Young taught it was the apostleship that provided the principal presiding authority in the Church.[6] Sidney Rigdon was a counselor to Joseph Smith in the First Presidency, but he was a high priest, not an apostle. For this reason, he could not have held the keys of the kingdom.

In his discourse delivered in Salt Lake City on April 6, 1853, President Young explained that the office of apostle, and not high priest, was the highest office in the Church, and that it was by virtue of the apostleship, not the high priesthood (i.e., the office of high priest) that Joseph Smith had been authorized to organize the Church. He further noted that neither he nor his first counselor, Heber C. Kimball, had ever been high priests. They were elders before being ordained to the apostleship.[7]

Wilford Woodruff echoed Brigham Young's statements, saying, "The highest office that any man has ever held on the face of the earth in this or any other generation is that of an apostle" (*Journal of Discourses* 13:319). On yet another occasion, Elder Woodruff declared:

> This Church has been established by raising up prophets, unto whom have been given the keys of the kingdom of God— the keys of the Holy Priesthood and apostleship of the Son of God, with power to organize the Church and kingdom of God on the earth, with all its gifts, graces, ordinances, and orders, as proclaimed by all the apostles and prophets who have lived since the world began. (*Journal of Discourses* 14:2-3)

---

6 Some of his statements on this matter were cited in Chapter 2, others in Chapter 11.

7 *Journal of Discourses* 1:134-37. Extracts from the discourse are included in the appendix.

The Presiding Quorums

It was Brigham Young who first made it clear that succession in the Presidency of the Church went from the First Presidency to the Quorum of the Twelve to the First Quorum of the Seventy and so on. This principle is based on D&C 107, which places these three quorums at the head of the Church and makes each equal with the other when in the presiding position. President Young's most important discussion of this matter is contained in a speech delivered on May 7, 1861:

> When the Twelve were called and ordained they possessed the same power and authority as the three First Presidents . . . The seventies possess the same power and authority; they hold the keys of establishing, building up, regulating, ordaining, and setting in order the kingdom of God in all its perfections upon the earth. We have a quorum of high priests, and there are a great many of them. They are a local body they tarry at home; but the seventies travel and preach; so also do the high priests, when they are called upon. They possess precisely the same priesthood that the seventies and the Twelve and the First Presidency possess; but are they ordained to officiate in all the authority, powers, and keys of this priesthood? No, they are not. Still they are high priests of God; and if they magnify their priesthood they will receive at some time all the authority and power that it is possible for man to receive . . .
>
> Suppose . . . there had been only Joseph Smith left of the First Presidency, would he alone have had authority to set in order the Kingdom of God on earth? Yes. Again, suppose that eleven of the Twelve had been taken away by the power of the adversary, that one apostle has the same power that Joseph had and could preach, baptize, and set in order the whole kingdom of God upon the earth as much so as the Twelve, were they all together. Again: If in the providence of God He should permit the enemy to destroy these two first quorums and then destroy the quorum of the seventy, all but one man, what is his power? It would be to go and preach, baptize, confirm, lay on hands, ordain, set in order, build up, and establish the whole kingdom of God as it is now . . .

Suppose the enemy had power to destroy all but one of the high priests from the face of the earth, what would that one possess in the power of his priesthood? He would have power and authority to go and preach, baptize, confirm, ordain, and set in order the kingdom of God in all its perfection on the earth. Could he do this without revelation? No. Could the seventies? No. Could the Twelve? No. And we ask, could Joseph Smith or the First Presidency do this without revelation? No; not one of them could do such work without revelation direct from God. I can go still further. Whoever is ordained to the office of an elder to a certain degree possesses the keys of the Melchizedek Priesthood; and suppose only one elder should be left on the earth, could he go and set in order the kingdom of God? Yes, by revelation. (*Journal of Discourses* 9:87-88)

President Joseph F. Smith confirmed this principle of succession to the Presidency of the Church, alluding to D&C 107:

I want here to correct an impression that has grown up to some extent among the people and that is, that the Twelve Apostles possess equal authority with the First Presidency in the Church. This is correct when there is no other Presidency but the Twelve Apostles; but so long as there are three presiding elders who possess the presiding authority in the Church, the authority of the Twelve Apostles is not equal to theirs. If it were so, there would be two equal authorities and two equal quorums in the priesthood, running parallel, and that could not be, because there must be a head. Therefore, so long as there is a First Presidency in the Church they hold supreme authority in the Church, and the Twelve Apostles are subject unto them and do not possess the same authority as they do as a presiding quorum. When the Presidency are not here, or when the Lord takes away the man who is called to be the President of the Church and the quorum of the three Presidents is thereby dissolved, then the quorum of the Twelve rises to the dignity of Presidents of the Church and NOT till then. Some people have thought also that the quorum of seventies possess equal authority with the First Presidency and the Twelve. So they would if there was no Presidency and no Twelve and only seven elders called seventies in the Church, but their authority is not equal to that of the First Presidency while the First Presidency lives, nor to that of the Twelve Apostles . . .

If the Presidency were to be killed off, then the Council of the Twelve Apostles would stand in their place and preside until the Presidency should be restored; and if they and the First Presidency were all killed off, then the seventies would come forward and they would establish the order of Zion and renew the order of the priesthood upon the earth; and if all the seventies were killed off, and yet there was one elder possessing the Melchizedek Priesthood, he would have authority to organize the Church, under the command of God and the guidance of His Holy Spirit as Joseph did in the beginning; that it should be re-established in its perfect form. So you can see that this organization is well-nigh indestructible.[8]

Other Church leaders have affirmed that this is the order of succession in directing the Church.[9] It is this view that may have led Wilford Woodruff to use the title "apostle" in reference to various officers of the Church, saying, "Let the Twelve Apostles, and the Seventy Apostles, and High Priest Apostles, and all other Apostles rise up and keep pace with the work of the Lord God" (*Journal of Discourses* 4:147).

Stakes and Wards

During the early Utah days, the only stake that resembled what we today call stakes was the one at Church headquarters. The Salt Lake Stake Presidency sat on the stand at General Conference and were sustained by the congregation along with the General Authorities. Salt Lake Stake priesthood quorum presidencies were also sustained in General Conference and exercised some jurisdiction over quorums in other stakes. Interestingly, the stake had a single large quorum of high priests and a stakewide quorum of elders. At its peak, the Salt Lake Stake had some fifty wards spread over several counties. And, for the first time, bishops actually presided over congregations and conducted Sunday services.

---

8 *Liahona,* or *Elders Journal* 4 (7 September 1895): 43, 45-46.
9 See the quotes included in the appendix.

Stakes or branches in outlying districts were quite different, often being smaller than many of today's wards, with a single presidency, a high council, a patriarch, and a single bishopric that did not preside or conduct Sunday services. This situation sometimes created problems.

These problems were discussed at length during the general conference of April 1862. At the conference, Brigham Young noted:

> From what has been remarked it appears that, in some instances, the President and the Bishop of a Branch infringe upon the rights of each other, perhaps honestly; and they think that they possess this power and authority, and thereby contention arises in the midst of this people, creating alienation of feeling and apostasy. What a pity it is that such circumstances should exist . . .
>
> The spiritual and the temporal cannot be separated, and, in the economy of the Framer of the Universe, are not designed to be . . .
>
> I will say a few words with regard to a Bishop. Except we find a literal descendant of Aaron, a man has to be ordained to the High Priesthood to administer as did Aaron and his sons. Suppose we then place the same man also as a President in a Branch, how are we going to divide his duties and labours? . . . as he has been ordained to the office of a High Priest, after the order of Melchisedek, to prepare him to act in the office of a Bishop in the Priesthood of Aaron, when he has baptized the people under the authority of his Bishopric, he has a right as a High Priest to confirm them into the Church by the laying on of hands. Bishops begin a contention in their branch, where they operate in their calling, when they amalgamate with their Bishop's office the office of the High Priesthood, when they try to bring the authority of the High Priesthood in the kingdom of God down to the capacity of the Priesthood that belongs to the office of an acting Bishop; here they make a grave mistake, and fall into perplexing errors.
>
> What are the duties of a President and a Bishop? We will first notice a duty that belongs to a President. For instance, he wishes a comfortable place prepared for the people to meet in, and he calls on the Bishop to marshal his forces to gather the material to build a house, and the house is prepared for the comfort and accommodation of all. In this instance you observe the duty and

office of a Bishop is attended to. In his capacity the Bishop knows nobody only as a member of the kingdom of God, and in the performance of this duty he calls upon the President and everyone else to aid in accomplishing the wishes of the President, to go to the canyon to get out timber, to quarry rock, make adobies, &c., &c., for everybody is entitled to pay Tithing. When the house is put up according to the President's direction, then the President calls on the Bishop to see that it is well seated, lighted and warmed . . .

On Monday morning the Bishop calls upon the President and everybody it concerns, to send their Tithing to the General Tithing Office. The President, who officiates as presiding officer on Sunday, is as subject to the Bishop on Monday as anybody else . . .

A Bishop sometimes officiates as a High Priest, and sometimes as a Bishop. (*Journal of Discourses* 9:279- 281)

In some branches, the offices of president and bishop had to be assigned to a single individual. President Young explained,

We have scores of branches of this Church in different parts of this country, and had we better now place officers, helps and governments in these branches, or wait till the people come to understanding, and learn to appreciate and honor such appointments? It is chiefly because of the ignorance of the people that we often concentrate in one man these different offices and callings, but when the people are sufficiently informed and have advanced further in the knowledge of the truth, it will not be so, but every branch will have its full quota of officers—a Patriarch, President, Bishop, High Council, and all officers that are necessary for the work of the Ministry, and the edifying of the body of Christ. Until the people can receive and honor these helps and governments, and be benefited by them, the different offices will be concentrated in as few men as possible, for men will contend for power, and as to which shall be the greatest, until they are better informed . . .

When the people come to sufficient understand, we shall not put the onerous task upon one man to act both as President and Bishop, but we will give you a full organization of helps, governments, &c; but at present we shall take a course to confine the offices of the Church in such a manner as to give the least cause for contention and trouble. (*Journal of Discourses* 10:97)

During the same conference, other Church leaders discussed the combining of the offices of president and bishop. Elder George A. Smith recalled a time when

> there were some Bishops sent out of Salt Lake City to explain to the country Bishops their duties. These brethren would go into a settlement where there were both a Bishop and a President, and they would go on and tell the Bishops what their duties were, and in doing so, embrace the whole circle of duties required of both Bishop and President, and never think that in that Branch of the Church, those duties were not united or centered in one man but divided between two." (*Journal of Discourses* 10:62)

Because of this, problems arose when the Salt Lake bishops, who presided over wards and were thus both bishops and presiding high priests, tried to instruct bishops in the smaller stakes who did not hold both offices. Elder Smith went on to note that friction between the local president and bishop sometimes necessitated that the General Authorities combine the two offices in one man.[10]

At the conference, Elder Orson Hyde suggested that it might be necessary to abolish the office of president in the "country branches" and allow the bishop to preside (*Journal of Discourses* 10:31). But Brigham Young saw a solution in having each priesthood holder magnify his own calling. He said, "as soon as Elders have wisdom sufficient to magnify their calling and Priesthood, we will give to every Branch, no matter how small the Ward, both a Bishop and a President" (*Journal of Discourses* 10:33).

The "country" stakes or branches were like the wards in the larger towns, but they varied considerably in their presiding authority. While some had both a presidency and a bishopric, which President Young preferred, others had a combined presidency/bishopric, blurring the distinction between wards and stakes in the outlying regions.

---

10 For a lengthier extract from Elder Smith's discourse, along with extracts from other discourses that dealt with the issue of president vs. bishop, see the appendix.

This is reflected as late as 1877 in a statement by Elder Lorenzo Snow, in which he spoke of "the man who acts as the presiding Elder of his ward" (*Journal of Discourses* 13:375).

Brigham Young was not content with the inconsistent way in which the outlying stakes were organized and considered that it did not work as efficiently as it should. At the October 1862 conference, he said,

> I sometimes think I would be willing to give anything, yes, almost anything in reason, to see one fully organized Branch of this kingdom—one fully organized Ward . . . is Zion organized? No. Is there even in this Territory a fully organized Ward? Not one. It may be asked, "Why do you not fully organize the Church?" Because the people are incapable of being organized. I could organize a large Ward which would be subject to that full organization by selecting families from the different Wards, but at present such [a] Branch of the Church is not in existence. (*Journal of Discourses* 10:20)

It was President Young's earnest desire to properly organize the Church. He declared,

> I have had visions and revelations instructing me how to organize this people so that they can live like the family of heaven, but I cannot do it while so much selfishness and wickedness reign in the Elders of Israel. Many would make of the greatest blessings a curse to them . . . There are so many great and glorious privileges for the people, which they are not prepared to receive. How long it will be before they are prepared to enjoy the blessings God has in store for them, I know not—it has not been revealed to me. I know the Lord wants to pour blessings upon this people, but were he to do so in their present ignorance, they would not know what to do with them. They can receive only a very little, and that must be administered to them with great care. (*Journal of Discourses* 9:269-70)

One of the problems, as President Young saw it, was that priesthood leaders often did not remain within the bounds of their own callings. Because there were not enough worthy men who could be called to leadership positions, it had become necessary sometimes to assign a high priest as both president and bishop. It was important for these brethren to understand that their presiding authority did not come from their ordination as bishop, but from the fact that they were high priests.

There is no retrograde movement in ordaining a High Priest to the office of a Bishop, for, properly speaking, he is set apart to act in that office. When we ordain a man to officiate in a branch of the Church as a Bishop, he does so according to the best of his knowledge; and now and then one believes that he has a right, when ordained as a Bishop, to officiate and preside over every temporal and spiritual interest in his district by virtue of his Bishopric; he believes that he ought to go into a Seventies' Council in his Ward and preside because he is a Bishop: and under this impression he dictates, guides and directs all things in his district; he baptizes, confirms and administers the sacrament as a Bishop, performing, under this impression, every spiritual and temporal duty. Were we to inquire of the Bishops of this Church what duties are assigned to the Aaronic Priesthood they hold, and what are assigned to the Melchizedek, those who could answer correctly are in the minority . . . The duties and powers of a Bishop cease the very moment he steps over the Aaronic Priesthood, which is to officiate in temporal things; when he passes this he immediately begins to officiate by the authority and power of the Melchizedek Priesthood, though he may not know it.

We have scores of branches of this Church in different parts of this country, and had we better now place officers, helps and governments in these branches, or wait till the people come to understanding, and learn to appreciate and honor such appointments? It is chiefly because of the ignorance of the people that we often concentrate in one man these different offices and callings, but when the people are sufficiently informed and have advanced further in the knowledge of the truth, it will have its full quota of officers—a Patriarch, President, Bishop, High Council, and all officers that are necessary for the work of the ministry and for the edifying of the body of Christ. (*Journal of Discourses* 10:95-96)

Another problem that concerned President Young and the other apostles was the disrespect that some of the high priests and seventies showed to their ward bishops, not respecting callings made by the bishops.[11] In May 1861, he declared,

> I want to inform the Seventies living in Bishop Miller's Ward (and what I now say applies to all the other Wards and Bishops,) if he calls on them to act as Teachers, it is their imperative duty to act as Teachers, seeking to benefit and bless the people . . . It is not the duty of a Seventy or High Priest, who is appointed a Teacher or a Bishop, to neglect the duties of those callings to attend a Seventies' or High Priests' meeting . . .
>
> When a Bishop calls upon a man to officiate as an assistant to him, he does not call upon him as a Seventy or as a High Priest, but as one of his own family—as a member of his Ward. . . . If Bishop Miller is not responsible for this Ward, to dictate to all this Ward, who is? He is the man that is appointed here to preside, and as a High Priest he has a right to meet with his brethren of that Quorum, and to baptize, confirm, bless children, administer to the sick, and perform all other duties pertaining to the office and calling of a High Priest. His being a Bishop does not take away any of his Priesthood or power. (*Journal of Discourses* 9:92-93)

A number of changes were made during Brigham Young's last years. At the general conference of April 1873, he chose five additional counselors and announced that "he had two counselors to aid him as President of the Church; he had the privilege of having seven brethren to assist him in this capacity" (*Millennial Star* 35:292). But the most important changes, designed to correct some of the problems he had seen in the Church, were instituted during a reformation that took place during the last year of his life.

---

11 See the comments by George A. Smith at the general conference of April 1862, in *Journal of Discourses* 10:61.

The 1877 Reformation

The forty-seventh annual General Conference of the Church was a joyous occasion, held not in Salt Lake City, but in Saint George, Utah. On April 6, 1877, as part of the proceedings, the Saint George Temple was dedicated, the first to be completed since the Saints left Nauvoo. On that same day, President Young announced a reformation intended to reorganize the stakes of the Church.

The Salt Lake Stake would no longer have "center stake" authority over the other stakes. Six members of the Quorum of the Twelve were released as stake presidents and were assigned to handle stake quarterly conferences. Stakes would now be organized with a full compliment of presidency and high council, and a bishopric of three high priests in each ward. Where a stake had sufficient numbers of priesthood holders, there should be more than a single quorum of elders, priests, teachers, and deacons.

Returning to Salt Lake City from Saint George, members of the First Presidency and the Twelve stopped at various settlements along the way to implement the reorganization of the stakes.

In May 1877, as the reformation began, Elder Orson Pratt again brought up some of the problems regarding bishops in outlying areas of the Church. Some had been appointed to serve as bishops without being ordained to that office. He indicated that

> the Lord has manifested unto the President of the Church, who is the proper authority, for the Twelve to go forth and set in order and organize more perfectly the various Branches that are located throughout all the Territory, and in adjoining Territories. And no doubt those few who are acting in the Bishopric without being ordained will receive their ordination, and there may be changes in order to introduce, in all its perfection, as far as we have knowledge and understanding, a more perfect organization through the Church.[12]

---

12 *Journal of Discourses* 18:365; for a lengthy extract from Elder Pratt's remarks, see the appendix.

A month later, John Taylor, then president of the Twelve, explained to the members of the Church assembled at Farmington what was intended in the reformation:

In the organization of a Stake of Zion, as revealed, there should be a President with two Counselors, to preside over all the officers, authorities and people of that Stake. There should also be a High Council consisting of Twelve Councilors presided over by the President of the Stake and his two Counselors. There should also be a High Priests' Quorum, with a President and two Counselors to preside over all the High Priests in the Stake.

The Elders' Quorum should be composed of ninety-six Elders, presided over by a President and two Counselors, and when more than ninety-six, other quorums should be organized.

The Priests' Quorum should be composed of forty- eight, presided over by a Bishop. The Teachers' Quorum should be composed of twenty-four, and the Deacons of twelve, each with their respective Presidents and Counselors. The Bishop necessarily presides over the whole of the lesser Priesthood in his Ward, and they are under his special guidance and direction, while he is presided over by the Presidency of the Stake, and the Presidents of the Stakes, in their turn are presided over by the First Presidency and the Twelve; thus all are amenable to proper authority in their various organizations and there is no schism in the body. All Bishops should be properly ordained with their Counselors, in order to be qualified and to act efficiently in their offices, and to be qualified to sit as common judges in Israel . . .

In relation to organizations, there has been a great deal of carelessness exhibited in many instances; we have failed to sense the importance of the serious responsibilities—responsibility that attaches itself to this Priesthood, this delegated power of heaven. We have found more or less confusion among the churches wherever we have gone; and hence the wisdom manifested by the President in requesting a more perfect organization seems the more to be appreciated . . . In the bishopric we find many irregularities. In some instances we have found that a Bishop has no Counselors, in others he has had one Counselor perhaps, and sometimes we have found the Bishop with two Counselors, but he himself nor ordained to the office, but had only been appointed, and in some instances we have found that the Counselors have not been properly authorized and qualified to act in their calling. Whereas there is a law regulating these things which we hope to comply with. Every Bishop should be ordained a High Priest, then set apart to the Bishopric by the proper authority; and the Bishop's Counselors, if not already ordained to the High Priesthood, should be, and then set apart to act in their capacity, as first and second Counselors to the Bishop. These three then form a quorum, and a court and are qualified to sit in judgment upon all matters that may come before the Bishop, as a common judge in Israel which pertains to his Ward . . .

And then if there is an appeal from this [Bishop's] court it goes to the High Council which is also composed of High Priests, set apart to this office, by the First Presidency or the Twelve, to be presided over by the Presidency of the Stake. For the lack of this more perfect organization all kinds of confusion has prevailed among the brethren in many instances; all kinds of little differences are taken to the High Council, which ought to be taken to the Bishop's court . . . Instead of having these little matters settled by the Teachers or Bishop in their own Wards, they occupy the time of the fifteen men composing the Council . . .

Such cases should not come before the High Council; they more properly belong to the lesser Priesthood, to the Priests and Teachers and to the Bishop's court. (*Journal of Discourses* 19:51-3)

In July, a First Presidency message indicated that young men should be ordained to Aaronic priesthood offices (the term was used of priests, teachers, and deacons) as training for the Melchizedek priesthood (previous to this time, these offices were held only by adult men).[13] This would make it possible to have a continuous supply of men prepared to preside over the wards and stakes of the Church.

---

13 Commenting on the apostle Paul's requirement in 1 Timothy 3 that deacons be married, Brigham Young declared in the general conference of October 6, 1854,

It is not the business of an ignorant young man, of no experience in family matters, to inquire into the circumstances of families, and know the wants of every person. Some may want medicine and nourishment, and to be looked after, and it is not the business of boys to do this; but select a man who has got a family to be a Deacon, whose wife can go with him, and assist him in administering to the needy in the ward. (*Journal of Discourses* 2:89)

.

Brigham Young died on August 29, 1877, but the reformation he envisioned had already been completed. Just over two months later, at the October general conference, Elder George Q. Cannon explained,

> It has been a fitting consummation to the labors of his [Brigham Young's] long life that he should be spared to organize the Church throughout these valleys in the manner in which it now is organized. It was remarked by brother Pratt, in his discourse, that at no time since the first organization of the Church have the Latter-day Saints been so well organized . . . He lived to receive Elder Taylor and the brethren of the Twelve who accompanied him after their return from organizing the last of the Stakes of Zion, and to confer with them. In a few hours afterwards he took his exit (*Journal of Discourses* 19:232)

At the same conference, Elder Orson Pratt declared,

> And near the close of his useful life, he was wrought upon by the spirit of God, and more especially on his last mission at St. George, to give counsel to the Twelve Apostles, to go into all parts of the Territory and more fully organize the people according to the revelations and commandments and institutions of heaven, as given by revelation, through the Prophet Joseph Smith . . . and finally having organized the Saints into Stakes, appointing Bishops, and having them ordained, in all parts of our Territory, having fulfilled and completed the work, the Lord has taken him home to himself. (*Journal of Discourses* 19:113)

At this conference, John Taylor, now the senior apostle, said,

> The Lord some time ago wrought on the mind of President Young to have a more complete organization in the Church, and the Twelve were called on to visit the settlements and explain the order of the Priesthood, etc.; to organize the Stakes with all the officers—President and Counsel, the High Council and [high] Priests under the President and the Counsel over the Stake—Bishops, Elders, the Lesser Priesthood, and all those called local authorities in their several places, and have everything in order; the Twelve went through the Territory, and

assisted by the Presidency, the work was accomplished, and has been for some time. (*Journal of Discourses* 19:146)

President Taylor further noted that there were some twenty stakes throughout the territory that had been completely organized along these lines.[14] In the same discourse, he noted the disappointment of the brethren that they had not been able to find enough qualified high priests to fill positions when they reorganized the stakes. He noted the requirement of D&C 124:134 that the office of high priest was

for the purpose of qualifying men for Presidents of the different Stakes scattered abroad. Many circumstances have occurred since the commencement of our recent organizations which show how little prepared the High Priests were to take upon themselves the duties of their office, in presiding over Stakes, Wards, etc. We have had to take hundreds from the Quorums of Seventies and Elders and ordain them High Priests and make Bishops, Bishops' Counselors, Presidents of Stakes and High Councilors of them. (*Journal of Discourses* 19:140)

This, he explained, was because the High Priests were not properly instructed "on the principles of Presidency." He further noted that the high priests

are a sort of normal school to prepare the people to preside; they have hardly fulfilled this; perhaps if they had been more active, and become acquainted with principles for which they are organized, we should not have to ordain so many High Priests from the Elders' Quorum to make Presidents of Stakes, Bishops, High Councils, etc.; but as it was we had to pick up the material where we could, and I hope we will have better material next time. (*Journal of Discourses* 19:147; see also 306)

---

14 *Journal of Discourses* 19:124. See the quotes in the appendix. Six years later, Elder Franklin D. Richards noted, "In the late organization of 1877, a score of Stakes were organized, a great many more Wards were instituted, many men were called and ordained to be Bishops in the Church (*Journal of Discourses* 24:283-4).

Chapter 13

THE UTAH PERIOD

I prophesied that the Saints would continue to suffer much affliction and would be driven to the Rocky Mountains, many would apostatize, others would be put to death by our persecutors or lose their lives in consequence of exposure or disease, and some of you will live to go and assist in making settlements and build cities and see the Saints become a mighty people in the midst of the Rocky Mountains. (Joseph Smith, August 6, 1843, History of the Church 5:85)

On August 29, 1877, Brigham Young died after having led the Church for three decades, twice as long as Joseph Smith. A few days later, on September 4, the Twelve, led by John Taylor, publicly assumed leadership of the Church. A month later, during general conference, President Young's first and second counselors, neither of whom had been members of the Twelve, were named "Counselors to the Twelve" (*Journal of Discourses* 19:115, 120).[1] In explanation of this rather unusual move, President Taylor said, "There has been a change of Presidency, and necessarily a change of administration" (*Journal of Discourses* 19:122).

Presiding Bishop Edward Hunter was also appointed "one of the counselors to the Trustee-in-Trust," President Taylor, because he was over "temporal things" in the Church. Thereafter, he met with the Twelve whenever "temporal matters" were discussed (*Journal of Discourses* 21:35). As was the case following the death of Joseph

---

1 At the time of Brigham Young's death in 1877, his son John Willard Young served as his first counselor, with Daniel Hammer Wells as second counselor. Serving as assistant counselors at the time were Lorenzo Snow, Joseph F. Smith, Brigham Young Jr., and Albert Carrington. Snow, Smith, and Young would later serve as presidents of the Twelve, with all but Young becoming president of the Church. When Brigham Young died, all of his assistant counselors returned to the Quorum of the Twelve from which they had been taken. Wells was not an apostle, and while John Willard Young had been ordained an apostle by his father, he had never been a member of the Twelve.

Smith, the Quorum of the Twelve was sustained as the First Presidency of the Church (*Journal of Discourses* 21:358-9, 362). It was not until October conference of 1880 that a separate First Presidency was reorganized (*Journal of Discourses* 22:40).

The Question of Succession

When the First Presidency was reorganized under Brigham Young in December 1847, the Quorum of the Twelve was left with only nine members. With the excommunication of Lyman Wight on December 3, 1848, that left only eight. The quorum did not reach its full complement of twelve until February 12, 1849, when four new members were called. At that time, the five senior members of the quorum were listed as Orson Hyde (president of the Twelve), Parley P. Pratt, Orson Pratt, Wilford Woodruff, and John Taylor. All three members of the First Presidency, Brigham Young, Heber C. Kimball, and Willard Richards, were also senior to John Taylor. By the time of the general conference of April 1861, Willard Richards and Parley P. Pratt had died. At that time, President Young explained,

> Brother Orson Hyde is the senior man in the Quorum of the Twelve Apostles, of those first chosen into that Quorum. This calls him, by his age, to be the President of that Quorum. Now, I will go a step further for your consideration. The oldest man— the senior member of the first Quorum will preside, each in his turn until every one of them has passed away. The next Quorum that comes into action may take the senior man for a president, but not until the first Quorum is gone. Brother Orson Hyde and brother Orson Pratt, senior, are the only two that are now left in the Quorum of the Twelve that brother Joseph Smith selected. Perhaps there are a great many here who never thought [about] these ideas, and never heard anything said about them. (*Millennial Star* 23 [1861], 370.

When the Twelve had first been called, Joseph Smith seated them by age and explained that the eldest of them would be president over the others (*History of the Church* 2:219-220). This was because they had all been called at the same time. As members of the Twelve died or left the Church, their replacements were ranked after the original members by age.[2] Thus, when John Taylor, John E. Page, Wilford Woodruff, and Willard Richards were called in the revelation of July 8, 1838 (D&C 118:6), the group of four was ranked by age, with Page (born 1799) ranked first, followed by Richards (born 1804), Woodruff (born 1807), and Taylor (born 1808). But this was not the order in which they were named in the revelation, nor the order in which they were ordained. Page and Taylor were ordained on December 19, Woodruff the following April 26. Richards, who was then a missionary in England, was not ordained until April 14, 1840, after the Twelve arrived in that country.

At the conference of October 1861, as John Taylor read out the names of the Twelve for a sustaining vote, he called the name of Wilford Woodruff, his senior in age, before his own,

> upon which President Young directed the clerk, J. T. Long, to place Brother Taylor's name above Brother Woodruff's as Elder Taylor was ordained four or five months before Elder Woodruff. It was suggested to the President that Elders Woodruff, Taylor, and Richards were called by revelation at the same time, and their places had been arranged from the date of calling, according to age, instead of the date of ordination. President Young said the calling was made in accordance with the date of ordination. He spoke of it now, because the time would come when a dispute might arise about it.[3]

Two decades later, President George Q. Cannon explained the circumstances by which John Taylor's position in seniority was changed:

> Other names had at one time preceded President John Taylor in the order of the Twelve. There were various reasons for this. Two of the Apostles had lost their standing and upon deep and heartfelt repentance had again been ordained to the Apostleship. In both instances this had occurred after the ordination of President Taylor to that calling. Still for many years their names

---

2 See the October 1877 comments by Elder Orson Pratt, in the appendix.

3 *History of Brigham Young*, October 1861, 437. The manuscript in the Church Historian's Office and is cited in Reed C. Durham, Jr., and Steven H. Heath, *Succession in the Church* (Salt Lake City: Bookcraft, 1970), 65.

were allowed to stand in their old places and preceded his in the published list of the Twelve. The revelation designating Presidents Taylor, Woodruff and Willard Richards to be ordained Apostles was given July 8th, 1838; John E. Page was called to the same office in the same revelation. He and President Taylor were ordained at Far West before the Saints were driven from there. Brother Woodruff being on a mission at the Fox Islands, was afterwards ordained on the corner stone of the Temple, April 26th, 1839. Brother Willard Richard, when he was called, was on a mission in England, and was ordained in that land after the Twelve went there on their mission. In this way, Brother Richards and Woodruff, though the seniors of President Taylor in years, were his juniors in the Apostleship; he had assisted in ordaining them Apostles. For some years attention was not called to the proper arrangement of the names of the Twelve; but some time before President Young's death they were arranged by him in their proper order. Not long before his death a number of the Twelve and leading Elders were in Sanpete when, in the presence of the congregation in the meeting-house, he turned to President Taylor, and said, "Here is the man whose right it is to preside over the council in my absence, he being the senior Apostle.

Therefore, as I have said, when President Young died there was no doubt in the minds of those who understood the principle as to who was the man—it was the then senior Apostle. He was the man who had the right to preside, he holding the keys by virtue of his seniority, by virtue of his position in the Quorum; and he became the President of the Twelve Apostles; and became President of the Church. (*Journal of Discourses* 23:364-5)

Changes were made in the order of seniority among the Twelve during a conference held in Sanpete, Utah, in June 1875. President Young noted that Orson Hyde and Orson Pratt, the two senior members of the quorum, had each been disfellowshipped and removed from the Twelve, but were later received back into the Church and into the Quorum of the Twelve. Several of the current apostles (John Taylor, Wilford Woodruff, and George Albert Smith) had been ordained before the two Orsons were re-ordained, and their names were consequently placed first in order of seniority. This was the order of succession presented to the Church at the October conference of 1875. However, John Taylor, though the senior apostle, was not sustained at that time as president of the Twelve.

The situation was explained by Elder George Q. Cannon at the October conference of 1877, just two months after President Young's death:

> By extraordinary providence he [John Taylor] has been brought to the front. Men have wondered at it, why it was so. It is easy of explanation. There was a time when [there were] three living Apostles, three Apostles who now live, whose names were placed above his in the Quorum of the Twelve. But when this matter was reflected upon, President Young was moved upon to place him ahead of one, and afterwards ahead of two others, until by the unanimous voice of the Apostles he was acknowledged the Senior Apostle, holding the oldest ordination without interruption of any man among the Apostles . . . President Young was led by the Spirit of God, as we do verily believe, to place him in his right position; and two years ago last June, in Sanpete, he declared in a public congregation that John Taylor stood next to him; and that when he was absent it was his right to preside over the Council. (*Journal of Discourses* 19:234)

As a consequence of Brigham Young's actions, John Taylor was sustained as president of the Twelve at the conference of October 1877.[4]

Apostles as Prophets, Seers, and Revelators

We noted in earlier chapters that the Twelve, beginning in Joseph Smith's day, were sustained as prophets, seers, and revelators, and that the Quorum of the Twelve were sustained as the First Presidency of the Church following the death of Joseph Smith and later following the death of Brigham Young. But in all of those circumstances, the senior apostle, whether Joseph Smith, Brigham Young, or John

---

4 For additional statements by early Church leaders on the topic of John Taylor's seniority in the Quorum of the Twelve, see the appendix.

Taylor, was the man to whom all the apostles looked as the Lord's mouthpiece.

At the October 1877 conference at which the Twelve were sustained as the presidency of the Church, Elder George Q. Cannon said,

Every man who is ordained to the fulness of the Apostleship, has the power and authority to head and guide the people of God whenever he is called to it, and the responsibility rests upon him. But there is a difference, as was explained by brother Pratt, that arises in some instances from seniority in age, in other instances from seniority in ordination. And while it is the right of all the Twelve Apostles to receive revelations, and for each one to be a Prophet, to be a Seer, to be a Revelator, and to hold the keys in the fullness, it is only the right of one man at a time to exercise that power in relation to the whole people, and to give revelation and counsel, and direct the affairs of the Church . . .

The Church . . . is governed by men who hold the keys of the Apostleship, who have the right and authority. Any one of them, should an emergency arise, can act as President of the Church, with all the powers, with all the authority, with all the keys, and with every endowment necessary to obtain revelation from God, and to lead and guide this people . . . but there is only one man at a time who can hold the keys, who can dictate, who can guide, who can give revelation to the Church. The rest must acquiesce in his action, the rest must be governed by his counsels, the rest must receive his doctrines. It was so with Joseph. Others held the Apostleship—Oliver received the Apostleship at the same time that Joseph did, but Joseph held the keys, although Oliver held precisely the same authority. There was only one who could exercise it in its fullness and power among the people. So also at Joseph's death, there was only one man who could exercise that authority and hold these keys, and that man was President Brigham Young, the President of the Quorum of the Twelve whom God had singled out, who by extraordinary providence had been brought to the front, although many were ahead of him according to ordination at one time and another.

Now that he has gone, one man only can hold this power and authority to which I refer, and that man is he whom you sustained yesterday, as President of the Quorum of the Twelve, as one of the Twelve Apostles and of the Presidency, John Taylor by name. When revelation comes to this people, it is he who has the right to give it. When counsel comes to this people, as a people, it is he who has the right to impart it; and while the Twelve are associated with him, one in power, one in authority, they must respect him as their President, they must look to him as the man through whom the voice of God will come to them, and to this entire people. (*Journal of Discourses* 19:233-34)

Similar thoughts were expressed in a revelation given to Elder Wilford Woodruff at Sunset, Arizona, on January 26, 1880, in which the Lord told him,

And while my servant John Taylor is your President, I wish to ask the rest of my servants of the Apostles the question, although you have one to preside over your Quorum, which is the order of God in all generations, do you, all of you, hold the Apostleship, which is the highest authority ever given to men on earth? You do. Therefore you hold in common the Keys of the Kingdom of God in all the world.

And while my servant John Taylor is your President, I wish to ask the rest of my servants of the Apostles the question, although you have one to preside over your Quorum, and over the Church which is the order of God in all generations, do you not all of you hold the Apostleship, which is the highest authority ever given to man on the earth? You do. Therefore you hold in common the Keys of the Kingdom of God in all the world. And each of you have power to unlock the veil of eternity and hold converse with God the Father and his Son Jesus Christ and to have the ministration of angels. It is your right, privilege and duty to inquire of the Lord as to his mind and will concerning yourselves and the inhabitants of Zion and their interests. And whenever any one of you receives the word of the Lord, let it be written and presented in your councils. And whatever by a united consent you deem wisdom to be presented unto the people, let it be presented by the President, my servant John Taylor, as the word of the Lord. In this way you will uphold him and strengthen his hands, as all the burden should not rest upon one man. For thus saith the Lord all of mine Apostles should be full of the

Holy Ghost, of inspiration, and revelation and know the mind and will of God and be prepared for that which is to come.[5]

Two years later, the Lord confirmed these words in a revelation to President Taylor:

> Verily, thus saith the Lord, I have instituted my Kingdom and my laws, with the keys and power thereof,
>
> And have appointed you as my spokesman and my Constitution, with President John Taylor at your head, whom I have appointed to my Church and my Kingdom as Prophet, Seer and Revelator unto my Church and unto my Kingdom, and to preside over my Church and over my Kingdom, and to be my mouthpiece unto my Church and unto my Kingdom.
>
> And I will honor him, and he shall speak forth the words that I will reveal unto him from time to time by the whisperings of my Spirit, by the revelation of my will and my word, or by mine own voice, as I will, saith the Lord; and ye shall listen to his words as my words, saith the Lord your God . . .
>
> And now, behold, I speak unto you through my servant John, whom you have acknowledged and shall acknowledge as my spokesman.[6]

In 1851, near the beginning of Brigham Young's presidency, John Taylor wrote,

> The First Presidency has authority over all matters pertaining to the Church. The next in order are the Twelve Apostles, whose calling is to preach the gospel, or see it preached, to all the world. They hold the same authority in all parts of the world that the First Presidency does at home, and act under their direction. They are called by revelation and sanctioned by the people. The Twelve have a president . . . This presidency is obtained by seniority of age and ordination. (*Millennial Star* 13 (15 November 1851): 337-338)

---

5 *Wilford Woodruff Journal,* December 28, 1880 and [repeated?] April 17, 1897, in LDS Church Historian's Office.

6 Revelation to John Taylor in Salt Lake City, on the anniversary of the death of the prophet Joseph Smith, June 27, 1882, John Taylor Papers, LDS Church Historian's Office.

From this, we see that the right of revelation for all the saints lies in the president of the Church, who is the senior apostle. Brigham Young noted:

> When the Lord wishes to give a revelation to His people, when He wishes to reveal new items of doctrine to them or administer chastisement, He will do it through the man whom He has appointed to that office and calling. The rest of the offices and callings of the Church are helps...to strengthen the hands of the Presidency of the whole Church. (*Journal of Discourses* 11:135-36)

Three years after John Taylor was sustained as president of the Twelve, that quorum reorganized the First Presidency. They were sustained at the general conference of the Church held October 10, 1880.

Reorganizing the Seventy

Following the death of Joseph Smith, Brigham Young and the Twelve authorized the ordination of a large number of seventies. Over the years their number had grown. At the April conference of 1878, John Taylor noted that there were seventy-six quorums of seventy in the Church (*Journal of Discourses* 19:307).

By 1883, President Taylor decided to reorganize the First Quorum of the Seventy. On April 13 of that year, the First Presidency drafted a letter to the Twelve and the First Presidents of the Seventy, which was presented to them the following day. It read, in part:

> In the organization of these quorums [of Seventy] in October, 1844, there were ten quorums, each provided with seven presidents, which presidents constituted the First Quorum of the Seventies, and of which the First Seven Presidents of the Seventies were members, and over which they presided. But as the Seventies have greatly increased, these regulations will not apply to the present circumstances; and furthermore, the First Quorum, according to the present organization, has not acted in a quorum capacity, but it would seem there are duties devolving upon its members, as a quorum, that may require their official action.

The First Quorum of Seventies may be composed of the First Seven Presidents of the Seventies, and the senior president of the first sixty-four quorums. These may form the Seventy referred to in the Book of Doctrine and Covenants, and may act in an official capacity as the First Quorum of Seventies.

The senior presidents of the other quorums, over and above the sixty-four, may meet with the First Quorum in their assemblies in any other than an official capacity; but in case of the absence of any of the members of the First Quorum, they can act in the place of such members with the First Quorum during such absence, in any cases of importance that may arise.[7]

The changes were unanimously endorsed by all present, after which President Taylor prayed, saying, "Show unto us Thy will, O Lord, concerning the organization of the Seventies." In response, he received the following revelation:

What ye have written is my will, and is acceptable unto me:

And furthermore, thus saith the Lord unto the First Presidency, unto the Twelve, unto the Seventies, and unto all my holy Priesthood, let not your hearts be troubled, neither be ye concerned about the management and organization of my Church and Priesthood and the accomplishment of my work. Fear me and observe my laws and I will reveal unto you, from time to time, through the channels that I have appointed, everything that shall be necessary for the future development and perfection of my Church, for the adjustment and rolling forth of my Kingdom, and for the building up and establishment of my Zion. For ye are my Priesthood, and I am your God. Even so, Amen.[8]

In the early Utah period, seventies (except for the First Council) belonged to the quorum in which they had been ordained. With so many families being sent to various parts of the western United States, this meant the various quorums were fragmented, scattered far and

---

7 James R. Clark, comp., Messages of the First Presidency of The Church of Jesus Christ of Latter-day Saints (Salt Lake City: Bookcraft, 1965-75), 2:347-49.
  8 *Ibid.*, 2:354.

wide. As part of the 1883 reorganization, the seventy were realigned along geographical lines, making it easier for them to meet on occasion in a body.

One of the reasons for reorganizing the seventies seems to be that many had been ordained to that office without actually serving as missionaries, which is the principal calling of a seventy. In 1880, speaking at a stake conference in the Ogden Tabernacle, President Taylor noted,

> According to your statistical report, which has been read, you have in this Stake 360 Seventies; and how many of these, if they were called to-day, are prepared to go to the nations of the earth to preach the Gospel? You are not prepared to do it any more than the High Priests were prepared to magnify their calling. The Twelve are commanded first to call upon the Seventies, but when they do so they frequently find they with one consent begin to make excuses . . . As there are other appendages to the Melchisedek Priesthood, the Twelve are obliged to call upon the Elders, and High Priests, and others, to go and perform duties which should be performed by the Seventies, but which they neglect to do. (*Journal of Discourses* 22:202; see also 19:141)

Nevertheless, until the latter part of the nineteenth century, most of the Church's full-time missionaries were seventies. It was not until 1904 that the number of elders serving in the mission field exceeded the number of seventies.

High Priests

John Taylor continued to be concerned that so many men had been ordained to the office of high priest but were not qualified to serve in bishoprics or stake presidencies. He frequently discussed the matter in meeting with the Saints (*Journal of Discourses* 21:359; 22:201). But a more serious problem also occupied his mind. There was much discussion among the seventies and high priests of the Church over which office was the greatest.

President Taylor addressed the subject just two months after Brigham Young's death. "I hear a great deal about which is the 'biggest' man," he said. "We have got a great number of Seventies, and the question has often arisen, Which is the biggest, they or the High Priests? I say I don't think it makes much difference as to which is the greater or smaller" (*Journal of Discourses* 19:147; see also page 141).

On another occasion, he said,

> There is a matter that has of late become a subject of a good deal of conversation, and it occurs to my mind to refer to it, namely that of the High Priesthood, or the place and calling of a High Priest . . . I do not think we should have taken so many men from among the Seventies and Elders to make them Presidents and Bishops and Councilors, as we have been obliged to do. But instead of the High Priests pursuing this source, many of them have indulged in much unnecessary talk about which was the biggest, a High Priest or a Seventy . . . And if they do this, magnifying their calling, then when other Stakes are to be organized and other changes made, all we will have to do will be to go to the High Priests for such persons to fill such offices that rightly belong to the High Priesthood. And the question that has agitated the minds of the Seventies and High Priests will no longer trouble them. (*Journal of Discourses* 19:242-3)

The topic was still current a decade and a half after John Taylor's passing. Speaking in the October 1903 general conference, President Joseph F. Smith asked,

> Which is the greater the high priest or the seventy, the seventy or the high priest? I tell you that neither of them is the greater, and neither of them is the lesser. Their callings lie in different directions, but they are from the same priesthood. If it were necessary, the seventy, holding the Melchizedek Priesthood as he does, I say if it were necessary he could ordain a high priest; and if it were necessary for a high priest to ordain a seventy, he could do that. Why? Because both of them hold the Melchizedek Priesthood. (*Conference Report*, October 1903, 87)

Auxiliary Organizations

During the latter part of the nineteenth century, what came to be known as the auxiliary organizations of the Church began to play a more central role in the teaching of members. The Relief Society was established by the prophet Joseph Smith in Nauvoo in 1842. After the Saints settled in Utah, Brigham Young ordained that relief society organizations should be established in each of the wards and branches. They were disbanded in 1857 during the Utah War, but in December 1867, President Young asked the bishops of the Church to re-establish this important organization.

The first LDS Sunday School was held in 1849 in Salt Lake City, and gradually spread to various wards throughout Utah. Ten years later, in 1869, Brigham Young, concerned for the education of his daughters and other young women, organized the Young Ladies' Retrenchment Association, later to become the Young Woman's Mutual Improvement Association (YWMIA). In 1875, the first Young Men's Mutual Improvement Association (YMMIA) was organized in the Salt Lake Thirteenth Ward. The following year, the Church formed a central committee to coordinate all of the YMMIA organizations in the wards. In 1878, the first Primary Association meeting was held in Farmington, Utah. The idea rapidly spread, and in 1880, a Church-wide organization was established.

The auxiliary organizations took over some priesthood functions, and while they accomplished much good in teaching the young people of the Church, President Joseph F. Smith was concerned that families and priesthood quorums had abdicated their duties to the YW, YMMIA and Primary organizations. At the April 1906 conference, he declared,

> We expect to see the day . . . when every council of the Priesthood in the Church of Jesus Christ of Latter-day Saints will understand its duty, will assume its own responsibility, will magnify its calling, and fill its place in the Church, to the uttermost, according to the intelligence and ability possessed by it. When that day shall come, there will not be so much necessity for work that is now being done by the auxiliary organizations, because it will be done by the regular quorums of the priesthood. The Lord designed and comprehended it from the beginning, and He has

made provision in the Church whereby every need may be met and satisfied through the regular organization of the Priesthood. (*Conference Report* April 1906, 3)

At the same conference, President J. Golden Kimball of the Seventy, in his typical fashion, spoke his mind on the subject:

> The auxiliaries have been urged forward with great enthusiasm, everywhere . . . The Priesthood quorums are apparently weary in well doing, and the officers and members seem to think that their organizations can run themselves . . . I am in favor of the Priesthood quorums taking their proper places, and if they do not do it, they ought to be ashamed of themselves, for they have the power and intelligence, and they have the authority. (*Conference Report*, April 1906, 19)

General Priesthood Committee

In an effort to reemphasize the responsibilities of the priesthood in governing the Church, President Smith established, in 1908, a General Priesthood Committee on Outlines to institute churchwide priesthood reform and reorganization.[9] From that time until their release in 1922, the committee studied various issues and made recommendations to the First Presidency. Initially, the committee comprised Rudger Clawson and David O. McKay of the Twelve and the Presiding Bishopric (Charles W. Nibley, Orrin P. Miller, and David A. Smith), but it was soon enlarged to nearly twenty members, half of whom brought experience as general board members of the Sunday School, the YMMIA, and other organizations. At the committee's inaugural meeting, Joseph J. Cannon noted that "the auxiliary organizations had been actually doing the work that the quorums should do."[10]

Prior to that time, priesthood activity and instruction was dependent on local bishops and stake presidents and their faithfulness.

---

9 For details, see William Hartley, "The Priesthood Reform Movement, 1908-1922," in *BYU Studies,* Winter 1973.

10 *Ibid.*, 141.

Practices varied widely from one place to another. For example, after 1877, it had become customary for boys age 12 to be ordained deacons, but there were no standard practices for advancing them to the offices of teacher and priest.

The new committee set standard ages for such ordinations. In accordance with this decision, the Presiding Bishopric issued a letter stating that if boys were worthy, they should be advanced,

> and unless there are special reasons to the contrary they should be advanced in the priesthood from deacon to teacher and from teacher to priest. There can be no set age when persons should be ordained to the various offices in the Aaronic Priesthood, but we suggest that as near as circumstances will permit boys be ordained as follows: Deacons at twelve, Teachers at fifteen and Priests at eighteen years of age."[11]

The committee also presented regular lessons for all quorums, comprising thirty-six lessons for each office. Under the new system, lesson manuals were screened by a reading committee, who referred questionable statements to the Twelve. Quorums were clearly told, however, that these books represented the authors' opinions and were not authoritative statements of Church doctrine.

Church leaders announced that all quorums except the seventies were to meet in Monday night ward priesthood meetings, with monthly stake priesthood meetings. The program was approved at the October 1908 general conference and then in special priesthood conventions held during November and December in every stake in the Church. The program was implemented in most wards early in 1909. When the seventies quorums asked to be included in the regular weekly meetings, this was allowed.

Because priesthood quorums did not always coincide with ward boundaries, there was much confusion at first between class and quorum activities, especially among high priests and seventies. Instructions for the seventies were forthcoming:

---

11 Presiding Bishopric, Circular Letter File, 1 January 1909, LDS Church History Department, cited in *ibid.*, 142.

For the convenience of men who belong to quorums that are widely scattered, and who could not come together frequently for instruction, owing to the distance to be traveled, a system of ward priesthood meetings has been introduced by the presiding authorities of the Church which divides quorums that are located in more than one ward into ward classes, but this arrangement does not contemplate excusing men from coming together in quorums as the Lord has commanded. (*Improvement Era* 14: [July 1911]: 841)

To further resolve the earlier debates about the role of bishops, in 1913 Church leaders reminded members that the bishops were the presiding high priests over all local priesthood matters, and that quorum loyalties were subordinate to his local needs and directives (*Improvement Era* 16 [April 1913]: 648).

In 1912, the First Presidency established a Correlation Committee to prevent unnecessary duplication of lesson materials, with David O. McKay as chair. In 1920, the Social Advisory Committee of the General Boards of the auxiliaries merged with the Correlation Committee. On April 14, 1921, the committee issued a major report that proposed correlating Priesthood and auxiliary activities. While some provisions were adopted early on, most of them were not implemented until the committee's first chairman, David O. McKay, became President of the Church in 1951.

Chapter 14

THE WORLDWIDE CHURCH

*For, verily, the sound must go forth from this place into
all the world, and unto the uttermost parts of the earth—
the gospel must be preached unto every creature, with
signs following them that believe. (D&C 58:64)*

The first LDS missionaries to serve outside the United States were
sent, beginning in 1837, to Great Britain, then to other parts of Europe
and finally to other places throughout the world. Most of their converts immigrated to the United States—first to Nauvoo, then to Utah.
They brought strength to the Church in its early years, but by the turn
of the century, the number of immigrants diminished considerably and
the Church began slow growth in outlying areas.

During the nineteenth century, most missionaries were mature
men, often seventies and usually married. As the Church moved into
the twentieth century, young unmarried elders were generally called
to serve. There were exceptions during wartime, when the number of
young men available for missionary service diminished.

For example, on April 6, 1942, with World War II in progress, the
First Presidency announced that it would call only high priests and
seventies on missions. On July 20, 1951, at the height of the Korean
War, the First Presidency called for seventies to serve. Many married
men subsequently filled full-time missions. During the Vietnam War,
a maximum quota was set for the number of missionaries that could
be sent from any given ward.

Another change in missionary work was the transfer of more and
more responsibility to local Church leaders. During the Brigham
Young era, missionaries' names were announced over the pulpit at
General Conference, along with their assignments. Those so called
generally had no prior notice, and therefore, little time in which to
prepare. Later, calls were issued by letter from the First Presidency,
sent from "Box B" in Salt Lake City. Again, the missionaries had lit-

tle or no advance warning, though the recommendation of names for mission calls came from the bishops.

During the twentieth century, it became the practice for bishops and stake presidents to interview prospective missionaries and send their recommendations to Church headquarters. A General Authority would conduct a third interview, then make his recommendation to the First Presidency. The missionary call continued to come by mail from the First Presidency. Missionaries were brought to the Mission Home in Salt Lake City to be trained and set apart by General Authorities and to receive their endowments in the temple. Upon returning from their missions, each would report to a General Authority.

This system became unwieldy as the Church grew in size and the time schedule of Church leaders became busier. On March 25, 1953, it was announced that returning missionaries would henceforth report to their stake presidency and high council instead of the General Authorities.

The decade of the 1960s saw a number of changes in the missionary program of the Church. In March 1960, the mission age for young men was lowered from 20 to 19 years. The following year, missions were organized into nine areas with a General Authority over each. In November of that year, the Language Training Institute was established at Brigham Young University to prepare missionaries for service in non-English-speaking countries. It became the Language Training Mission in 1963.

On September 9, 1978, the Mission Training Center was announced. It was located in Provo and replaced the Language Training Mission there and the Mission Home in Salt Lake City. By this time, General Authorities were no longer regularly involved in the interview of prospective missionaries. This had become the province of the stake presidents, who also set the missionaries apart to their new callings.

More recent changes have been the construction of mission training centers in other parts of the world and the calling of retired couples to serve as missionaries. By the end of the twentieth century, more than 53,000 missionaries were serving worldwide.

With increased missionary work and rapid growth in the number of members, the Church has moved from a regional organization to international status. On March 27,1960, the first stakes outside the North American continent were organized in England and Australia. The first non-English-speaking Stake was established in the Netherlands on March 12 of the following year.

Latter-day Saints have lived in Mexico since the beginning of the twentieth century and several English-speaking stakes were organized there. The first Spanish-speaking stake was organized in Mexico City on December 3, 1962. On May 1, 1966, the first South American stake was established in Sao Paulo, Brazil. The first Asian stake was organized in Tokyo on March 15, 1970, seven days before the establishment of the first African stake, in the Transvaal region of South Africa. On February 18, 1979, the Church organized its one thousandth stake, at Nauvoo, Illinois, where the westward trek began in 1846. With Spanish now the Church's second language, closely followed by Portuguese (mostly in Brazil) and Tagalog (Philippines), it was appropriate that the two thousandth stake should be organized in Mexico City on December 11, 1994.

It took 121 years for the Church to reach one million members in 1951. Just 46 years later, in 1997, it reached ten million, with more than half living outside the United States. The tremendous surge in Church membership has required organizational changes to meet the needs of people living in more than 160 nations and territories, speaking 175 different languages.

The Correlation Program

With continued growth of the Church, it became apparent that local Church authorities would have to take more responsibility for members in their area in order that General Authorities might devote their time to matters of concern to all. It was also clear that these local leaders could not simply go their own way in matters of doctrine. It was important that members of the Church be united in the faith.

President David O. McKay, who headed the Church's Correlation Committee early in his apostleship, decided to institute more of the correlated activities suggested in the 1908-1922 study. In March 1960, the First Presidency asked the General Priesthood Committee (chaired by Harold B. Lee of the Council of the Twelve) to study the various programs and curricula of the Church and suggest ways to provide for better correlation between them. Elder Lee gave his first public report of the correlation work on September 30, 1961. In the years that followed, correlation committees were organized to provide curricula and programs for children, youth and adults, under the direction of the priesthood leaders of the Church.

The correlation program is, in essence, the means whereby members of the Church can be taught the principles of the Gospel from the scriptures in a manner that is consistent and organized. Initially, this required that all the children of a given age group throughout the world, whatever their cultural or linguistic background, receive the same instruction. For youth and adults, it meant that the lessons taught in Priesthood and Relief Society (or Young Women's groups) were designed to dovetail with those being taught during the same year in Sunday School. All lessons were centered on the Standard Works rather than on theological lesson books as in the past. The adult curriculum began with an eight-year cycle, then became a four-year cycle, devoting one year each to the Old Testament, New Testament, Book of Mormon and Doctrine and Covenants.

Along with a correlated curriculum, the program was designed to make effective use of Church publications, auxiliaries, the ward teaching (renamed home teaching) program, family home evening activities, welfare/social services, etc. A new home teaching program was instituted in January 1964, after being presented in stake conferences during the last half of 1963. The following January, the Church reemphasized the family home evening program that began in the time of President Joseph F. Smith, and made a manual available to assist parents. In order to standardize the program, in October 1970, Monday night was set aside for the activity and all Church units were forbidden to schedule activities on that evening. Even temples closed their doors on Monday afternoon or didn't open at all during that day.

Ultimately, the correlation program instituted ward priesthood executive committee meetings in which the bishopric and quorum leaders could coordinate local priesthood efforts. Another new organization was the ward council, which consisted of the priesthood executive committee and the leaders of the auxiliary organizations. A similar council was established at the stake level.

Aaronic Priesthood Programs

The practice of ordaining young men to offices in the Aaronic Priesthood had already been in practice for some time when, in January 1937, the First Presidency officially adopted age guidelines. Young men could be ordained deacons at age twelve, teachers at age fifteen, and priests at age seventeen. On August 31, 1954, the First Presidency approved a plan revising these ages and allowing bishops to authorize the ordination of teachers at age fourteen, and priests at sixteen.

With teenage boys being ordained as priests, teachers, and deacons, it became necessary to provide a separate program for men ordained to these offices. This was part of the 1916 recommendation of the General Priesthood Committee on Outlines. In 1936, the Church's Adult Aaronic Priesthood program was instituted. A circular letter issued by the Presiding Bishopric on October 6, 1952 introduced a new Senior Aaronic Priesthood program, with men over twenty-one years of age organized into separate Aaronic Priesthood quorums. Subsequently, special weekday classes were encouraged to prepare these men for the Melchizedek Priesthood and the Temple.

On February 24, 1935, the General Superintendency of the Young Men's Mutual Improvement Association (YMMIA) was released in order to allow the General Authorities serving therein to devote more time to their other callings. Three new men were called to head the organization. On July 1, 1950, responsibility for the LDS Girls' Program was transferred from the Presiding Bishopric to the Young Women's Mutual Improvement Association (YWMIA), where it remained until 1974. In November 1972, the MIA was reorganized into Aaronic Priesthood (through age eighteen) and Melchizedek Priesthood MIA and placed under priesthood leadership.

Two years later, on June 23, 1974, the Aaronic Priesthood MIA name was changed to the Aaronic Priesthood and Young Women's organizations. On May 14, 1977 (one day before the anniversary of the restoration of the Aaronic Priesthood by John the Baptist), in an effort to further implement the correlation program, the Young Men's program was restructured. A new Young Men's presidency was called to serve under the youth division of the Priesthood Executive Committee. They were placed over Aaronic Priesthood curriculum, leadership training, quorum work, Young Men activities (including Scouting) and combined Young Men-Young Women activities.

The Presiding Bishopric

The role of the Presiding Bishopric has varied from time to time throughout the history of the Church. The reason for this is that the Doctrine and Covenants assigns three basic roles to bishops: (1) oversight of the temporal affairs of the Church, (2) presidency of the Aaronic Priesthood, and (3) the responsibility of judging members of the Church.

In the case of local (ward) bishops, these three duties have remained fairly constant. In the nineteenth century, the bishop was charged with oversight of the law of consecration. Today, he continues to collect tithes and offerings and to determine the temporal welfare needs of his flock. The bishop is president of the priests quorum in his ward and president over all the Aaronic Priesthood. He continues to sit in judgment on the members of his ward, both in matters of transgression and of worthiness for Church callings and temple recommends.

But the Presiding Bishop is far removed from most of these activities. For example, there is no general "priests quorum" for the entire Church over which he presides. While the First Presidency may (and sometimes has) asked that he preside over all the Aaronic Priesthood of the Church, only a literal descendant of Aaron, of the firstborn line, has an inherent right to this presidency, and even he must be called by the First Presidency. The Presiding Bishop has, from time to time, been charged with fiscal responsibilities in the Church, but his position precludes the possibility of being directly involved in providing welfare services to its millions of members. This must remain in the hands of local bishops. Since he does not preside over a ward, the only judgment the Presiding Bishop might be called upon to perform is in the case of transgression on the part of a member of the First Presidency.

As a consequence, the Presiding Bishop's role has changed from time to time, depending upon the needs of the Church, as determined by the First Presidency and Quorum of the Twelve. For example, through 1976, the Presiding Bishopric held presidency over the

Aaronic Priesthood and was responsible for all of its programs. Under the new correlation program (discussed above), this changed.

On February 5, 1977, the First Presidency announced that the Twelve would be responsible for overseeing ecclesiastical matters, including curriculum, activity programs and Scouting, while the Presiding Bishopric would be over temporal programs of the Church. This announcement was preceded on January 14 by the calling of the first Presiding Bishopric area supervisor, who was charged with the responsibility of directing Church temporal affairs in Mexico (mostly supervision of properties). On June 4, eight more area supervisors were announced for the USA and Canada.

Patriarch to the Church

The office of Patriarch to the Church has had an unusual history, due in large measure to the fact that the office was always held by a member of Joseph Smith's family. It passed from Joseph Smith Sr. to his son Hyrum, then to Hyrum's brother William, until his rebellion against the Twelve and excommunication from the Church. During the early days of Brigham Young's presidency, John Smith, brother of the Church's first patriarch, served in the position. He was replaced by his namesake, John, the eldest son of Hyrum.

When John's half-brother Joseph F. Smith became President of the Church in 1901, there were some modifications to the office. President Smith had the patriarch ordain him as president of the Church and began the practice of having him sustained as "Presiding Patriarch" rather than "Patriarch to the Church." From contemporary records, it is clear that the two brothers felt that the office had presiding authority in the Church because Hyrum had been second to his brother Joseph. This was not the understanding of other Church leaders, who pointed out that Hyrum held two positions simultaneously— that of Patriarch and that of Assistant President of the Church.

After the younger John Smith's death, Hyrum Gibbs Smith was sustained as Presiding Patriarch. Taking that title literally, he began issuing printed instructions to the Church's patriarchs, along with all patriarchal ordination certificates. He even ordained some of the patriarchs. He was the last to be sustained as "Presiding Patriarch." For a full decade following his death in 1932, George F. Richards, one of the Twelve, served as Acting Patriarch to the Church. The last Patriarch to the Church, still alive at this writing, was Eldred G. Smith, who was named an emeritus General Authority at the October 1979 general conference.[1]

Help for the Twelve

On April 6, 1941, Elder Marion G. Romney was sustained as the first of several Assistants to the Twelve. The new position was considered to fall under the category of "helps and for governments, for the work of the ministry and the perfecting of my saints" (D&C 124:143; verbiage drawn from 1 Corinthians 12:28). Assistants to the Twelve were assigned to stake conferences in the same manner as the Twelve and the First Council of Seventy.

With increased growth in the Church during the 1960s, it became clear that the Assistants to the Twelve were insufficient in number to fill all the needs of the stakes being organized around the world. On September 19, 1967, the First Presidency announced the calling of some sixty-nine regional representatives of the twelve. Initially, these officers were called to assist the Twelve in coordinating activities with the various stakes. They continued with their current employment. Stakes were also clustered together within regions, with regional representatives of the Twelve helping Church leaders fulfill their assignments.

On April 3, 1976, President Spencer W. Kimball announced that Regional Representatives would be given limited line authority to enhance their ability to serve the needs of the stakes. Of the twenty-four new regional representatives named at the October 1979 general conference, seven were called to serve full-time in Europe or the Americas. It was clear that the growth of the Church required more full-time attention.

---

1 For a detailed, though slightly biased, history of the office of Patriarch to the Church, see Irene M. Bates and E. Gary Smith, *Lost Legacy: The Mormon Office of Presiding Patriarch* (Urbana and Chicago: University of Illinois Press, 1996). Gary Smith is the son of Eldred G. Smith, the last Patriarch to the Church.

The Seventy

During much of the twentieth century, seventies continued to operate out of the stakes, while still under the direction of the First Council of the Seventy. In April 1936, the various stake missions, begun over the years under stake presidents in Utah and California, were transferred to the First Council of Seventy, and were thereafter organized in all of the stakes.

Some stakes had only a few seventies, not enough to qualify for the organization of a quorum. It was announced at the October 1974 conference that thereafter each stake would have a quorum of seventies, regardless of how many members were available to serve in the quorum. At the same time, stake mission presidencies were reorganized. The previous presidencies consisting of three men were replaced by the seven presidents of the seventy for that stake.

All this was to change over the next few years. The First Presidency and the Twelve asked the First Council of the Seventy[2] to study the possibility of reorganizing the First Quorum. Their report recommended not only that the First Quorum be reconstituted, but that seniority be abolished in the quorum and even in its presidency. They further recommended that membership in the Seventy need not be a lifetime appointment, as it is for the First Presidency and the Twelve. All of these recommendations were ultimately implemented.

On October 3, 1975, President Spencer W. Kimball announced the organization of the First Quorum of Seventy which, except for its seven presidents, had ceased to function in the time of President John Taylor. Three members of that quorum were sustained and added to the seven presidents (*Ensign* 5/11 [November 1975], 3). A year later, on October 1, 1976, all the Assistants to the Twelve were added to the First Quorum of the Seventy,[3] and the quorum's presidency was reorganized (*Ensign* 6/11 [November 1976], 9). The quorum then had thirty-nine members.

---

2 The seven presidents who, as General Authorities, presided over all the stake quorums of seventy.

3 This was in accordance with the instructions in D&C 107:38 that the Twelve were "to call upon the Seventy, when they need assistance, to fill the several calls for preaching and administering the gospel, instead of any others."

On September 30, 1978, a new emeritus status was instituted for General Authorities (except the First Presidency and Twelve), and seven of the Seventy were so designated (*Ensign* 8/11 [November 1978], 16). In the years that followed, others were called to fill up the quorum and, by the end of the April 1987 general conference, there were (counting those holding "emeritus" status) 67 members of the First Quorum of the Seventy—nearly a full quorum.

During the general conference of October 4, 1986, President Ezra Taft Benson announced the discontinuance of all seventies quorums in the stakes, instructing the members of those quorums to return to the elders quorums.[4]

At the April 1984 conference, the first seventies designated for short-term service (three to five years) as General Authorities were sustained (*Ensign* 14/5 [May 1984], 4-5). Five years later, at the April 1989 conference, a second quorum of seventy was created for those who had been called to temporary service, now standardized at five years (*Ensign*19/5 [May 1989], 17).

Regionalization

The ever-increasing growth of the Church has, over time, necessitated the clustering of stakes and missions into larger organizations. In January 1947, Elder Matthew Cowley was appointed by the First Presidency as President of the Pacific Mission, comprising seven separate missions. The European Missions were similarly grouped in the early 1960s, and divided into the European and West European Missions. At the mission presidents' seminar held in June 1960, all missions in the world were organized into nine areas, with a General Authority over each. In June 1965, twelve missionary areas replaced these nine.

On May 3, 1975, the First Presidency announced the organization of "areas" outside the USA and Canada. Six of the Assistants to the Twelve were assigned to oversee Church activities in these areas. This was increased to eight in number later in the year. Two weeks later, the Church announced a supervisory program for missions in the USA and Canada, with the Twelve as advisors and other General Authorities as

---

4 For the complete text of his statement, see the appendix.

supervisors over the twelve new areas. Because of continued growth, the areas were renamed "zones" on July 1, 1977, and the eleven zones then existing were subdivided into areas, with members of the First Quorum of the Seventy as zone advisers and area supervisors.

The first area presidencies were created in June 1984, when members of the Seventy were called to serve in thirteen major geographical areas of the Church, seven of them in the United States and Canada.

Still, the workload increased. At the April 1995 conference, President Gordon B. Hinckley announced the release of all regional representatives and "the call of a new local officer to be known as an area authority," who would "continue with their current employment, reside in their own homes, and serve on a Church-service basis . . . for a period of approximately six years" under the direction of the area presidencies. In making the announcement, President Hinckley referred to the provision of D&C 107:98 for "other officers of the church, who belong not unto the Twelve, neither to the Seventy . . . notwithstanding they may hold as high and responsible offices in the church" (*Ensign* 25/5 [May 1995], 52).

Two years later, at the April conference of 1997, President Hinckley announced the assignment of the area authorities to three new quorums, the Third through the Fifth Quorums of Seventy, and a new designation "Area Authority Seventy." Those called to this position would be authorized to "(*a*) preside at stake conferences and train stake presidencies; (*b*) create or reorganize stakes and set apart stake presidencies; (*c*) serve as counselors in Area Presidencies; (*d*) chair regional conference planning committees; (*e*) serve on area councils presided over by the Area Presidency; (*f*) tour missions and train mission presidents; and (*g*) complete other duties as assigned" (*Ensign* 27/5 [May 1997], 5-6).

To those who were members of the Church prior to the calling of Assistants to the Twelve, the trend is clear: As the Church begins to fill the world, responsibilities once filled only by the First Presidency and the Twelve Apostles are being delegated to area officers.

Where Do We Go From Here?

With so many changes in the structure of the Church over the last 170 years, there are some things that remain the same. The head of the Church is, as always, Christ himself. He manifests his will through divinely appointed apostles and prophets, as he has from the beginning. Just as Christ has delegated his authority to those apostles and prophets, he has authorized them to delegate others to serve in regional and local positions.

Delegation is the way priesthood keys operate. The Church is growing so rapidly we should expect to see even more delegation in the future. This delegation entails not only the areas, stakes, missions, districts, wards, and branches of the Church, but its temples. The First Presidency served as presidency of the Kirtland Temple when it was dedicated in 1836, while the Twelve Apostles were the presidency of the Nauvoo Temple. During the latter part of the nineteenth century and even into the twentieth century, members of the Twelve were occasionally designated to preside over the temples in Utah. With the construction of temples in other states and nations, that authority has been delegated to others.

More recently, as the Church has tried to bring temples closer to its members in the massive effort spearheaded by President Gordon B. Hinckley, the authority to seal for time and all eternity is being delegated to an even larger cadre of faithful priesthood bearers. Blessings that were once available only at the headquarters of the Church will soon be within easy traveling distance for every deserving member of The Church of Jesus Christ of Latter-day Saints.

As we conclude this survey of the history of the restored priesthood, the best advice we can give to readers is this: Do not close the door on the Lord's revelations! He will continue to direct the leaders of his Church in how best to bring his blessings to every nation, kindred, and people.

We believe all that God has revealed, all that He does now reveal, and we believe that He will yet reveal many great and important things pertaining to the Kingdom of God. (Article of Faith 9)

Appendix
ADDITIONAL SOURCES

There are many more statements about the topics covered in this book than could have been included in the various chapters without disrupting the flow of the narrative. It seemed appropriate to include some of the more interesting and important material in an appendix. They are presented here, with minimal commentary, in the order in which the topics are discussed in the preceding chapters.

Chapter 1. The Calling of Joseph Smith

Joseph Smith Foreordained to the Priesthood

A number of early Church leaders who were personally acquainted with Joseph Smith testified that he had been foreordained to the priesthood. Here are some of their statements on the subject.

> You will be thankful, every one of you, that Joseph Smith, junior, was ordained to this great calling before the worlds were. I told you that the doctrine of election and reprobation is a true doctrine. It was decreed in the counsels of eternity, long before the foundations of the earth were laid, that he should be the man, in the last dispensation of this world, to bring forth the word of God to the people, and receive the fulness of the keys and power of the Priesthood of the Son of God. The Lord had his eye upon him, and upon his father, and upon his father's father, and upon their progenitors clear back to Abraham, and from Abraham to the flood, from the flood to Enoch, and from Enoch to Adam. He has watched that family and that blood as it has circulated from its fountain to the birth of that man. He was foreordained in eternity to preside over this last dispensation. (Brigham Young, October 9, 1859, in *Journal of Discourses* 7:289-290)

The Lord called Joseph Smith because he was foreordained before the world was to build up this Church and Kingdom, and he came through the loins of ancient Joseph . . . he lived . . . until he received every key held by every Prophet and Apostle that ever lived in the flesh from the days of Adam down to his day, which belonged to this dispensation . . . Peter, James, and John, who were Prophets . . . came and ordained Joseph Smith to the Apostleship. (Wilford Woodruff, September 12, 1875, in *Journal of Discourses* 13:118)

When Joseph died he had embodied in him all the keys and all the authority, all the powers and all the qualifications necessary for the head of a dispensation, to stand at the head of this great last dispensation . . . There is no man in this dispensation can occupy the station that he, Joseph did, God having reserved him and ordained him for that position, and bestowed upon him the necessary power. (George Q. Cannon, October 29, 1882, in *Journal of Discourses* 23:362)

George Q. Cannon believed that Joseph and other Church presidents had received their callings in the pre-existence. In a discourse delivered on December 5, 1869, he stated that "long before he was born, yes, probably before the earth was organized, Joseph Smith and Brigham Young were chosen, the same as Jeremiah was." After quoting the Lord's statement to Jeremiah (Jeremiah 1:5), he added that this was his "opinion about the leaders of Israel in the latter days. I believe they were chosen" (*Journal of Discourses* 13:52).

Chapter 2. The Restoration

Restoration of the Priesthood

Oliver Cowdery has left accounts of the restoration of the priesthood in 1829, one of which is published in the *Pearl of Great Price* as a footnote to Joseph Smith-History 1:71. Here, we cite two other accounts recorded by Oliver:

The Lord, who is rich in mercy, and ever willing to answer the consistent prayer of the humble, after we had called upon

Him in a fervent manner, aside from the abodes of men, conde-
scended to manifest to us His will. On a sudden, as from the
midst of eternity, the voice of the Redeemer spake peace to us,
while the veil was parted and the angel of God came down
clothed with glory, and delivered the anxiously looked for message, and the keys of the Gospel of repentance. What joy! What
wonder! What amazement! While the world was racked and dis-
tracted—while millions were groping as the blind for the wall,
and while all men were resting upon uncertainty, as a general
mass, our eyes beheld, our ears heard, as in the "blaze of day";
yes, more—above the glitter of the May sunbeam, which then
shed its brilliancy over the face of nature! Then his voice, though
mild, pierced to the center, and his words, "I am thy fellow-ser-
vant," dispelled every fear. We listened, we gazed, we admired!
'Twas the voice of an angel from glory, 'twas a message from the
Most High! And as we heard we rejoiced, while His love enkin-
dled upon our souls, and we were wrapped in the vision of the
Almighty! Where was room for doubt? Nowhere; uncertainty
had fled, doubt had sunk no more to rise, while fiction and
deception had fled forever!

But, dear brother, think, further think for a moment, what joy
filled our hearts, and with what surprise we must have bowed,
(for who would not have bowed the knee for such a blessing?)
when we received under his hand the Holy Priesthood as he said,
"Upon you my fellow-servants, in the name of Messiah, I confer
this Priesthood and this authority, which shall remain upon earth,
that the Sons of Levi may yet offer an offering unto the Lord in
righteousness!" (*Times & Seasons* 2/1 [November 1, 1840]: 200-
202; later added as a footnote to Joseph Smith History 1:71)

Because God called upon his son Joseph, and ordained him
to this power, and delivered to him the keys of the kingdom, that
is, of authority and spiritual blessings upon the church. He was
ordained by the angel John, unto the lesser or Aaronic
Priesthood, in company with myself, in the town of Harmony,
Susquehanna County, Pennsylvania, on Friday the 15th of May,
1829 . . . And we diligently sought for the right of the fathers and
the authority of the Holy Priesthood, and the power to administer in the same; for we desired to be followers of righteousness

and the possessors of greater knowledge, even the knowledge of the mysteries of the kingdom of God. Therefore we repaired to the woods, even as our father Joseph said we should, that is, to the bush, and called upon the name of the Lord, and he answered us out of the heavens: And while we were in the heavenly vision the angel came down and bestowed upon us this priesthood; and then, as I have said, we repaired to the water and were baptized. After this we received the high and Holy Priesthood: but an account of this will be given elsewhere, or in another place. (Oliver Cowdery's preface to the patriarchal blessing given by Joseph Smith to his father, Joseph Smith Sr., at Kirtland, December 18, 1833; Patriarchal Blessings Book, 1:8, in LDS Church Historian's office)

In the preface to the history he prepared in 1832, Joseph Smith spoke of the events leading up to the restoration of the Church, beginning with the first vision and going through the ordinations received under the hands of divine messengers:

<firstly> he receiving the testamony from on high seccondly the ministering of Angels thirdly the reception of the holy Priesthood by the ministering of Aangels to administer the letter of the Gospel—<—the law and commandments as they were given unto him—> and the ordinencs, forthly a confirmation and reception of the high Priesthood after the holy order of the son of the living God power and ordinence from on high to preach the Gospel in the administration and demonstration of the spirit the Kees of the Kingdom of God confered upon him and the continuation of the blessings of God to him &c (Dean C. Jessee, *The Papers of Joseph Smith, Volume 1, Autobiographical and Historical Writings* [Salt Lake City: Deseret, 1989], 3; original spelling retained).

The Apostleship

Several early Church leaders commented on the restoration of the apostleship. Some of their comments are included here.

The Twelve had then received their endowments. Joseph gave them the endowments, and keys and power were placed upon them by him, even as they were placed upon him by Peter, James, and John, who ordained him. That is true, gentlemen, because they held the Apostleship last, and had authority to confer it upon him, or any whom the Father had chosen. Brother Joseph called and ordained the Twelve Apostles of the last days, and placed that power upon them. Five of those men who received that authority from under his hands are now living. (Heber C. Kimball, October 8, 1852, in *Journal of Discourses*1:206)

I know [error for *knew*?] that Joseph received his Apostleship from Peter, James, and John, before a revelation on the subject was printed, and he never had a right to organize a Church before he was an Apostle.

I have tried to show you, brethren, as briefly as possible, the order of the Priesthood. When a man is ordained to be an Apostle, his Priesthood is without beginning of days, or end of life, like the Priesthood of Melchisedec; for it was his Priesthood that was spoken of in this language, and not the man. (Brigham Young, April 6, 1853, in *Journal of Discourses* 1:137).

Joseph Smith was the first Apostle of this Church, and was commanded of Jesus Christ to call and ordain other Apostles and send them into all the world . . . These other Apostles are Apostles of Jesus Christ, and of Joseph Smith the chief Apostle of this last dispensation.

Joseph Smith has laid the foundation of the kingdom of God in the last days; others will rear the superstructure. (Brigham Young, August 31, 1862, in *Journal of Discourses* 9:364-5)

We believe that the Lord called Joseph Smith and ordained him an Apostle and Prophet to this generation, giving him the keys and power of the Holy Priesthood. (Brigham Young, October 6, 1862, in *Journal of Discourses* 10:21)

Peter, James and John . . . laid their hands upon the head of Joseph Smith and sealed upon him every power, principle, ordinance and key belonging to the apostleship. (Wilford Woodruff, October 8, 1873, in *Journal of Discourses* 16:266)

In what manner was the Priesthood restored to this earth in our day? Angels ministered from heaven—men who had died holding the Priesthood of the Son of God . . . and conferred the Priesthood upon our first Apostles, Joseph Smith and Oliver Cowdery . . . they continued to receive commandments from time to time, to ordain other Apostles and other Elders. (Parley P. Pratt, September 7, 1856, in *Journal of Discourses* 5:200)

About the 1st of September, 1830, I was baptized by the hand of an Apostle of the Church of Jesus Christ, by the name of Oliver Cowdery . . .

A meeting was held the same evening [for confirmation] . . . After which I was ordained to the office of an Elder in the Church . . . (Parley P. Pratt in Parley P. Pratt, Jr., ed., *Autobiography of Parley Parker Pratt* [Salt Lake City, 1873; 3rd ed., Deseret, 1938], 42)

[Peter, James and John came to Joseph Smith and Oliver Cowdery] and gave them the Melchisedec Priesthood, and the holy apostleship, which is equivalent to that Priesthood. (Orson Pratt, December 19, 1869, in *Journal of Discourses* 13:68)

In these last days the Lord called upon Joseph Smith, gave him power and authority to organize His Church and kingdom again upon the earth, and gave him the Holy Priesthood and the keys of the kingdom of God. Joseph was ordained to the Apostleship under the hands of men holding the keys of the kingdom of God in the days of Jesus—namely, Peter, James and John. (Wilford Woodruff, September 5, 1869, in *Journal of Discourses* 13:320)

Peter, James, and John, who were Prophets . . . came and ordained Joseph Smith to the Apostleship. (Wilford Woodruff, September 12, 1875, in *Journal of Discourses* 13:118)

When Joseph Smith and Oliver Cowdery were ordained Apostles, they received the Apostleship by the laying on of the hands of the men who had held that authority in the flesh. (George Q. Cannon, May 8, 1881, in *Journal of Discourses* 22:267)

Peter, James and John . . . came to him and laid their hands upon him and ordained him to the Apostleship, the same authority that they themselves held, and authorized him to go forth and to build up the Church of Christ as it was built up in ancient days. (George Q. Cannon, May 27, 1883, in *Journal of Discourses* 24:135)

Peter, James and John . . . administered unto him [Oliver Cowdery] at the same time that they administered unto Joseph, upon the same occasion, and he became an Apostle with Joseph, being the second Apostle in the Church of Jesus Christ of Latter-day Saints . . . favored to receive the Melchisedec Priesthood and Apostleship at the same time with the Prophet. (George Q. Cannon December 2, 1883, in *Journal of Discourses* 24:363)

Another early revelation given to Joseph Smith confirms that he and others were to be "especial witnesses to bear testimony of this land, upon which the Zion of God shall be built up in the last days, when it is redeemed" (letter from W. W. Phelps to Brigham Young, dated August 12, 1861, Joseph Smith Collection, LDS Church Historian's Office). The term "especial witnesses," in other revelations given to the prophet Joseph, refers to the apostles (D&C 27:12; D&C 107:23, 26).

We claim . . . that John the Baptist, who held the keys of authority to baptize, restored the Aaronic Priesthood and bestowed it upon Joseph Smith and Oliver Cowdery, also that Peter, James and John, Apostles of the Lord Jesus Christ, restored the higher or Melchizedek Priesthood by ordaining these same men to the apostleship." (Heber J. Grant, *Millennial Star* 97:355, May 12, 1935)

Organizing the Church

A revelation given to Oliver Cowdery in 1829 is closely related to D&C 20. It notes, for example, that the elder or priest is to bless the sacrament, and lists the prayers to be offered. Other relevant passages include:

> And ye are also called to ordain Priests and Teachers according to the gifts and callings of God unto men and after this manner shall ye ordain them. Ye shall pray unto the Father in my name and then shall ye lay your hand upon them and say: In the name of Jesus Christ I ordain you to be a priest or if he be a teacher I ordain you to be a teacher to preach repentance and remission of sins through Jesus Christ by the endurance of faith on his name to the end. Amen. And this shall be the duty of the Priest; He shall kneel down and the members of the Church shall kneel also, which Church shall be called: The Church of Christ and he shall pray to the Father in my name for the Church . . . And after that ye have prayed to the Father in my name ye shall preach the truth in soberness casting out none from among you but rather invite them to come. (Revelation through Oliver Cowdery, 1829, in the Joseph Smith Collection, LDS Church Historian's Office)

Priesthood as a Prerequisite to Organizing the Church

> I speak thus to show the order of the Priesthood. We will now commence with the Apostleship, where Joseph commenced. Joseph was ordained an Apostle—that you can read and understand. After he was ordained to this office, then he had committed unto him the keys of the Priesthood, which is after the order of Melchisedec—the High Priesthood, which is after the order of the Son of God. And this, remember, by being ordained an Apostle.

> Could he have built up the Kingdom of God, without first being an Apostle? No, he never could. The keys of the eternal Priesthood, which is after the order of the Son of God, are comprehended by being an Apostle. All the Priesthood, all the keys, all the gifts, all the endowments, and everything preparatory to entering into the presence of the Father and of the Son, are in, composed of, circumscribed by, or I might say incorporated within the circumference of, the Apostleship . . .

> We begin with the First Presidency, with the Apostleship, for Joseph commenced always, with the keys of the Apostleship, and he, by the voice of the people, presiding over the whole

community of Latter-day Saints, officiated in the Apostleship, as the first President . . .

Joseph as an Apostle of the Lamb, with the keys of the eternal Priesthood committed unto him by Peter, James, and John. What for? To build up the Kingdom of God on the earth . . .

We see this Apostle with the keys of the Priesthood, to build up the Kingdom. (Brigham Young, April 6, 1853, *Journal of Discourses* 1:134-5)

And when they [Joseph Smith and Oliver Cowdery] were ordained Apostles, they proceeded then to lay hands upon each other, the one ordained the other, having received authority from God to do this. In virtue of this Apostleship they proceeded to organize the Church under the command of God. (George Q. Cannon, May 8, 1881, *Journal of Discourses* 22:266-67)

Chapter 3: The Kirtland Period

The Bishop

After the Church moved to Utah, Brigham Young and some of his associates discussed how the office of bishop came to be instituted in Kirtland. In a discourse delivered October 10, 1880, Elder Orson Pratt said,

By and by, after the Church was organized and there being no Bishops the Lord saw that it was necessary to introduce some kind of a plan in relation to the property of His people in the State of New York. What did the Lord say to us under those circumstances, when we were not fully organized? Said He to the Church in the State of New York, in the General Conference, through the mouth of His servant Joseph, in a revelation given on the 2d day January, 1831 . . . No Bishop to take charge of the properties. The Lord said, Let certain men among you in the State of New York be appointed to take charge of the properties of my people, that which you cannot dispose of or sell in time to flee out; let them have charge of it to sell it in after times for the benefit of the Church. Here, then, was a revelation appointing certain men without ordination, without the Bishopric, to handle properties, to do that which Bishops were afterwards required to perform. Now, here is a lesson for us. Because the Lord does one thing in the year 1831, and points out certain men according to the circumstances in which people are placed, that is no evidence that He will always continue the same order. The Lord deals with the children of men according to circumstances, and afterwards varies from that plan according to His own good will and plea-sure. When these men had fulfilled their duties in relation to the properties of the Saints, and the Saints had gathered out from New York and Pennsylvania to the land of Kirtland, then it became necessary for a regular Bishop to be called and ordained, also his Counselors. Did the Lord point out that these Bishops should be taken from the High Priesthood? No.

"And again, I have called my servant Edward Partridge, and give a commandment, that he should be appointed by the voice of the Church, and ordained a Bishop unto the Church." And with regard to choosing his Counselors, the Lord said they should be selected from the Elders of his Church. Why did He say the Elders? Because the High Priests at that time had not been ordained; that is, they had not been ordained under that name. Although the Apostleship had been conferred upon Joseph and Oliver, even they were called Elders; the word High Priest was not known among them to be understood and comprehended until a long time after Bishops were called; and that is the reason why the Lord said to Bishop Partridge, "select from the Elders of the Church." "But," says one who has read the Doctrine and Covenants, "you will find in the revelation given on the 6th of April, 1830, something about Bishops, High Priests, etc." . . .

I was saying that at the time that Bishop Partridge was called and ordained a Bishop, on the 4th of February, 1831, that at that time there were no High Priests, they were not known under that name, but were known under the name of the Apostleship, etc., and hence Elders were specified to be called as Counselors. I was also saying that in the revelation given on the 6th day of April, 1830, there was nothing said about High Priests at the time the revelation was given; neither about Bishops. But you will find two paragraphs in that revelation [D&C 20:65-67] which mention them, which paragraphs were placed there sever-

al years after the revelation was given, which the Lord had a perfect right to do . . .

Well, after the first Bishop had been chosen, and two Elders
selected by him to operate with him, his duties began to be more
fully made manifest . . . he was required to go out from Kirtland
about a day's journey to the southeast, and organize the
Colesville branch in the town of Thompson. The Lord told him
how to organize the people, and that there was a man in the
Church whose name was Leman Copley, who had a large tract
of land, and he covenanted before God that if the Colesville
Branch would go upon his land, they might have their inheritances, etc., and that they might enter into the Order of God, as
should be pointed out by the Prophet. And when the Prophet
Joseph went to Thompson and undertook to organize the Branch
according to this promise and covenant that was made, Bishop
Partridge was there, and he had it pointed out to him how he
should deal with that particular organization, that they should all
be made equal, and should receive their stewardships, and
should consecrate all of their property into the hands of the
Bishop." (*Journal of Discourses* 22:31-33)

Elder Pratt went on to say that in July and August of 1831, the
Lord instructed Bishop Partridge to go to Missouri with the Colesville
group that fled Thompson because of Copley's broken covenant, and
to give their inheritances by the law of consecration.

On April 6, 1853, Brigham Young gave an account of the establishment of the apostleship and the bishopric in the early Church. He
found it particularly significant that the office of apostle holds the
keys of the spiritual blessings of the Church, while the office of bishop holds the keys of the temporal blessings.

We begin with the First Presidency, with the Apostleship, for
Joseph commenced always, with the keys of the Apostleship,
and he, by the voice of the people, presiding over the whole
community of Latter-day Saints, officiated in the Apostleship, as
the first President.

What comes next in the Church? I will now refer you directly to the building up of the Kingdom of God in the last days.
What do we see next? Joseph as an Apostle of the Lamb, with

the keys of the eternal Priesthood committed unto him by Peter, James, and John. What for? To build up the Kingdom of God on the earth. Next grows out of office pertaining to the temporal affairs of this Kingdom, the keys of which are committed to man on the earth, preparatory to its establishment, preparatory to its spreading, growing, increasing, and prospering among the nations. The next step we see then by the Lord, is to provide for the body, therefore some person must be appointed to fill this office, to stand side by side with this Apostle, this first President. Who was it? It was not brother Hunter. Who was it? It was brother Partridge. We see brother Partridge was called to fill that place before there was an Elders' Quorum, or a High Priests' Quorum was in existence, yea, before the thing was talked of, and also before the Twelve Apostles were chosen, not, however, before the revelation was given to signify there would be such a Quorum.

We see this Apostle with the keys of the Priesthood, to build up the Kingdom . . . Him the Lord told to call a Bishop. So the Bishop was the next standing authority in the Kingdom of God. (*Journal of Discourses* 1:135)

High Priests

How came these Apostles, these Seventies, these High Priests, and all this organization we now enjoy? It came by revelation . . . In the year 1831 the Prophet Joseph Smith went to Ohio . . . and arrived in Kirtland sometime in May. They held a General Conference, which was the first General Conference ever called or held in Ohio. Joseph then received a revelation, and ordained High Priests . . . When he received this revelation in Kirtland, the Lord revealed to him that he should begin and ordain High Priests; and he then ordained quite a number, all whose names I do not recollect; but Lyman Wight was one; Fathers Cahoon and Morley, John Murdock, Sidney Rigdon, and others were also then ordained. These were the first that were ordained to this office in the Church. I relate this to show you how Joseph proceeded step by step in organizing the Church. At that time there were no Seventies nor Twelve Apostles.

Twenty-seven years ago, on the 5th of this month, in the year 1834, a company started for Kirtland to redeem the land of Zion.

Brother Heber C. Kimball and my brother Joseph were in that camp. There had not been ordained any Twelve Apostles, nor any Seventies, although there was a revelation pertaining to the Apostles and Seventies. There were High Priests, but no High Priests' Quorum . . .

I relate these circumstances to show you that a person who is ordained to the office of an Elder in this kingdom has the same Priesthood that the High Priests, that the Twelve Apostles, that the Seventies, and that the First Presidency hold; but all are not called to be one of the Twelve Apostles, nor are all called to be one of the First Presidency, nor to be one of the First Presidents of all the Seventies, nor to be one of the Presidents of a Quorum of Seventies, nor to Preside over the High Priests' Quorum. (Brigham Young, May 7, 1861, *Journal of Discourses* 9:88-89)

President Young, who was not baptized until the following year, was evidently mistaken about the date when the first high priests were ordained in Kirtland (end of April 1831). All other witnesses attest to the month of June as being the first instance of such ordinations (see Chapter 3). David Whitmer wrote, "In Kirtland, in June, 1831 . . . the first High Priests were ordained" (David Whitmer, "An Address to All Believers in Christ" [Richmond, Missouri, 1887], 64). President Young's misstatement may have resulted from the fact that the ordinations took place at a general conference of the Church. During his presidency these conferences were held in April rather than June.

David Whitmer, in his 1887 pamphlet, "An Address to All Believers in Christ," took exception to the introduction of the office of high priest in the Church. Extracts from what he wrote are included here. It should be noted that, by the time he penned these words, Whitmer was an elderly man who had been out of the Church for half a century. While he affirmed his testimony of the Book of Mormon, he chose not to follow Joseph Smith's successors. His account is useful for its presentation of historical events if not for his misguided opinion about them.

As to the High Priesthood, Jesus Christ himself is the last Great High Priest, this too after the order of Melchisedec, as I understand the Holy Scriptures. ("An Address to All Believers in Christ," 9)

The next grievous error which crept into the church was in ordaining high priests in June, 1831. This error was introduced at the instigation of Sydney [sic] Rigdon. The office of high priests was never spoken of, and never thought of being established in the church until Rigdon came in. Remember that we had been preaching from August, 1829, until June, 1831—almost two years—and had baptized about 2,000 members into the Church of Christ, and had not one high priest. During 1829, several times we were told by Brother Joseph that an elder was the highest office in the church . . . In Kirtland, Ohio, in 1831, Rigdon would expound the Old Testament scriptures of the Bible and Book of Mormon (in his way) to Joseph, concerning the priesthood, high priests, etc., and would persuade Brother Joseph to inquire of the Lord about this doctrine and that doctrine, and of course a revelation would always come just as they desired it. Rigdon finally persuaded Brother Joseph to believe that the high priests which had such great power in ancient times, should be in the Church of Christ to-day. He had Brother Joseph inquire of the Lord about it, and they received an answer according to their erring desires. ("An Address to All Believers in Christ," 35)

In another part of this pamphlet I devote a chapter to the subject of High Priests. I will remark here, that in that chapter I give you the solemn news—at least, news to many of you—that when the first high priests were ordained at Kirtland, Ohio, in June, 1831, the devil caught and bound two of the high priests as soon as they were ordained . . . thus showing that God's displeasure was upon their works when they ordained the first high priests in the church. ("An Address to All Believers in Christ," 36)

Rigdon who showed him that high priests and other offices should be added to "elders, priests and teachers" . . .

I will also show you by a revelation in the Book of Commandments—afterwards changed in the Doctrine and Covenants—that we had no high priests, etc. in the beginning; as if God had organized his church at first with "elders, priests and teachers," and after we had preached almost two years, and had baptized and confirmed about 2000 souls into the Church of

Christ, then God concluded he had not organized it right, and decided to put in high priests and other offices above the office of an elder. ("An Address to All Believers in Christ," 57)

For further details, see Whitmer's chapter entitled "High Priests" ("An Address to All Believers in Christ," 62-67). The reader should note that, at the time he wrote his remarks, David Whitmer had come to believe that all of Joseph Smith's revelations except those given "through the stone" were false. On pages 59-60 of his work, he criticizes the addition of high priests, bishops, and high councilors to section 17 of the 1835 Doctrine and Covenants (today's section 20). He evidently did not understand that it was the Lord's intention to augment the organization of the Church as it grew in numbers and expanded geographically.

The High Priesthood

There are many examples of the term "high priesthood" in early LDS Church documents used in the later sense of "high priest" or "high priests."

In D&C 84:111, we read of the office of "high priest." But the corresponding passage in the revelation as recorded in the Kirtland Revelation Book (page 30) reads "highpriesthood," with the "-hood" part crossed out, apparently in preparation for publication.

On July 6, 1840, "a General Conference" was held in Manchester, England, with seven of the apostles present, including Parley P. Pratt, who was chosen President of the Conference. "Three persons were then ordained to the high Priesthood . . . also [seven others] were ordained Elders; seven individuals were ordained to the lesser Priesthood."[1]

At a conference held in Manchester, England, on April 6, 1841, with nine of the Twelve present, "Eleven persons were chosen and ordained to the High Priesthood during this Conference, and twelve persons were ordained Elders."[2]

---

1 Parley P. Pratt (Jr.), ed., *Autobiography of Parley Parker Pratt* (Salt Lake City, 1873; 3rd ed., Salt Lake City: Deseret, 1938), 308.

2 *Ibid.*, 314.

In the official history, the wording "high priesthood" in the earlier version in the *Millennial Star* was sometimes changed to "high priest" or "high priests" in the later *History of the Church*. Here are some examples:

Date	Millennial Star	History of the Church
September 10, 1834	"High Priesthood" (15:183)	"High Priest" (2:164)
January 12, 1836	"High Priesthood" (15:582)	"High Priests" (2:366)
January 21, 1836	"High Priesthood" (15:621)	"High Priests' Quorum" (2:383)
January 28, 1836	"High Priesthood" (15:631)	"High Priests' Quorum" (2:386)
April 6, 1836	"High Priesthood . . ."	"High Priests . . ."
	"High Priests" (15:849)	"High Priests' Quorum" (2:476)
October 7, 1841	"High Priesthood" (18:696)	"High Priest" (4:430)

Chapter 4: Government of the Early Church

Patriarchs

Oliver Cowdery recorded the first patriarchal blessings given by Joseph Smith on December 18, 1833. The blessing pronounced on the head of Joseph Smith Sr. is found in Patriarchal Blessings Book, 1:8 (in the LDS Church Historian's Office). Some of Oliver's introductory remarks read as follows:

> The following blessings by the spirit of prophecy were pronounced by Joseph Smith, Jr., the First Elder, and first Patriarch of the Church.
>
> For although his Father laid hands upon, and blessed the fatherless, thereby securing the blessings of the Lord unto them and their posterity, he was not the first elder.
>
> Because God called upon his son Joseph, and ordained him to this power, and delivered to him the keys of the kingdom, that is, of authority and spiritual blessings upon the church . . .

After recounting the restoration of the Aaronic and Melchizedek Priesthoods, Oliver continued:

> Let it suffice that others had authority to bless, but after these blessings were given, of which I am about to write, Joseph Smith Sen. was ordained a president and patriarch under the hands of

his son Joseph, myself, Sidney Rigdon, and Frederick G. Williams, presidents of the church.

Then follows the blessing on the head of Joseph Smith Sr., of which the following is part:

> Blessed of the Lord is my father, for he shall stand in the midst of his posterity and shall be comforted by their blessings when he is old and bowed down with years, and shall be called a prince over them [cf. D&C 107:54-55], and shall be numbered among those who hold the right of patriarchal priesthood, even the keys of that ministry:
>
> For he shall assemble together his posterity like unto Adam; and the assembly which he called shall be an ensample for my father, for this it is written of him: [quotes revelation in D&C 107:56, then continues:]
>
> So shall it be with my father: he shall be called a prince over his posterity; holding the keys of the patriarchal priesthood over the kingdom of God on earth, even the church of the Latter Day Saints.
>
> And he shall sit in the general assembly of patriarchs, even in council with the Ancient of Days, when he shall sit and all the patriarchs with him, and shall enjoy his right and authority under the direction of the Ancient of Days . . .
>
> His counsel shall be sought for by thousands, and he shall have place in the house of the Lord; for he shall be mighty in the council of the elders.

The implication in this blessing is that Joseph Smith, Sr. had a right to the patriarchal office by virtue of his lineage.

In the same record, Oliver Cowdery recorded (under the date of October 3, 1835) the blessing he pronounced on the head of Joseph Smith on September 22, 1835 (Patriarchal Blessings Book, 2:28). To this, too, he added a preface, of which the following is an extract:

> The reader will remember the remarks made at the commencement of the foregoing blessings, pronounced by the first patriarch, and first elder in this church, Joseph Smith Jr.
>
> I said that he had authority to bless: this is so.

Then, in the blessing itself, Oliver wrote:

> And thus shall it be recorded of him, that the generation to come may bless his name, in Israel, saying, "The Lord make thee as Joseph the Seer, who was of the house of Ephraim the brother of Manasseh:
>
> "The Lord do thee good, and bring peace and blessings among thy house as he brought them upon the house of Joseph the Seer, who was raised up of a choice vine from the stem of Jacob through the root of Joseph, even that Joseph who was separated from his brethren" . . .
>
> In his hands shall the Urim and Thummim remain and the holy ministry, and the keys of the evangelical priesthood also, for an everlasting priesthood forever, even the patriarchal; for, behold, he is the first patriarch in the last days.
>
> He shall sit in the great assembly and general council of patriarchs, and execute the will and commandment under the direction of the Ancient of Days, for he shall have his place and act in his station.

Brigham Young was evidently unaware of the timing of the first patriarchal blessings and of the ordination of Joseph Smith, Sr., as first patriarch in December, 1833. In a discourse delivered on June 23, 1874, President Young said:

> At the time that Zion's Camp, as it is called, went up to Missouri, in 1834, so far as I am aware, Joseph had never received any intimation as to there being a Patriarch in the Church. On onr [sic; read "our"] return home from Missouri, my brother Joseph Young, while conversing with me, asked if it would be right for our father to give us a blessing. Said he "I feel just as though I want my father to give me a patriarchal blessing." When we reached Kirtland we talked with Joseph on the subject, and he said, "Certainly," and finally we appointed a day, and brother Joseph, the Prophet, came to where we met and ordained my father a Patriarch, and he was the first man ordained to the office of Patriarch in the Church, and he blessed his children; and soon after this Joseph ordained his father a patriarch and his father called his children together and blessed them.

Then Joseph had another revelation, that a record should be kept, and when this was revealed to him, he then had his father call his house together again, and blessed them over and a record was kept of it. (*Journal of Discourses* 13:240-241)

Chapter 5. Organizing the Church

The High Council

Following the calling of the first bishop and the introduction of the office of high priest, the first high council was organized in February 1834. The following year, when the Book of Commandments was revised, what is now section 20 was modified to include the calling of high priests, bishops, presiding elders and high councilors, none of which existed in 1830 when the Church was organized. The high council was also added to D&C 42:34 when the Book of Commandments (44:29) underwent its revision in 1835 (Section 13:10). These additions were noted a century later by Elder Orson Pratt, who saw them as positive, and by David Whitmer, who, having left the Church in 1838, saw them in a negative light.

In the revelation given on the 6th day of April, 1830, there was nothing said about High Priests at the time the revelation was given; neither about Bishops. But you will find two paragraphs in that revelation [D&C 20:65-67] which mention them, which paragraphs were placed there several years after the revelation was given, which the Lord had a perfect right to do" (Orson Pratt, October 10, 1880, *Journal of Discourses* 22:32).

Two paragraphs have been added to it, having been thrust into the middle of it: Paragraphs 16 and 17 is the part added, which part speaks of high priests and other high offices that the church never knew of until almost two years after its beginning: As if God had made a mistake in the first organization of the church, and left out those high important offices which are all above an elders; and as if God had made a mistake and left these high offices out of that revelation when it was first given . . . This revelation as it is in the Book of Commandments, speaks of the duties of all the spiritual officers in the church; of elders, priests and teachers; but does not mention a word about the office of high priest, president of the high priesthood, high counselors, etc. The part added to this revelation was put there to give the duties of these high officers in ordinations. I repeat that the church never heard of or thought of having in it any of these offices, until we moved to Kirtland, Ohio, in the days of Sidney Rigdon. The Church of Christ upon either continent had no such offices in it, and Christ told us through the stone that he would establish his church "LIKE UNTO THE CHURCH WHICH WAS TAUGHT BY MY DISCIPLES IN THE DAYS OF OLD" . . .

Now brethren, the Church of Christ of old had in it only elders, priests and teachers . . .

I will now quote the two paragraphs which have been added to the revelation above mentioned:

"No person is to be ordained to any office in this church, where there is a regularly organized branch of the same, without the vote of that church; but the presiding elders, traveling bishops, high counselors, high priests and elders, may have the privilege of ordaining, where there is no branch of the church, that a vote may be called. Every president of the high priesthood (or presiding elder), bishop, high counselor and high priest, is to be ordained by the direction of a high council, or general conference."

In all the teachings of Christ, these high offices are not even mentioned as being in the Church of Christ." (David Whitmer, "An Address to All Believers in Christ," 59-60)

I want to say a few words here in regard to section 17 [now 20] in the Doctrine and Covenants. This revelation was published in *The Evening and Morning Star* in 1832, before the Book of Commandments was published, and was put in that paper as, "The Articles and Covenants of the Church of Christ, with a few items from other revelations." This revelation was received in June, 1830, and these two paragraphs were added in June, 1832, in that paper. Now I will explain why they did not print this revelation in the Book of Commandments in 1833, with these added parts in it. It is this: The heads of the church had not yet become sufficiently blinded to change a revelation that was given in 1830, and print it *changed* in God's Book of

Commandments in 1833. W. W. Phelps is the one who printed this revelation in that paper with the "items" (Paragraphs 16 and 17), added to it." ((David Whitmer, "An Address to All Believers in Christ," 61-62)

During the early days of the Church, the high council at the head-quarters of the Church was considered superior to other high councils. The precedent was set during the Kirtland era, when the First Presidency directly presided over the Church's first high council. John Taylor later spoke of this, as follows:

> In Kirtland, Ohio, we had many things revealed through the Prophet Joseph; we had the First Presidency over the High Council, and another in Missouri. Joseph Smith and his Counsel presided over that in Kirtland." (John Taylor, October 21, 1877, *Journal of Discourses* 19:147)

> In Kirtland, Ohio, a great many things were revealed through the Prophet. There was then a First Presidency that presided over the High Council, in Kirtland; and that High Council and another which was in Missouri, were the only High Councils in existence. As I have said, the High Council in Kirtland was presided over by Joseph Smith and his Counselors. (John Taylor, October 21, 1877, *Journal of Discourses* 19:242-43)

Zion's Camp

Nearly four decades after the events of July 1834, David Whitmer explained why he and Joseph Smith disagreed on some matters (notably on the printing of the *Book of Commandments*), then wrote:

> To show you that Brother Joseph and myself still loved each other as brethren, after this, I will tell you that he had so much confidence in me that in July, 1834, he ordained me his successor as "Prophet Seer and Revelator" to the Church. He did this of his own free will and not at any solicitation whatever on my part. I did not know what he was going to do until he laid his hands upon me and ordained me.

Now, bear in mind, brethren, that I am not claiming this office; as I have told you, I do not believe in any such an office in the church. I was then in error in believing that there was such an office in the Church of Christ. I suppose this is news to many of you—that Brother Joseph ordained me his successor—but it is in your records, and there are men now living who were present in that council of elders when he did it, in the camp of Zion, on Fishing River, Missouri, July, 1834.

This is why many of the brethren came to me after Brother Joseph was killed, and importuned me to come out and lead the church. I refused to do so. *Christ* is the only leader and head of his church. (David Whitmer, "An Address to All Believers in Christ," 55)

Chapter 6. The Presiding Quorums

The addition of the Twelve and the Seventy to the First Presidency in 1835 brought the Church to a level of organization that has remained the pattern for general authorities of the Church until today, with few modifications. It is interesting that, despite the small size of the Church at the time, the Lord inspired Joseph Smith to establish all of the leading quorums as a pattern for the future.

The Twelve Apostles

In 1829, nearly a year before the organization of the Church, the Lord designated Oliver Cowdery and David Whitmer, two of the three witnesses to the Book of Mormon, to select the twelve apostles who would be chosen (D&C 18:37). Though he did not leave the Church until two years after the calling of the Twelve, David Whitmer contended in 1887 that there should be no apostles in the restored Church. He protested that the original revelation used the term "disciples," not "apostles." This criticism has no merit, for the twelve apostles selected by Jesus in the Old World are more often termed "disciples" than "apostles."

> . . . in the Book of Mormon . . . Christ chose "twelve" and called them disciples or elders, not apostles, and the "twelve" ordained elders, priests and teachers. These are all the spiritual

offices in the Church of Christ, and their duties are plainly given. (David Whitmer, "An Address to All Believers in Christ," 29)

The Book of Mormon is full and plain on the doctrine of Christ. Christ chose "twelve" and called them disciples, or elders (not apostles); and the "twelve" ordained elders, priests, and teachers. These are all the spiritual offices in the church: that is, the officers who are ordained to officiate in spiritual ordinances; as baptism, laying on of hands for the gift of the Holy Ghost; ordaining other officers, administering the Lord's supper, etc. The office of a Bishop is to administer in temporal things. He is the business man of the church. The church has a right to appoint officers who act in a temporal capacity; this is outside of the spiritual offices. We see that the disciples at Jerusalem appointed temporal officers. Acts vi:2-3: "Then the twelve called the multitude of the disciples unto them, and said: It is not reason that we should leave the word of God and serve tables. Wherefore, brethren, look ye out among you seven men of honest report, full of the Holy Ghost and wisdom, whom we may appoint over this business." So they appointed the seven deacons . . . Concerning the spiritual offices in the church, Elders, Priests and Teachers, with their duties as given in the Book of Mormon, they comprise the officers who are qualified to act in all spiritual matters, and there is no need of any more spiritual offices than these in the church, as we can plainly see from the scriptures ...

The twelve at Jerusalem are called in the written word "Apostles." They are apostles because they were special witnesses to the sufferings of Christ, His death, burial and resurrection; but the twelve which Christ chose on this land are called disciples or elders, and are not once called apostles in the Book of Mormon. In the revelation which came through the stone in June, 1829, to Oliver Cowdery and myself to search out the twelve, they are also called disciples, and not apostles; and the revelation says "disciples" in the Book of Commandments to-day. But it has been changed in the Doctrine and Covenants to read "apostles." The heading to this revelation in the Book of Commandments says: "Making known the calling of twelve 'Disciples' in these last days." In the Doctrines [sic] and Covenants it reads: "Making known the calling of twelve

'Apostles' in these last days." In 1 Nephi iii:26, where reference is made to the twelve at Jerusalem and the twelve upon this land, each twelve are called by their respective names: "Behold the twelve 'Disciples' of the Lamb, who are chosen to minister unto thy seed. And he (the angel) said unto me, thou remembereth [sic] the twelve 'Apostles' of the Lamb? Behold they are they who shall judge the twelve tribes of Israel: wherefore, the twelve ministers of thy seed shall be judged of them." The twelve on this land are called disciples, and not in any place are they called apostles. When Christ was teaching the twelve on this land, in giving them instructions He refers to the way His twelve apostles did at Jerusalem in the laying on of hands, saying to them: "For thus do mine apostles."

In 1 Cor. xii:28, it says: "And God hath set some in the church, first apostles, secondarily prophets," etc. He did so, placing the twelve apostles first, which he chose at Jerusalem: they are to judge the twelve tribes of Israel, and they are to judge the twelve disciples whom Christ chose on this land among the Nephites. Therefore, we see from the written word that they are placed first.

When it is God's own due time to gather up the scattered fragments of his kingdom which has been laid waste by men, then we suppose that God will place at the head of his church twelve disciples; but we of the Church of Christ will not place them there, unless God so commands us. This is God's work and not man's work. We do not believe in twelve man-made disciples. (David Whitmer, "An Address to All Believers in Christ," 50-51)

Whitmer is wrong on two counts. First, his statement that Christ called the twelve Nephites "elders" is incorrect. He never called them "elders," only "disciples." Second, contrary to Whitmer's statement, the account in Acts 6 never calls the seven men chosen in Jerusalem "deacons." Since one of them, Philip, served as a missionary among the Samaritans, performing miracles and baptizing people (Acts 8:5-13) and later baptized the Ethiopian man (Acts 8:26-38), he clearly was not a deacon. Whitmer may have been misled by the fact that the page header in some editions of the King James Bible says they were deacons. However, the actual text does not.

A few statements made in later years by leaders of the Church suggest that Joseph Smith actually ordained the Twelve in 1835. We know from contemporary records that he participated in at least some of the ordinations of the Twelve, though it is not always clear who was voice.

> The Twelve had then received their endowments. Joseph gave them the endowments, and keys and power were placed upon them by him, even as they were placed upon him by Peter, James, and John, who ordained him. That is true, gentlemen, because they held the Apostleship last, and had authority to confer it upon him, or any whom the Father had chosen. Brother Joseph called and ordained the Twelve Apostles of the last days, and placed that power upon them. Five of those men who received that authority from under his hands are now living. (Heber C. Kimball, October 8, 1852, *Journal of Discourses* 1:206)

The context of this statement may indicate that President Kimball referred not to the ordination of the Twelve, but to Joseph Smith giving them the keys in Nauvoo. However, note the following statement from Elder Parley P. Pratt:

> In the year 1835, in Kirtland, Ohio, they [Joseph Smith & Oliver Cowdery] ordained our President, Brigham Young, also Heber C. Kimball, your servant that is now addressing you, and many others by the word of the Lord. Thus our President and others received the keys of the Apostleship. (Parley P. Pratt, September 7, 1856, *Journal of Discourses* 5:200)

It may be these brethren spoke in general terms and that, in fact, Joseph merely authorized the ordination of the Twelve by others. In 1869, George Q. Cannon stated:

> By virtue of the ordination he received, Joseph had the right and the authority to confer this Priesthood upon others. He called Twelve Apostles, and they were ordained under his authority by the direction of the Lord, and those twelve were endowed with the keys. (*Journal of Discourses* 13:49)

Another possible explanation is that President Kimball had reference to the fact that Joseph Smith and his counselors also laid hands on the twelve after their ordination by the three witnesses. During the Nauvoo era, he declared, "After we had been thus ordained by these brethren, the First Presidency laid their hands on us and confirmed these blessings and ordinations" (*Times and Seasons* 6/7 (April 15, 1845): 868, cited in a note to *History of the Church* 2:188.).

In 1843, Joseph Smith wrote "of the Twelve Apostles chosen in Kirtland and ordained under the hands of Oliver Cowdery, David Whitmer and myself" (*History of the Church* 5:412). It is interesting that he omitted the name of Martin Harris but includes the other two men who, prior to February 1835,, were ordained to the apostleship along with him, and who are the only two charged in D&C 18:37 with seeking out the twelve.

Upon his return to the Church, Oliver Cowdery addressed a meeting held at Mosquito Creek, Council Bluffs, Iowa, on October 21, 1848, at which he said:

> I laid my hands upon that man—yes, I laid my right hand upon his head—(pointing to brother Hyde) and I conferred upon him this Priesthood, and he holds that Priesthood now.
>
> He was also called through me, by the prayer of faith, an Apostle of the Lord Jesus Christ. (Reuben Miller Diary, October 21, 1848, in LDS Church Historian's Office; see also *Deseret News,* April 13, 1859)

The Traveling High Council

In a revelation given to Wilford Woodruff at Sunset, Arizona, on December 25, 1880, the Lord said:

> And as I the Lord ordained mine Apostles who were with me in my ministry, and promised them that they should sit upon twelve thrones, judging the Twelve Tribes of Israel, so I say unto you mine Apostles, whom I have raised up in these last days, that I have ordained you to bear record of my name, and of the gospel of Jesus Christ, to the Gentiles first, and then to the House of Israel.

I have also ordained you to sit upon thrones and judge the Gentiles and all of the inhabitants of the earth unto whom you have borne testimony of my name in the day and generation in which you live.

Therefore how great is your calling and responsibility before me. (Wilford Woodruff Journal, December 28, 1880 and [repeated] April 17, 1897; in LDS Church Historian's Office)

Chapter 8. The Church in Zion

During the years 1837-38, there were serious problems among the leading quorums of the Church, with a number of the brethren being excommunicated for apostasy. In this section, we examine some of the things these men had to say.

The Missouri Presidency

In his "An Address to All Believers in Christ," 27-28, David Whitmer wrote of his departure from the Church, "I had to leave the Latter Day Saints; and, as I rode on horseback out of Far West, in June, 1838, the voice of God from heaven spake to me as I have stated above. I was called out to hold the authority which God gave to me." His comment about "authority" given by God is ironic, in view of the fact that, in the same monograph, he declares that he did not believe God restored the office of high priest to which he was ordained and over which he had been made a president.

During 1838, while Joseph Smith was in Liberty Jail, Elder William E. M'Lellin of the Twelve fell away and tried to reorganize the church with David Whitmer as President, because he was ordained by Joseph Smith as his successor in 1834 (*History of the Church* 3:31-32 note). After the death of Joseph Smith in 1844, some expected that Whitmer would come forth and claim a right to the presidency by virtue of his ordination as Joseph's successor ten years earlier. Of this, he wrote:

Many of the Reorganized Church have wondered why I have stood apart from them. Brethren, I will tell you why. God commanded me by his own voice to stand apart from you. Many of you think that I have a desire to lead—to lead a church that believe as I do. I have no such desire . . . After Brother Joseph was killed, many came to me and importuned me to come out and be their leader; but I refused. (David Whitmer, "An Address to All Believers in Christ," 28)

In a discourse delivered on April 7, 1852, Brigham Young stated, "Joseph Smith, Oliver Cowdery, and David Whitmer were the first Apostles of this dispensation, though in the early days of the Church David Whitmer lost his standing, and another took his place" (*Journal of Discourses* 6:320).

Chapter 9. The Nauvoo Era

To a certain extent, Church organization as we know it today can be traced to the Nauvoo era. The number of stakes organized during that time was greater than during the previous decade, and the role of the bishopric came a step closer to what it is today.

Reorganizing in Nauvoo

In the Church today, we think of two kinds of bishops only: the local ("ward") bishop, who presides over a congregation, and the Presiding Bishop of the Church. Edward Partridge is often considered to have been the first "Presiding Bishop" of the Church. Though he was the first bishop called in this dispensation, he was more a "region-al" than a "presiding" bishop, until the saints settled in Nauvoo, when he became bishop over a local territory called a "ward." In a discourse delivered October 10, 1880, Elder Orson Pratt referred to Edward Partridge as a "general Bishop," then noted that, in December 1831, the Lord called Newel K. Whitney as "another general Bishop," one being over Jackson County and surrounding territory and the other over the states of Ohio, Pennsylvania and New York. He continued:

> Their duties were pointed out, but neither of them was a Presiding Bishop . . . they were general bishops. By and by, after the Church of God was driven from the State of Missouri, it became necessary to have a Presiding Bishop; and the Lord gave a revelation saying:
> "Let my servant Vinson Knight, and my servant Shadrick [*sic*] Roundy, and my servant Samuel H. Smith, be appointed as Presidents over the Bishopric of my Church."

Here, then is the first intimation that we have of a Presiding Bishop. Neither Bishop Partridge nor Newel K. Whitney at that time was a presiding Bishop, but each one held distinct jurisdiction, presiding in a distinct locality, neither presiding over the other. But when Vinson Knight, in years afterwards, was called, it was his duty to preside over all of the Bishops that were then appointed. Was there any general Bishop after the death of Bishop Partridge? Yes:

"Let my servant, George Miller, receive the Bishopric which was conferred upon Edward Partridge, to receive the consecrations of my people," etc.

He was ordained to the same calling, and called to the same Bishopric; not to the Presiding Bishopric.[*sic*] but to the same Bishopric conferred upon Edward Partridge . . . Here, then, were two distinct orders of Bishops, so far as their duties, jurisdiction and responsibilities were concerned, but as Bishops they held the same calling as others. By and by, in the process of time, as the Church increased and multiplied upon the earth, it became necessary that there should be local Bishops; hence arose Bishops over this town and over that town, not general Bishops, but Ward Bishops, the same as you have throughout your respective Stakes.

Now the duties of these three distinct callings of those that are termed Bishops are very different, so far as their duties are concerned. The jurisdiction of a Ward Bishop does not go beyond his Ward . . . The office of the Presiding Bishop still continues, but for some reason we have not at the present time, so far as I am aware, any traveling or general Bishop like Bishop Ed. Partridge, and like Bishop Newel K. Whitney, who afterwards did become a Presiding Bishop. A traveling Bishop in his jurisdiction would not be limited to a Ward; it would be his duty if so called and appointed to travel through the various Stakes of Zion to exhort the people to do their duty, to look after the temporal interests of the Church, to humble the rich and the proud and lift up the low and meek of the earth.

There is another class of Bishops. We find in every Stake of Zion what is termed a Bishop's Agent. Does he hold the Bishopric? He should have that office conferred upon him. Why? Because it is his duty to administer in temporal things.

Does his jurisdiction extend beyond that of a Ward Bishop? It does. Why? By appointment, by selection, by being sent by the Presidency of the High Priesthood after the order of Melchizedek to administer in the special duties of his office in any or in all the Stakes of Zion, as the case may be according to the nature of his appointment, and by the authority of the Presiding Bishop. (Orson Pratt, *Journal of Discourses* 22:34-35)

President John Taylor, speaking on August 8 of the same year, discussed the calling of the bishop. After reading from D&C 68, he said:

If we had among us a literal descendant of Aaron who was the firstborn, he would have a right to the keys, or presiding authority of the Bishopric. But then he would have to be set apart and directed by the First Presidency, no matter what his or their claims might be, or how clear their proofs. The same would have to be acknowledged by the First Presidency. These claims of descent from Aaron would have to be acknowledged by the First Presidency and, further, the claimant would have to be set apart to his Bishopric by them, the same as in the case of a High Priest of the Melchisedek Priesthood called to fill the same office . . .

A Bishop of this kind, holding the keys of this Priesthood, must be set apart by the First Presidency and, should occasion arise, must also be tried by the First Presidency. This, however, does not apply to all Bishops, for there are a variety of Bishops, as for instance Bishop Partridge, who presided over the land of Zion, and whose duty was . . . to preside in the capacity of Bishop, not to act as President over a district of country that was then called Zion, but as a general Bishop. George Miller was afterward appointed to the same Bishopric. Newel K. Whitney was appointed also a general Bishop, and presided over Kirtland and all the churches in the eastern country. The calling of these men, you will perceive, was very different from that of a Bishop over one of the Wards of a Stake, for he can only preside over his own Ward . . . While the calling of the former was general, that of the latter is local. And there were Bishops' agents appointed formerly. There was Sidney Gilbert; he was a Bishop's agent appointed to assist Bishop Partridge in his duties; and Bishop

Whitney also had his assistants or agents to assist him in his administrations, the one presiding as Bishop over the affairs of the Church in the West, the other over the affairs of the Church in the east. But neither of them was presiding Bishop of the Church at that time. But you will find that afterwards George Miller was appointed to the same Bishopric that Edward Partridge held; and that Vinson Knight was appointed to the Presidency over the Bishopric, with Samuel H. Smith and Shadrach Roundy as his counselors . . .

Now, these general Bishops had to be appointed by the First Presidency; they had to be tried by the First Presidency as the presiding Bishopric, because they were general Bishops, and were appointed by the First Presidency. But Stake Bishops stand in another capacity. They have a presidency over them. (*Journal of Discourses* 21:361-362)

Chapter 10. Joseph and Hyrum

Choosing a Trustee

Elder Parley P. Pratt, one of the apostles instrumental in thwarting Sidney Rigdon's effort to take the leadership of the Church after the death of Joseph Smith left the following account of the events of July and August 1844:

We were enabled to baffle all the designs of aspiring men, such as Rigdon and others (who strove to reorganize and lead the Church, or divide them), and to keep the Church in a measure of union, peace and quiet till the return of President Young and the other members of the quorum.

Elder Rigdon arrived from Pittsburgh soon after my arrival, and with the aid of Elder Marks, local President of the Nauvoo Stake, and others, attempted to worm himself in as President of the whole Church. A public meeting was actually called and appointed for that purpose; the call being made and the day appointed by President Marks on the public stand." Parley P. Pratt (Jr.), ed., *Autobiography of Parley Parker Pratt* (Salt Lake City, 1873; 3rd ed., Salt Lake City: Deseret, 1938), 334.

The Twelve and the Keys

In the spring of 1844, Joseph Smith assembled the Twelve Apostles and a few others in Nauvoo and gave them their endowments and some instruction. John Taylor testified, "Before the Prophet Joseph departed, he said, on one occasion, turning to the Twelve, 'I roll the burden of this kingdom on to you,' and, on another occasion, he said their place was next to that of the First Presidency (*Journal of Discourses* 19:139).

Heber C. Kimball declared,

> He [Brigham Young] has the same authority that brother Joseph had. That authority was in the Twelve, and since brother Joseph stepped behind the vail [*sic*], brother Brigham is his lawful successor. I bear testimony of what brother Joseph said on the stand at Nauvoo, and I presume hundreds here can bear witness of the same. Said he, "These men that are set here behind me on this stand, I have conferred upon them all the power, Priesthood, and authority that God ever conferred upon me." There are hundreds present this day who heard him utter words to that effect, more than once.
>
> The Twelve had then received their endowments. Joseph gave them the endowments, and keys and power were placed upon them by him, even as they were placed upon him by Peter, James, and John, who ordained him. That is true, gentlemen, because they held the Apostleship last, and had authority to confer it upon him, or any whom the Father had chosen. Brother Joseph called and ordained the Twelve Apostles of the last days, and placed that power upon them. Five of those men who received that authority from under his hands are now living. (*Journal of Discourses* 1:206)

Wilford Woodruff testified of the events of that day:

> And when they received their endowments, and actually received the keys of the kingdom of God, and oracles of God, keys of revelation, and the pattern of heavenly things; and thus addressing the twelve he exclaimed, 'Upon your shoulders the kingdom rests, and you must round up your shoulders and bear

it, for I have had to do it until now.'" (*Times and Seasons* 5/20 [November 2, 1844]: 698)

Elder Woodruff repeated the story in a discourse delivered on December 12, 1869:

> Joseph Smith was what he professed to be, a prophet of God, a seer and revelator. He laid the foundation of this Church and kingdom, and lived long enough to deliver the keys of the kingdom to the Elders of Israel, unto the Twelve Apostles. He spent the last winter of his life, some three or four months, with the Quorum of the Twelve, teaching them. It was not merely a few hours ministering to them the ordinances of the Gospel; but he spent day after day, week after week and month after month, teaching them and a few others the things of the kingdom of God. Said he, during that period, "I now rejoice. I have lived until I have seen the burden, which has rested on my shoulders, rolled on to the shoulders of other men; now the keys of the kingdom are planted on the earth to be taken away no more for ever." But until he had done this, they remained with him; and had he been taken away they would have had to be restored by messengers out of heaven. But he lived until every key, power and principle of the holy Priesthood was sealed on the Twelve and on President Young, as their President. He told us that he was going away to leave us, going away to rest. Said he, "You have to round up your shoulders to bear up the kingdom. No matter what becomes of me. I have desired to see that Temple built, but I shall not live to see it. You will; you are called upon to bear off the kingdom." . . . He said this time after time to the Twelve and to the Female Relief Societies and in his public discourses. (*Journal of Discourses* 13:164)

At the MIA conference of June 2, 1889, President Woodruff repeated the story in these words:

> We had had our endowments; we had had all the blessings sealed upon our heads that were ever given to the Apostles or Prophets on the face of the earth. On that occasion the Prophet Joseph rose up and said to us, 'Brethren, I have desired to live to

see this temple built. I shall never live to see it, but you will. I have sealed upon your heads all the keys of the Kingdom of God. I have sealed upon you every key, power, principle that the God of heaven has revealed to me or sealed upon me. Now, no matter where I may go or what I may do, the Kingdom rests upon you. (*Contributor* 10:381-2)

Elder Erastus Snow said,

The mighty strides that seemed to take in the last years of his [Joseph's] life; the force with which he seemed to push forward the work that was upon him, and the feeling that hurried him forward to confer upon the Apostles and a few others the keys of the Priesthood and the Holy Endowments, which God had revealed unto him, and his efforts to set in order all things pertaining to the Priesthood . . .

The Prophet Joseph Smith has organized the quorums, has set in order the Priesthood, and conferred the keys and powers thereof upon his brethren, and said to the Twelve Apostles, "Upon your shoulders shall rest the burden of this kingdom, to bear it off in all the world. The Lord is going to let me rest." (*Journal of Discourses* 19:100-101)

Elder George Q. Cannon expressed similar thoughts in a talk delivered on December 5, 1869:

By virtue of the ordination he received, Joseph had the right and the authority to confer this Priesthood upon others. He called Twelve Apostles, and they were ordained under his authority by the direction of the Lord, and those twelve were endowed with the keys. Previous to his death, the Prophet Joseph manifested great anxiety to see the temple completed, as most of you who were with the Church during his day well know. "Hurry up the work, brethren," he used to say, "let us finish the temple; the Lord has a great endowment in store for you, and I am anxious that the brethren should have their endowments and receive the fullness of the Priesthood." He urged the Saints forward continually, preaching unto them the importance of completing that building, so that therein the ordinances of life and salvation might be administered to the whole people, but especially to the quorums of the holy Priesthood; "then", said he, "the Kingdom will be established, and I do not care what shall become of me."

These were his expressions oft repeated in the congregations of the Saints, telling the brethren and sisters of the Church, and the world that he rolled the Kingdom on to the Twelve, and they would have to round up their shoulders and bear it off, as he was going to rest for awhile, and many other expressions of a like nature, the full meaning of which the Saints did not realize at the time.

Prior to the completion of the Temple, he took the Twelve and certain other men, who were chosen, and bestowed upon them a holy anointing, similar to that which was received on the day of Pentecost by the Twelve, who had been told to tarry at Jerusalem. This endowment was bestowed upon the chosen few whom Joseph anointed and ordained, giving unto them the keys of the holy Priesthood, the power and authority which he himself held, to build up the Kingdom of God in all the earth and accomplish the great purposes of our Heavenly Father; and it was by virtue of this authority, on the death of Joseph, that President Young, as President of the quorum of the Twelve, presided over the Church. (George Q. Cannon, *Journal of Discourses* 13:49)

Some years later, Elder George Q. Cannon reprised the subject:

Impressed by the Spirit and power of God, he [Joseph Smith] called together our leading men, and he bestowed upon the Twelve Apostles all the keys and authority and all the power that he himself possessed and that he had received from the Lord. He gave unto them every endowment, every washing, every anointing, and administered unto them the sealing ordinances . . . And filled with the power of God, he blessed them and placed those keys and this authority upon them, and told them that he had thus ordained them to bear off the kingdom. There was no key that he held, there was no authority that he exercised that he did not bestow upon the Twelve Apostles at that time. Of course, in doing this he did not divest himself of the keys; but he bestowed upon them these keys and this authority and power, so that they held them in their fullness as he did, differing only in this respect, that they exercised them subordinate to him as the head of the dispensation. He ordained them to all this authority, without withholding a single power or ordinance that he himself had received.

Thus you see these men whom God chose to hold the Apostleship received all this authority from Him. Hence he told the people before he was taken, "I roll this kingdom off on to the shoulders of the Twelve." Probably there are some in this room who heard him talk in this manner. I was but a boy at this time, but I remember it very distinctly. He evidently wanted his brother Hyrum also to be preserved, and for some time before his martyrdom talked about him as the Prophet. But Hyrum, as you know, was not desirous to live away from Joseph; if he was to be exposed to death, he was resolved to be with him. (George Q. Cannon, *Journal of Discourses* 23:362-3)

Benjamin F. Johnson, who was present at the Nauvoo meeting, has also left his testimony:

So here I will leave this subject for your further interrogations and proceed to give you, so far as I can remember the Prophet Joseph's Last Charge to the Quorum of twelve apostles. It was in Nauvoo early in 1844 in an assembly room common to the meeting of a Council or Select Circle of the Prophet's most trusted Friends including all the Twelve, but not all of the constituted authorities of the Church, for Presidents Rigdon, Law or Marks—the High Council nor Presidents of Quorums were not members of that Council, which at times would exceed Fifty in number . . .

And now returning to the Council and the "Last Charge"—let us remember that by revelation he had Reorganized the Holy Priesthood and by command of the Lord D&C 124:123 [124]—had taken from the first presidency his brother Hyrum to hold as Patriarch the sealing power, the first and highest honor due to Priesthood. That he had turned the Keys of Endowments to the last Anointing and Sealing together with keys of Salvation for the dead, with the eternity of the Marriage Covenant and the power of Endless Lives—all these Keys he held and under these then Existing conditions, he stood before that association of his Select Friends—including all the Twelve and with great feeling and animation he graphically reviewed his life and persecution, Labor and

Sacrifice for the Church and Kingdom of God—both of which he declared were now organized upon the earth; the burden of which had become too great for him longer to carry. That he was weary and tired with the weight he so long had borne and he then said with great vehemence "And in the name of the Lord I now shake from my shoulders the responsibilities of bearing off the Kingdom of God to all the world—and here and now I place that responsibility with all the Keys powers and privilege pertaining there too [sic] upon the shoulders of you the Twelve Apostles in connection with this Council." (Letter from Patriarch Benjamin F. Johnson to George F. Gibbs, October 1903, 17-25, 43, in LDS Church Historian's Office; see also *BYU Studies,* Winter 1976, 206)

Chapter 12. Brigham Young

Apostle and Prophet

On July 29,1843, while Joseph was yet alive, Brigham Young for the first time explained a subject that he would discuss on a number of occasions after he became President of the Church, i.e., the difference between a prophet and the Presidency:

> The first principle of our cause and work is to understand that there is a Prophet in the Church, and that he is the head of the Church of Jesus Christ on earth. Who called Joseph to be a Prophet? Did the people or God? God, and not the people called him. Had the people gathered together and appointed one of their number to be a Prophet he would have been accountable to the people; but inasmuch as he was called by God, and not the people, he is accountable to God only and the angel who committed the Gospel to him, and not to any man on earth" (*History of the Church* 5:521).

Elder George Q. Cannon, who was called to the Twelve during Brigham Young's presidency, had the following to say about Joseph Smith's status before his ordination:

> He was a prophet, it is true, but a man may be a prophet and yet not have authority to administer in the Priesthood. The

prophetic gift, to some extent, is distinct from the Priesthood. Joseph had received the prophetic gift and he exercised it and he acted as such prior to his ordination. (*Journal of Discourses* 13:47)

Later, as a member of the First Presidency, Elder Cannon reiterated what he had said twelve years earlier:

Now it is a remarkable fact that Joseph Smith had gifts before he was ordained. He was a Seer, for he translated before he was ordained; he was a Prophet, for he predicted a great many things before he was ordained and before the Church was organized; he was a revelator, for God gave unto him revelations before the Church was organized. He therefore, was a Prophet, Seer and Revelator before he was ordained in the flesh. Did you ever think of it? Brother Joseph Smith was a Prophet, Seer and Revelator before he ever received any Priesthood in the flesh . . . He was ordained a Prophet, doubtless, before he came here; but that ordination did not give him the right to immerse men and women in the waters of baptism, neither did it give him the power to lay on hands for the gift of the Holy Ghost. He had to await the authority from on high. (*Journal of Discourses* 22:267)

Brigham Young explained the difference between the offices of high priest and apostle in a discourse delivered at the general conference held on April 6, 1853. Here are extracts from his remarks.

Let me ask the High Priests' Quorum a question, in order to bring out the thing I wish to lay before you. I ask the High Priest, from whence does the Apostleship grow? Does it grow out of the High Priesthood? [i.e., the office of high priest] . . . Now recollect that the High Priesthood, and the Lesser Priesthood, and all the Priesthood there is, are combined, centered in, composed of, and circumscribed by the Apostleship . . .

I speak thus to show you the order of the Priesthood. We will now commence with the Apostleship, where Joseph commenced.[3] Joseph was ordained an Apostle . . . After he was

---

3 I.e., Joseph was ordained an apostle by Peter, James, and John in the summer of 1829, while the office of high priest was not introduced until June 1831, more than a year after the restoration of the Church.

ordained to this office, then he had the right to organize and build up the kingdom of God, for he had committed unto him the keys of the Priesthood, which is after the order of Melchisedec,—the High Priesthood, which is after the order of the Son of God. And this, remember, by being ordained an Apostle . . .

Could he have built up the Kingdom of God, without first being an Apostle? No, he never could. The keys of the eternal Priesthood, which is after the order of the Son of God, are comprehended by being an Apostle. All the Priesthood, all the keys, all the gifts, all the endowments, and everything preparatory to entering into the presence of the Father and of the Son, are in, composed of, circumscribed by, or I might say incorporated within the circumference of, the Apostleship . . . We begin with the First Presidency, with the Apostleship, for Joseph commenced, always, with the keys of the Apostleship, and he, by the voice of the people, presiding over the whole community of Latter-day Saints, officiated in the Apostleship, as the first President . . . I will now refer you directly to the building up of the Kingdom of God in the last days. What do we see next? Joseph as an Apostle of the Lamb, with the keys of the eternal Priesthood committed unto him by Peter, James, and John. What for? To build up the Kingdom of God on the earth . . .

The Apostleship . . . circumscribes every other Priesthood, for it is the Priesthood of Melchisedec, which is after the order of the Son of God.

To say a man is an Apostle, is equal to saying that a man is ordained to build up the Kingdom of God from first to last; but it is not so by saying he is ordained a High Priest . . .

The Lesser Priesthood . . . comes within the purview of the Apostleship, because a man that holds it has a right to act or officiate as a High Priest, as one of the High Council, as a Patriarch, as a Bishop, Elder, Priest, Teacher, and Deacon, and in every other office and calling that is in the Church, from first to last, when duty demands it . . .

The Apostleship circumscribes everything in the Church of God on earth . . .

Now will it cause some of you to marvel that I was not ordained a High Priest before I was ordained an Apostle? Brother Kimball and myself were never ordained High Priests

. . . In our early career, in this Church, on one occasion, in one of our Councils, we were telling about some of the Twelve wanting to ordain us High Priests, and what I said to brother Patten when he wanted to ordain me in New York State: said I, brother Patten wait until I can lift my hand to heaven and say, I have magnified the office of an Elder. After our conversation was over in the Council, some of the brethren began to query, and said we ought to be ordained High Priests; at the same time I did not consider that an Apostle needed to be ordained a High Priest, an Elder, or a Teacher. I did not express my views on the subject, at that time, but thought I would hear what brother Joseph would say about it. It was William McLellin who told Joseph, that I and Heber were not ordained High Priests, and wanted to know if it should be done. Said Joseph, "Will you insult the Priesthood? Is that all the knowledge you have of the office of an Apostle? Do you not know that the man who receives the Apostleship, receives all the keys that ever were, or that can be, conferred upon mortal man?" (*Journal of Discourses* 1:134-37)

The Presiding Quorums

A number of Church leaders have affirmed that all those who have been ordained as apostles, seventies, high priests, and elders, have a stake in the organization of the Church and that, if the necessity arose through the death of the Church's leaders, there is provision for reorganizing the leading quorums. Here is a selection of statements on this subject.

President Heber C. Kimball noted that the order, after the First Presidency, was "then the Twelve, the Seventies, High Priests, and other officers" (*Journal of Discourses* 5:134). On another occasion, he said, "Suppose the Gentiles were to try to put it down, and to kill brother Brigham, and me, and brother Daniel, and the Twelve Apostles, still there are some fifty or sixty Quorums of Seventies that are capable of spreading abroad this kingdom" (*Journal of Discourses* 5:8). He further noted that, after the First Presidency,

The Twelve Apostles come next . . . for no person has the right to dictate to them, except brother Daniel, brother Heber, and brother Brigham, because they form a Quorum next in authority to the First Presidency, and hold the keys of the kingdom to all men and nations upon the earth. They should be one in spirit with the First Presidency, and the Seventies should be one with the Twelve and with us.

The First Presidency of the Seventies, Joseph Young and his six counsellors, form another body holding power and authority, and where did they receive this power and authority from? They sprang from the Twelve. Then there are seven Presidents to each Seventy, and each Seventy is a branch, and they are all joined to the vine, their seven first Presidents are the junction by which the Seventies are connected to the vine. (*Journal of Discourses* 4:275-6)

At the October 1903 general conference, President Joseph F. Smith declared:

If it were necessary—though I do not expect the necessity will ever arise—and there was no man left on earth holding the Melchizedek Priesthood, except an elder, that elder, by the inspiration of the Spirit of God and by the direction of the Almighty could proceed, and should proceed, to organize the Church of Jesus Christ in all its perfection, because he holds the Melchizedek Priesthood. (*Conference Report*, October 1903, 87)

Half a century later, his son and namesake, Joseph Fielding Smith, wrote:

The twelve are equal in authority and power to the three members of the First Presidency. The fact that it is also stated that the Seventies hold equal authority, has caused some misunderstanding. It is impossible, of course, for two, much less three councils, to have equal authority and power at the same time. If that were the case, there could be no head. The interpretation of these statements is that the Twelve Apostles hold all the authority and power that is vested in the First Presidency. But, it cannot be exercised as long as the First Presidency is intact. On the death of the President of the Church, the First Presidency is dissolved, and then the Council of the Twelve Apostles exercises all the authority that was vested in the First Presidency, and this continues until the First Presidency is organized again and becomes the Presiding Council in the Church. If the time should ever come, which is improbable, when both the First Presidency and the entire Quorum of the Twelve Apostles should be destroyed, then, and only then, would the First Council of the Seventy have the power and the authority mentioned in the revelation. In no other way are these three councils equal in authority, and the First Presidency holds the keys of authority while the President of the Church is living. (*Improvement Era*, November 1956, 788)

Stakes and Wards

At the April conference of 1862, a number of Church leaders discussed the fact that, in some stakes or branches, it became necessary to confer the offices of president and bishop on a single individual. Here are some of the comments made at the conference:

This is illustrated very clearly in the organization of the several Branches, settlements, and stakes of Zion throughout Deseret. To use a figure, in almost all the branches containing from one hundred to three hundred families, it has been found necessary to combine all the authority of Presidency in one man, at least I will say this has been the case in many instances; there are a few exceptions to this rule, but not many. A Bishop while he presides at the meetings looks after the spiritual welfare of the settlements; he preaches in the Sabbath day, gives counsel to the people, spiritual and temporal; he gives counsel in relation to the donations, public buildings, the erection of school-houses; and almost everything is made to devolve upon the head of the Bishop.

In the first instance many of these places were organized with a President and Bishop who were expected to act in concert, and, with their counselors, work and exert themselves for the general good of the people, and with a strong hand all pull together and strive to strengthen each other. And when for the time these men ought to have been teachers they have proven that they required to be taught, for the very first question that would arise, was "which of us is the biggest man, for it is important that we should know the precise line between our authority, to know where the jurisdiction of the one ends and the other begins." A man of this disposition and feeling would want a rule and tape-line to draw his line of jurisdiction on the ground and stake it out. Then it would be, Bishop you must toe this line, and President you must keep your side of it. No familiarity. You must not tread on my toes, remember that . . .

At one place, containing about three hundred families, the President held the doctrine that the Bishop was a mere temporal officer, and therefore he had no right or business to talk on the Sabbath day on temporal matters. If he wished to talk about donations, emigration, teams, building meeting-houses, or of Tithing, he was told that that was temporal business and that he must call a meeting on a week day. Elder E. T. Benson and myself went to that place after they had been contending upon this subject, and it had become well understood that no man must talk there on temporal subjects on the Sabbath day . . . We asserted that a certain amount of temporal preparation was necessary in order that a man might enjoy his religion . . . Now, all this was the result of ignorance. If that Presidency had known their duties they would never have closed a meeting without asking the Bishop if he had anything to say, or any business to attend to; it was a matter of courtesy and of duty also; and instead of pulling against each other they should have united and all pulled together for the accomplishment of the same object. For this reason we have had to organize several Branches with a Bishop and his counsellors only . . . for if we set another man to assist him, men are so ignorant, they have learned so little that they will immediately start up and strive for the mastery, and hence contentions have risen among the brethren acting in the capacity of Bishops and Presidents . . .

I will here say that there have been places where these two organizations have existed for years without any difficulty, and there are other places where the two have existed at the same time, and the matter has been taken up by the people and worked at until it has been found necessary to reduce the organization by uniting the Presidency and Bishopric in one person . . .

There was one settlement where the people got so very wise that the Bishop had to have two sets of counsellors, and they had to be selected according to the wishes of the parties that took sides with the President, or rather that were in favor of having one, and then those who were willing to be contented with a Bishop had to have their choice, and thus was formed what I call an unlimited democracy . . . a few years ago, there were some Bishops sent out of Salt Lake City to explain to the country Bishops their duties. These brethren would go into a settlement where there were both a Bishop and a President, and they would go on and tell the Bishops what their duties were, and in doing so, embrace the whole circle of duties required of both Bishop and President, and never think that in that Branch of the Church, those duties were not united or centered in one man but divided between two. And in some instances, there would be a sort of half sharp-looking fellow get up and ask what the President was to do, if all those explained and fully defined duties were centered in the Bishop. "O," they would say, "we were not sent to instruct anybody but the Bishops;" and as might be expected, the result was a contention, if not among the authorities, among the people, and I had some of these difficulties to settle, and I found that the best way to do it was to dispense with one of the officers. (George A. Smith, April 7, 1862, *Journal of Discourses* 10:59-62)

It has been in my mind to remark that the office of both President and Bishop are in our President, and therefore he has the undoubted right to place these two offices on one man, or to ordain two separate men as he may see proper. There may possibly arise circumstances that may appear to cause the authority of these two to conflict . . . I am happy to inform you that I have never heard of any feeling of difficulty between the President and Bishop at Spanish Fork . . . My reason for desiring to have this matter brought here was to have the duties of Bishops and Presidents defined, thinking that probably the result of the investigation would be the abolishment of the office of President for the present in the country Branches. (Orson Hyde, April 7, 1862, *Journal of Discourses* 10:31)

At the October conference of 1865, Brigham Young again discussed the situation in the smaller stakes:

> Wherever a man is appointed to preside, he should preside in the dignity of his office, and be able to discriminate between his duties as a presiding officer in a branch, he being a high priest we will say, and the duties of the bishop. I am gratified to say that such a thing does exist in the midst of this people that one man can preside as a president and another as a bishop, in the same ward, and not quarrel with each other; each one has the privilege for himself of knowing his duty by the revelations of the Lord Jesus Christ. And if all presidents and bishops were inspired by this spirit, they never would have any difficulty, but they would see eye to eye. (*Journal of Discourses* 11:135)

The 1877 Reformation

The reformation of 1877 began soon after the April general conference. On May 13, Elder Orson Pratt explained the background:

> In the early days of this Church the Lord, through a revelation, set forth the various appendages of the higher Priesthood, the duties of its several offices and their callings; also how they should officiate . . .
>
> It seems that since these revelations were given, the Church, during its history, has passed through a variety of circumstances, wherein a perfect organization according to the rules and laws, as laid down by modern revelation, have not been entered into . . . Some, by virtue of the Priesthood, have officiated, without being set apart in certain callings that pertain to those who should be selected and set apart for that purpose . . . if we have literal descendants of Aaron, they have the right, through their obedience to the Gospel of the Son of God, to the bishoprick, which pertains to the lesser Priesthood. It is the presiding authority over the lesser Priesthood, they have the right to claim it, and to all the keys and powers pertaining to it, they have the right to be ordained and set apart to that calling and to officiate therein, and that too without the aid of two counselors . . . But as we have none at present to our knowl-

edge that belong to the seed of Aaron, that has the right to this by lineage, the Lord has pointed out that those who are ordained to the higher Priesthood have the right, by virtue of this higher authority, to administer, when set apart by the First Presidency, or under their direction and according to their instruction, as Bishops to officiate in the Presidency of the lower Priesthood . . . with the exception of one condition, that is, he must have two counselors ordained from among the high Priests of the Church . . . In some portions of our Territory, instead of this organization having been carried out in all its perfection, we have acted, in some few instances, for the time being, by appointing a person to that position when he had not been previously set apart to that special calling. We might refer to persons in some few of our settlements, both north and south, who have acted as Bishops by virtue of appointment only, and not ordination.

I understand now that the Spirit of the Lord has manifested unto the President of the Church, who is the proper authority, for the Twelve to go forth and set in order and organize more perfectly the various Branches that are located throughout all the Territory, and in the adjoining Territories. And no doubt those few who are acting in the Bishopric without being ordained will receive their ordination, and there may be changes in order to introduce, in all its perfection, as far as we have knowledge and understanding, a more perfect organization throughout the Church in these mountains. (*Journal of Discourses* 18:364-5)

At the October 1877 conference, John Taylor, president of the Twelve, noted the effects of the reformation that President Young ordained before his death. Here are some of his comments:

As has been referred to, the President was operated upon to organize the Church throughout the Territory more completely; the Twelve were called upon to visit every part of the Territory and organize it, which they have done. There are now twenty different Stakes fully organized with their Presidents and Counselors, with their High Councils, with Bishops and their Counselors, who operate as common judges in Israel, and with

High Priests, Seventies, Elders, and the lesser Priesthood, that they may administer in all things in their several Stakes under the direction of the Twelve. (*Journal of Discourses* 19:124)

Two weeks later, as he was conducting one of the reorganizations, he said, "The various quorums of the Priesthood, which have been presented to you this afternoon, give a more perfect representation of your Stake than has been given before. And I am pleased to say that this extended organization of the Priesthood exists among all the Stakes some twenty in all—throughout the Territory (*Journal of Discourses*19:241).

13. The Utah Period

The Question of Succession

When the first members of the Twelve were called, they were ranked by age rather than by date of ordination. Those called to the Twelve thereafter were first ranked by date of calling, but later by date of actual ordination. This brought John Taylor to the head of the quorum in 1875. He was sustained as its president upon the death of Brigham Young in August 1877. At the following October conference, Elder Orson Pratt, who had previously been listed as President Taylor's senior, explained,

> The original Twelve, first chosen, were all made equal, by the Prophet Joseph Smith. And he said to them in the basement of the Temple as they were to be sent as a Council on their first mission, that the oldest should preside in the first Conference, in the following Conferences, the next in seniority, and so on, until all had taken their turns in presiding. And you shall be equal, showing respect to the oldest. They were arranged according to their ages, while all their successors were arranged, according to the date of their respective ordinations. (*Journal of Discourses*19:118)

John Taylor's succession to the presidency of the Church was due mostly to Brigham Young's clarification of seniority among the twelve Apostles. President Young declared in 1861 that seniority should be by actual date of ordination rather than by the date of a man's calling. In 1875, he made John Taylor senior over Orson Hyde and Orson Pratt because both of these men had been excommunicated. They returned shortly thereafter and were re-ordained apostles, but Elder Taylor and others were ordained to the apostleship before their return. During John Taylor's presidency, a number of brethren discussed the situation. Here are quotes from John Taylor and his counselor George Q. Cannon to supplement those already included in chapter 13.

Orson Hyde and Orson Pratt had both of them been disfellowshipped and dropped from their quorum, and when they returned, without any particular investigation or arrangement, they took the position in the quorum which they had formerly occupied, and as there was no objection raised, or investigation had on this subject, things continued in this position for a number of years. Some ten or twelve years ago, Brother George A. Smith drew my attention to this matter. I think it was soon after he was appointed as a counselor to the first presidency [1868]; and he asked me if I had noticed the impropriety of the arrangement. He stated at the same time that these brethren having been dropped from the quorum could not assume the position that they before had in the quorum; but that all those who remained in the quorum when they had left it must necessarily take the precedence of them in the quorum. He stated, at the same time, that these questions might become very serious ones, in case of change of circumstances arising from death or otherwise; remarking also, that I stood before them in the quorum.

I told him that I was aware of that, and of the correctness of the position assumed by him, and had been for years, but that I did not choose to agitate or bring up a question of that kind. Furthermore, I stated that, personally, I cared nothing about the matter, and, moreover, I entertained a very high esteem for both the parties named; while at the same time, I could not help but see, with him, that complications might hereafter arise, unless the matters were adjusted. Some time after, in Sanpete, in June, 1875, President Young brought up the subject of seniority and stated that John Taylor was the man that stood next to him, and that where he was not, John Taylor presided. He also made the statement that Brother Hyde and Brother Pratt were not in their right positions in the quorum. Upon this statement, I assumed the position indicated.

Thus our positions at that time seemed to be fully defined; and what had been spoken of by Elder George A. Smith, without any action of mine, was carried out by President Young. I occupied the senior position in the quorum, and occupying that position, which was thoroughly understood by the quorum of the twelve, on the death of President Young, as the twelve assumed the presidency, and I was their president, it placed me in a position of president of the church, or, as expressed in our conference meeting: "As president of the quorum of the twelve apostles, as one of the twelve apostles, and of the presidency of the Church of Jesus Christ of Latter-day Saints." (John Taylor, "The Organization of the Church," *Millennial Star* 13/22: 337; later included in John Taylor, *Succession of the Presidency* [Salt Lake City, 1882], 16-17)

But who thought then [at the time of the Martyrdom] that he [John Taylor] would be the senior Apostle who would preside over this Church? There were a number his seniors. In consequence of a misunderstanding and his being senior in age, Brother Woodruff recognized all the time that he and Willard Richards were not his seniors in ordination. President Taylor had been ordained to the Apostleship before them, and when this matter was brought before the President of the Church (President Young) the names were put in proper order. Brother Woodruff recognized this as being correct, and if Willard Richards had lived, doubtless he would have had the same feeling. But then there stood Orson Hyde and Orson Pratt as seniors in the quorum. Their names preceded his. But had their names the right to stand in that position? No, they had not, for reasons I need not dwell upon here, which ought to be familiar to every Elder in this Church. Therefore, I will merely say this: that President John Taylor, Wilford Woodruff, and George A. Smith were bearers of the apostleship at a time when Orson Hyde and Orson Pratt did not hold that power. Therefore they were by right their seniors; and President Young providentially, prompted by the Spirit of God, made a ruling which the Twelve accepted—every man knowing the true state of the case—as correct, and placed the names in their order some time before his death, making John Taylor, Wilford Woodruff and George A. Smith, seniors of Orson Hyde and of Orson Pratt. In this manner God has brought forward to the front the man whom He chose to be President of the Church. (George Q. Cannon, August 12, 1883, *Journal of Discourses* 24:275-6)

14. The Worldwide Church

The Seventy

During the priesthood session of the general conference held October 4, 1986, President Ezra Taft Benson announced a change in the status of seventies in the stakes. Here is the text of his announcement:

> In harmony with the needs of the growth of the church across the world, the First Presidency and Council of the Twelve Apostles have given prayerful consideration to the role of the stake seventies quorums in the church and have determined to take the following action relative thereto:
>
> 1. The seventies quorums in the stakes of the church are to be discontinued, and the brethren now serving as seventies in these quorums will be asked to return to membership in the elders quorums of their wards. Stake presidents, in an orderly fashion, may then determine who among such brethren should be ordained to the office of high priest.
>
> This change does not affect the First Quorum of the Seventy, members of which are all general authorities of the church.
>
> 2. Particular emphasis is to be given in stake missions to cooperating with full-time proselyting missionaries by finding, friendshipping, fellowshipping and fostering member participation in all missionary activities. A missionary-minded elder or high priest will be called as the stake mission president with his counselors being selected from among the elders or high priests.
>
> Additional detailed instructions regarding this announcement will be provided local priesthood leaders by letter from the First Presidency.

At this time, we commend all who have served both past and present as members of stake seventies quorums of the church and who have so ably given of their time, talents and resources in spreading forth the gospel of Jesus Christ. (Deseret News, October 5, 1986; *Ensign* 16/11 [November 1986], 48)

Index

E

Elder's School; 60-61

Elias (as forerunners); 115-117, 119

Endowments; 27, 34, 73-74, 85, 103, 175-177, 192, 193, 199, 200, 204, 248, 266, 290-292, 294

Evangelist(s); 104, 158

Excommunications; 24, 55, 68, 69, 78, 93, 94, 129, 131, 142, 162, 163, 205, 232, 253, 285, 306

F

Far West Record; 19, 55

Fielding, Joseph; 143, 147

Finances; 47, 67, 149, 169

First President; 76, 84, 94-96, 100-105, 108, 132, 162

First Elders; 22, 26, 32-35, 51, 61, 67, 274

First Presidency; 16, 52-58, 71, 96

Fuller, Amos; 171

G

Garn, Daniel; 170

Gause, Jesse; 53-55, 80, 162

Gee, Salmon; 52

Gibbs, George F. 295

Gilbert, Algernon Sidney; 47, 63, 74

Gladden, Bishop; 68, 94, 95

Grant, Jedediah M.; 182

Grover, Thomas; 186

H

Hancock, Levi; 140

Hancock, Solomon; 74, 75, 203

Harris, George W.; 155

Harris, Martin; 43, 49, 54, 79, 284

Haun's Mill; 141

Higby, James; 68

High Priesthood; 42-43, 46, 52-53

M

N

O

P

R

S

Y

Z